MW00483816

BRIDGE AND TUNNEL BOYS

BRIDGE AND TUNNEL BOYS

BRUCE SPRINGSTEEN, BILLY JOEL, AND THE METROPOLITAN SOUND OF THE AMERICAN CENTURY

JIM CULLEN

RUTGERS UNIVERSITY PRESS

New Brunswick, Camden, and Newark, New Jersey
London and Oxford

Rutgers University Press is a department of Rutgers, The State University of New Jersey, one of the leading public research universities in the nation. By publishing worldwide, it furthers the University's mission of dedication to excellence in teaching, scholarship, research, and clinical care.

Library of Congress Cataloging-in-Publication Data

Names: Cullen, Jim, 1962– author.
Title: Bridge and tunnel boys : Bruce Springsteen, Billy Joel, and the metropolitan sound of the American century / Jim Cullen.
Description: New Brunswick : Rutgers University Press, 2023. |
    Includes bibliographical references and index.
Identifiers: LCCN 2023007691 | ISBN 9781978835221 (hardcover) |
    ISBN 9781978835238 (epub) | ISBN 9781978835245 (pdf)
Subjects: LCSH: Popular music—United States—1971–1980—History and criticism. |
    Rock music—United States—1971–1980—History and criticism. |
    Popular music—United States—1981–1990—History and criticism. | Rock
    music—United States—1981–1990—History and criticism. | Joel, Billy—
    Criticism and interpretation. | Springsteen, Bruce—Criticism and interpretation.
Classification: LCC ML3477 .C85 2023 | DDC 781.640973—dc23/eng/20230418
LC record available at https://lccn.loc.gov/2023007691

A British Cataloging-in-Publication record for this book is
available from the British Library.

rutgersuniversitypress.org

For Peter Mickulas
Who provided the onramp

CONTENTS

PREFACE

You See? I Was Right!

The writing of history is a bid for vindication.

Of course, the writing of history is many things: an expression of a deeply human desire for storytelling; an effort to understand; an act (sometimes implicit or even unconscious) of love. But whatever else they may be, histories are efforts to say, in effect: This—this *topic*, this *question*, this *explanation*, whatever—*matters*. It matters to me, but more importantly, it should matter to *you*. The document you're encountering, produced with some degree of exertion, seeks to capture a particular time and place, a time and place that may be described in personal terms but which is always to some degree collective, and that's precisely *why* it matters. To the extent that a writer of history will succeed in engaging a reader, that reader will agree: yes, it *does* matter, because I, perhaps instinctively, share it, too. In choosing to pay the historian in the currency of attention, the reader (viewer, listener, whatever—modalities may vary) has a moment of recognition that while the historian is describing phenomena in the past, such phenomena are in some sense ongoing, even if only as a matter of the reader understanding the urges that led the historian to write in the first place. That bond, however finite or fragile, is one of imagined communion: you see, I was *right* to care, because you care, too. We have, for a moment, transcended time. Together.

This book is about the most evanescent of human experiences: popular music. Created in a moment to express a moment, hit records—a peculiar expression of twentieth century American capitalism—are meant to capture an eternal now, not only in the moment of their composition, but also in the lives of their listeners: my senior year of high school; the summer I started dating Susie; that job I had in town. The pleasure these songs—these records of experience—confer is a function of their simultaneous specificity and collectivity (yes, I was in high school then too, or no, I wasn't, but I understand because I had a Susie of my own). We all have a special affection for the music we think of as being a part of our time, broadly construed, but its value comes from a recognition that its uniqueness has boundaries. We both widen and deepen our experience by considering those before and after moments and what makes them so, which is what history is all about.

In the larger sweep of human experience, the particular times and places considered in these pages are not especially important ones. The setting of this story is the United States in the closing decades of the twentieth century, what might be termed the Indian Summer of the American Empire—a time in which a nation, having experienced intimations of decline, flowered in a moment of mortal splendor expressed in the music of a pair of musicians of similar backgrounds and comparable temperaments who managed to express shared feelings with unusual acuity and durability. If the perceptions recorded here are imperfect (what perceptions are not?), they may nevertheless be useful in the construction of subsequent understanding and meaning. With that in mind, let's drop the needle and listen.

AUTHOR'S NOTE I: GAUGING SUCCESS

WHAT MAKES A piece of popular culture count as popular? The answer can be surprisingly complicated, especially in the case of popular music—a term that can also be difficult to define. For the purposes of this book, "popular music" or "pop," refers to what might be imagined as a virtual town square in which many musical genres jostle for musical currency in mainstream media culture. At any given time, a particular genre may dominate—jazz in the 1930s, for example, or hip-hop in the 1990s—even as others (country music, for example, or Broadway tunes) proceed in parallel fashion, with individual performers crossing over from relative margins to mainstream success. To make matters even more complicated, there is itself a genre that can be considered pop in its own right—songs conceived from the outset for mainstream success as understood in a particular moment, which can endow such music with a sense of novelty, but sometimes lead it to seem deracinated (though of course no music can entirely escape a timestamp of its origins). In the period covered in this book, the dominant genre in popular music was rock & roll, the one to which Billy Joel and Bruce Springsteen pledged their musical allegiance, and from which they garnered their most durable audience. But they actively sought, and for a season succeeded, in crossing over to pop success, success that involved an implicit endorsement of their choices and values as musicians—and, to a lesser extent, as people.

But how is such success measured? Is it a matter of record sales? (Not anymore.) Radio airplay? Comparative currency over time? The answer, of course, is it depends. However, there has long been consensus over the quantitative arbiter of who is a star and what is a hit: *Billboard* magazine. Founded in 1894 to cover various aspects of the entertainment business, this trade publication began publishing weekly charts in 1945 that measured the success of individual songs in terms of a series of metrics that included sheet music sales and jukebox presence. Over time, *Billboard* diversified its charts, not only in terms of proliferating genres—it maintained a center with its famed "Hot 100," though the emphasis was often on the "Top 40"—but also in terms of record sales and radio airplay. It's important to note that *Billboard's* rankings were not purely objective: they relied on sampling and a methodology we now understand in common parlance as an algorithm (much in the same way the *New York Times* bestseller lists also rely on proprietary methodology). Since the 1990s, *Billboard* has used more precise measures of sales by using SoundScan sales data furnished A.N. Nielsen Company, best known for its television ratings, and since 2007 has incorporated data from streaming services into its charts. Numbers, of course, do not tell the whole story, and numbers themselves are rarely as objective as they seem to be. But when you see references in the pages that follow that use terms like "number one," "top ten," or some such phrase, you can assume they come from *Billboard,* which for a long time issued periodic catalogs of pop hits edited by Joel Whitburn. Today this information is widely available online, and is the primary index used by Wikipedia, for example.

By these standards, among others, Billy Joel and Bruce Springsteen were major stars and big hitmakers.

AUTHOR'S NOTE II: HISTORICAL RECORDS

BILLY JOEL AND BRUCE SPRINGSTEEN are many things to many people: celebrities, live performers, songwriters, real or imagined lifelong companions. (Perhaps only the Grateful Dead has more obsessive collectors of live recordings and concert lore than Springsteen does.) In this study, however, the focus is on the eleven studio albums Joel released between 1971 and 1993, and the twenty-one Springsteen released between 1973 and 2022. While any number of live shows, some actually released as recordings, are of note, and both artists recorded individual songs that are durable gems, it's clear that they regarded their albums of original material as the fullest expression of their artistry, and where they placed their greatest hope for their legacies. To at least some degree, this desire reflects the cultural forces that shaped them—an explanation for which forms the core of this project—and why their careers are resonant artifacts in the larger history of American popular music.

BRIDGE AND TUNNEL BOYS

FIGURE 1. The (West) Village Green, which sits on the border between Hicksville and Levittown on Billy Joel's Long Island. Joel made the site a setting for a high school romance in his famous 1977 song "Scenes from an Italian Restaurant." (*Photo by Jim Cullen*)

Introduction

Margin and Center

There's a little bit of an inferiority complex,
which I find charming.
—Billy Joel on Long Island life, 2010

We, who bear the coolness of the forever uncool.
—Bruce Springsteen, New Jersey Hall of Fame
induction speech, 2008

OUR STORY BEGINS in December of 1977, at architect, designer, and man-about-town Sam LeTulle's party for his friend Harriet de Rosiere, a vivacious American woman married to a French vicomte. The party is crowded—about eighty people that include a couple of Vanderbilts and Manhattan doyenne Nan Kempner, entertained by an ensemble of Brazilian musicians performing a bossa nova—but the host had difficulty limiting the guest list. "All of New York is here," exults one participant.

"There are too many people I love," LeTulle explains as he squeezes his way through the reception rooms, the foyer, the staircases, and the nooks and crannies of his three-story townhouse. "I never know when to say no."

A *New York Times* reporter at the scene explains this is not a problem for one of the guests, Steve Rubell, co-owner of the famously exclusive Studio 54 nightclub in Manhattan. Indeed, Elizabeth Fondaras, a pillar of the city's social elite, confesses she's never gone to

1

Studio 54, for fear of being turned away. "On the weekends, we get all the bridge and tunnel people who try to get in," Rubell explains by way of the club's stringent admission gauntlet. Fondaras doesn't understand the reference, so Rubell elaborates: "The people from Queens and Staten Island and those places." He tells her that if she lets him know in advance, he will make sure she will be admitted.[1]

Bridge and tunnel. The phrase refers to the fact that those who live on the periphery of Manhattan—which, as everyone knows, is really the heart of New York City—must cross bodies of water by ferry, rail, or car to reach the island, though its connotations extend more widely. It's not a nice term. But it's a highly elastic one in which the disdain stretches in more than one direction. These days, one often hears it in the context of Broadway culture—theater insiders who lament the bland tastes of suburbanites who flock to dismayingly middlebrow musicals instead of more challenging fare, predilections all the more galling because the city's theatrical culture depends on the economic infusions those suburbanites provide. But the condescension takes on other forms as well. The bridge and tunnel crowd is not simply lacking in taste or wealth; it also evinces a host of other vices for which contempt, veiled or not, is understood to be justified. Environmental despoliation. Selfish fiscal libertarianism. And, of course, racism.

Like most stereotypes, these are not without foundation. For the last century, suburban sprawl *has* contributed to climate change. Those on the urban periphery often *do* take a skeptical, if not hostile, stance toward government programs in which they are not direct beneficiaries. White flight really *is* one of the major demographic facts of American life since World War II, a form of racial segregation, which, unlike that of the pre-1960s South, has been all the more insidious for its successful resistance to legal and political challenges. Those who inhabit these spaces can be charged with a form of bad faith: extracting the best of what the city has to offer while distancing themselves, literally and figuratively, from that which they don't like.

However, the picture is a little more complicated than that. Many of the people who inhabit Greater New York—a term that encompasses the four outer boroughs of the city (Brooklyn, Queens, the Bronx, and Staten

Island) and the surrounding counties of the tri-state area (New York, New Jersey, and Connecticut)—simply can't afford to live in Manhattan. A host of factors ranging from tax incentives to educational opportunities anchor them on the edge. And while racial segregation remains an important reality, these habitats—sometimes urban themselves, as well as suburban and even rural, with economies that are mixed and promote traffic in multiple directions—have substantially diversified in recent decades, achieving varying degrees of racial pluralism even as they segregate in other ways at the same time. It also must be noted that these faults are hardly theirs alone. Those who point fingers are often doing little more than signaling their virtue from perches of privilege.

The people we're talking about here are what might be termed a middling sort—generally not impoverished, but generally not wealthy, either. The term "middle class" may be one of the most elusive and even evasive in the English language, but it serves a purpose in capturing a reality, however imprecise. There's an accompanying reality as well: that within this middling sort that has long been an element— maddeningly hard to pin down—of socioeconomic mobility (in more than one direction). It has waxed and waned. And it has been at the center, whether as a matter of expectation or experience, of what it has been understood to be an American.

This book explores the careers of two figures with strikingly parallel experiences who embodied this metropolitan experience—of city and hinterland as a sometimes uneasily integrated geographic and demographic unit—in the second half of the twentieth century. They too were of a middling sort: people of modest backgrounds from the urban fringe who came of age at a time of unusual mobility and who experienced more mobility than most. That they could do so reflects a series of tendencies, from urbanization to relative national affluence, that go back centuries. But their lives were also the product of a highly unusual moment, one whose likes had never really happened before and are unlikely to happen again, a moment of unusual hope and promise for a great many Americans. We should understand that at the outset.

𝄞

On February 17, 1941, about ten months before Pearl Harbor, *Time* published a long essay by the magazine's publisher, Henry Luce, urging his fellow Americans toward a more engaged approach toward World War II. It was a tough sell; the war in Europe had been raging for a year and a half by then, and if there was one thing Americans tended to agree on, it was that they wanted no part of it there or anywhere else. There was consensus that Adolf Hitler was a very bad man, and that England, which had prevailed in the Battle of Britain, needed and should get American help. But anything beyond that was a mistake.

For Luce, it was this view that constituted the real mistake. Americans needed to accept the arrival of what the headline of his story called "The American Century," and to take a leading role in the world. Luce argued that while Americans were reluctant to recognize it—a reluctance which, in the aftermath of the First World War, helped bring about the Second—the American Century had actually started decades earlier. "The fundamental problem with America has been, and is, that whereas their nation became in the 20th century the most powerful and the most vital nation in the world, nevertheless Americans were unable to accommodate themselves spiritually and practically to that fact," he wrote. "Once we cease to distract ourselves with lifeless arguments about isolationism, we shall be amazed to discover that there is already an immense internationalism. American jazz, Hollywood movies, American slang, American machines and patented products are in fact the only things that every community in the world, from Zanzibar to Hamburg, recognizes in common."[2]

Luce was certainly right about this cultural internationalism— which, unlike other measures of U.S. imperial preeminence, persists to this day—but it's worth noting that all global forces have local roots. While the examples he cites are national in scope (Los Angeles movies; Detroit cars), the American Century is in many respects a New York City century, a time when Gotham, a polyglot archipelago with Dutch roots, became the financial and cultural capital of the world.

New York, of course, had already been a major player on the continental landscape for centuries by that point: a commercial and industrial powerhouse and a crossroads of the world for immigrants as well as migrants from other parts of the country. But the city entered a new chapter in its life in 1898 with the creation what we now know as the Greater New York of the five boroughs. Part of eastern Queens broke off from this arrangement the following year to form Nassau County, which, along with neighboring Suffolk, formed what we know collectively as Long Island (a misnomer, since Queens and Brooklyn are actually on Long Island as well). By the 1920s, the first waves of suburban sprawl had already taken root there, as well as across Long Island Sound into Westchester County. The sprawl crossed state lines into Fairfield County in Connecticut as well as a series of counties stretching from Bergen to Ocean in New Jersey. The Great Depression and the outbreak of the Second World War interrupted this sprawl, but it revived with unprecedented intensity in the decades after the war, as an urban housing shortage, growing affluence—and, above all, the automobile—transformed the region as part of a larger national pattern of demographic growth. When two of New York's professional baseball teams, the Giants of Manhattan and Dodgers of Brooklyn, decamped for California in the late 1950s, city fathers in 1962 created a new team which adopted the colors of both: the New York Metropolitans, whose stadium sits on the border between Queens and Nassau. We know them as the Mets. (The city's football teams would soon play at New Jersey venues in an ecosystem known as the Meadowlands.)

Metropolitanism—aggregated communities of people living, working, and moving within and between a cluster of urban and suburban, industrial and residential settings—became one of the most important developments of American life in the twentieth century, rearranging the nation's economics and politics. It also created a distinctive culture, specifically a musical culture, notable for its emphasis on sauciness, variety, and a strong tendency for integration. Indeed, it was there, more than any other realm of national life, where that aspiration was most nearly realized, however imperfectly. This sound is a subject that will be further explored in the chapter that follows.

That said, it's worth elaborating a little at the outset about the meaning of the term "metropolitan sound" as it applies to the topic at hand. Our focus here is on rock & roll, but this is only one in a series of musical forms that rested on a paradox in which the most historically oppressed people on the planet laid the foundation for a series of powerful musical cultures, among them jazz and hip-hop, that conquered the globe. Each of these musical genres branched into a series of idioms (in the case of jazz, for example, that would mean swing, bop, and fusion, among others) that also took on a series of regional inflections (East vs. West Coast rap, Trap, and so on). To greater or lesser degrees, the evolution of these musical cultures was the result of a fundamental sociological dynamic: the interplay between country and city. It is one of the more curious aspects of American popular music—at bottom, a democratic one—that so much of it originated in the nation's hinterlands but was refracted and ultimately transformed as part of a larger process of urbanization. The African Americans who left the rural South and migrated to Chicago over the course of the twentieth century, for example, brought their music with them. But the exigencies of their lives—like experiencing it in downtown nightclubs rather than front porches—required amplification for it to be heard, changing the musical form we know as the blues in the process. But not beyond comforting familiarity. "The city's sounds are brutal and oppressive, imposing themselves on anyone who comes into its streets," begins British music historian Charlie Gillett's classic 1970 study *The Sound of the City*. "Many of its residents, committed by their jobs to live in the city, measure their freedom by the frequency and accessibility of departures from it."[3]

As Gillett noted, this sociological dynamic of less-than-complete transformation played out across the Western world, from Los Angeles to London. But its configuration was unique, and uniquely powerful, in New York City. That's in part because of the confluence of the sheer variety of musical cultures that flowed into the city: not only that of African Americans surging there as part of the Great Migration, but also a variety of ethnic influences from recent immigrants, show tunes from the Broadway stage, and other idioms. As we all know, any number of racial and class tensions divided those who lived in and around the city, but culture in general and music in particular became a realm in which these musical forms blended distinctively in a metropolis at the very center of the nation's media infrastructure. From there, they were projected into the nation at large, inaugurating subsequent cycles.

Perhaps it would be useful to illustrate how these somewhat abstract forces played out by offering a specific example. In 1960, Carole King and Gerry Goffin, a married Jewish couple from Brooklyn, collaborated to write "Will You Still Love Me Tomorrow?" The song was recorded by the Shirelles, an African American "girl group" (in the language of the time) from Passaic, New Jersey—notwithstanding the objections of lead singer Shirley Owens, who felt it was "too country." (She was mollified by the addition of a string arrangement.) Though not direct, the topic of the song—premarital sexual intercourse—can be plainly inferred from its title, giving its otherwise dreamy rendering a worldly edge. "Will You Still Love Me Tomorrow?" went to the top of the *Billboard* pop chart in 1961, the first time a song performed by African American women had ever done so. As such, it is a quintessentially metropolitan story.[4]

Carole King, of course, made the song a hit again a decade later when she recorded it herself in her classic 1971 folk-rock album *Tapestry*. That same year, a ten-minute soulful, heavy-metal version of the song was performed live by a band by the name of Dr. Zoom and the Sonic Boom at Newark State College in Union, New Jersey. The band's lead singer later described the girl groups from New York "as a big part of my background," citing "the Ronettes, the Shirelles, the Crystals, the Chiffons, who put out a lot of great music at the time." His name was Bruce Springsteen.[5]

𝄞

Billy Joel and Bruce Springsteen are not the most successful popular musicians of all time. They're not even the most successful musicians of their time (their contemporaries Michael Jackson and Elton John have sold more records). But each has sales in the neighborhood of 150 million records,[6] has scored dozens of hit songs on various *Billboard* charts, and both have been staples of radio playlists for half a century. In this timespan they have been household names and have enjoyed the esteem of their peers—and, in some cases, like Johnny Cash (Springsteen) and Frank Sinatra (Joel), their elders as well. Their lives and work have been richly chronicled across multiple media, and there is now a substantial critical literature on each. Both have been the subject of academic symposia and the subject of scholarly articles with titles like "Our Butch Mother, Bruce Springsteen," and Springsteen fandom has become a subject of ethnographic study in its own right, most recently among women.[7] Springsteen himself is now the author of a number of books, including his 2016 memoir *Born to Run*; Joel, who planned a memoir of his own, instead cooperated with the publication of longtime *Rolling Stone* writer Fred Schruers's authorized biography in 2014.[8]

Which is why one might legitimately wonder about the efficacy of this study. One could also note, given the climate of elite opinion in the 2020s, that Springsteen and Joel have a number of strikes against them: White, male, Baby Boomer. (The only time Springsteen had a primarily Black audience was when he did a show in Ivory Coast in 1988, which he remembers fondly, as he does sharing the stage with Jay-Z in a benefit concert for Barack Obama twenty years later.[9]) Such aging stars have sucked up a lot of cultural oxygen for a long time now, and one can fairly decide to focus one's attention elsewhere. But the appeal of both extends beyond their assigned demographics. Both have significant followings among a diverse array of women, and both have managed to attain a measure of finite intergenerational appeal. Sarfraz Manzoor's Springsteen-saturated 2007 memoir of his Pakistani childhood in Britain, *Greetings from Bury Park*, became the basis of the 2019 movie *Blinded by the Light*. Journalist Fareed Zakaria realized a longtime dream of interviewing Joel, an idol since his youth in India, for a 2022 CNN documentary.[10] In her 2021 hit single "Déjà Vu," Olivia Rodrigo grimly imagines a former partner whom she taught the lyrics of Billy Joel's "Uptown Girl" singing the song to his new paramour. Rodrigo and Joel sang a duet of the song together in 2022.[11]

Both men have managed to retain an element of cultural currency well into their seventies. Joel has not released a studio album since 1993 but remains a favorite on the concert circuit. Since 2014 he has had a monthly residency at New York's Madison Square Garden that has consistently sold out. He commutes to these shows from his Long Island home by helicopter, earning in excess of a million dollars a night.[12] Springsteen also remains a high-profile performer globally (he's more popular in Europe than the United States), and has been a remarkably prolific recording artist. In 2020, he became the first pop star to have a top-five album over six decades.[13] Admittedly, many of those records struggle to sell hundreds of thousands of copies in contrast to the tens of millions of his biggest hits. But his consistency is truly remarkable, and his productivity stands in notable contrast to Joel, who on more than one occasion has described songwriting as a painful encounter with "this big black beast with 88 teeth."[14]

Actually, there are some who, granting that both are figures of great notoriety, may have trouble accepting the notion that Billy Joel—even if he's sold more records—can really be accepted as Springsteen's peer. (The two can be plausibly described as friends, appearing together at least a dozen times since 1974; Joel built a motorcycle for Springsteen that broke down near Springsteen's home in New Jersey in 2016.)[15] Bruce Springsteen is one of the most admired musicians—one of the most admired people—in American life. Billy Joel, well, not so much.

Indeed, while Joel has garnered a fair share of approbation—including rapid entry into the Rock & Roll Hall of Fame upon eligibility in 1999 and Kennedy Center Honors at the White House in 2013—it is also true that he has been the subject of some truly striking critical venom. This was true when Joel was in his recording heyday—leading Joel, unwisely, to read bad reviews aloud and tear them up onstage—but, perhaps remarkably, such disdain has intensified in the years since. In 2002, Chuck Klosterman, a Generation X critic best known for his 2003 book *Sex, Drugs and Cocoa Puffs*, in which there is a chapter-long reappraisal of Joel that praises him with faint damnation, published a long profile of Joel in the *New York Times Magazine* in which he quotes the self-appointed dean of rock critics, longtime *Village Voice* writer Robert Christgau. "He just doesn't get it," Christgau told Klosterman. "The person I compare Billy Joel to is Irving Berlin; that's the positive side of what he does." [Berlin's legacy for Joel and Springsteen will be further explored in chapter 1.] "But Billy Joel also has a grandiosity that Irving Berlin never got near. That's what's wrong with him. If he wanted to be a humble tunesmith—a 'piano man,' if you will—he would be a lot better off. But he's not content with that. He wants something grander. And that pretentious side infects not only his bad and mediocre work, but also his best work." A similarly mixed-to-negative appraisal came from music critic Jody Rosen, who wrote of Joel's "squandered genius" in a 2005 essay in *Slate*.[16]

A good deal less temperate is Ron Rosenbaum's 2009 takedown of Joel, also in *Slate*, which bears the headline, "the worst pop singer ever." Rosenbaum eviscerates Joel for what he calls "the unearned contempt" that laces through his music—and not, as Joel has sometimes claimed, because he's not an especially photogenic or charismatic person. But Rosenbaum is not content to leave it there. "He *was* terrible, he *is* terrible, he always *will be* terrible. Anodyne, sappy, superficial, derivative, fraudulently rebellious," the critic, a native Long Islander, writes. "Billy Joel, they can't stand you because *of your music*; because of your stupid, smug attitude; because of the way you ripped off your betters to produce music that rarely reaches the level even of mediocrity. It's not that they dislike anything *exterior* about you. They dislike you because of who you really are inside. They dislike you for being you. At a certain point, consistent aggressive badness justifies profound hostility. They hate you just the way you are."[17]

Hostility toward Joel can also seep into hostility toward his fans. His work has been described "the musical equivalent of the strip mall—just one more reason the great unwashed can't be trusted to think for themselves," Washington *Post* writer Fred Ahrens noted of attitudes toward Joel's constituency in 1998. "Left to their own devices, they'll choose imitation over authenticity. Between the lines of the intellectuals' criticism is, at best, a sense of paternalism toward the common man. At worst, a disdain."[18]

Springsteen, by contrast, was a critical darling from the outset, and Springsteen fandom regarded as membership in an elect. He rose to national attention thanks to pioneering rock critics Peter Knobler and Greg Mitchell, who wrote a piece "Who Is Bruce Springsteen, and Why Are We Saying All These Wonderful Things About Him?" for the beloved rock magazine *Crawdaddy* in 1973. He developed an early friendship with biographer Dave Marsh, a member of the "rock critic establishment," a term coined, and whose membership is described, in a 1976 piece that Christgau wrote for the *Village Voice*.[19] There has always been something of a literary flavor to Springsteen, an autodidact who, if he came of age at an earlier time, might well have ended up a short story writer. (Joel almost certainly would have ended up a Tin Pan Alley composer.) In the seventies and early eighties, Springsteen came across as what Marxists would call an organic intellectual for his incisive working-class vernacular. Since the mid-eighties he has tended to speak in what seem to be well-practiced epigrammatic sentences.

Springsteen has not been without his critics, beginning with Henry Edwards's notorious 1975 piece for the *Times*, "If There Hadn't Been a Bruce Springsteen, Critics Would Have Made Him Up." Perhaps not surprisingly, what may be the most incisive critique came from a woman and a non-American, Canadian filmmaker Mary Harron. In a 1982 piece for the British magazine *New Statesman*, Harron noted a dismaying vein of passivity in Springsteen's vision. "The poor suffer because that is how things are, men become unemployed and rob and get caught because that is how things are, and psychopaths go on the rampage because that is how things are," she wrote of his album *Nebraska*, in a critique that could be applied more broadly in what tends to be an overlooked conservatism at the heart of Springsteen's musical ideology.[20]

Whether or not one accepts such criticism—Harron is clearly further to the left than most Springsteen fans—Springsteen comes off as a more extroverted, appealing figure than Joel, whose melancholy suffuses his life and work, charming hits like "Uptown Girl" notwithstanding. "There is a large component of the loner in all of Billy's music," choreographer Twyla Tharp, who adapted Joel's work for a Broadway show, has said. Joel himself has noted, "I've only felt content a few times in my life, and it never lasted."[21] In fact, both men have battled depression, which Joel has tended to treat with alcohol, while Springsteen has treated with antidepressants. And both men have struggled to achieve mature adult attachments, with tempers that can erupt when their prerogatives are not honored.[22] Still, after prolonged study of their life and work, it's hard to avoid a conclusion that Springsteen has grown more, and managed his demons better, than Joel has.

That, however, is not the point of this study. Nor is it to make an argument for the quality of one man's work relative to the other, though it does seem fair to say that Joel is overall the better musician and Springsteen is overall the better lyricist. Instead, this book tries to do two things. The first is to carefully document an almost uncanny, and illuminating, set of parallels in Springsteen's and Joel's lives. Here are two men born within a few months of each other on opposite sides of, and about the same distance from, Manhattan. Both were signed to the same record label; both released their first albums on that label the same year. Despite high hopes, both underperformed expectations in the years following their debuts, and both were in danger of losing their careers by the mid-1970s. Both managed to spring back with breakthrough albums in the latter half of that decade. Both peaked in their dominance of the pop charts in the mid-1980s, when both married models (whom both later divorced). Both faded as pop stars in the early 1990s, though they retained their followings and augmented them into the twenty-first century. Both are remembered as icons of their era.

That's intrinsically interesting, but not quite sufficient. For it raises the question of what Springsteen and Joel were icons *of*, and why that matters *now*. The answer, as this introduction has tried to lay out as concisely and explicitly as possible, is that both were embodiments of a certain kind of metropolitan culture that emerged and flourished in the late twentieth century, a culture that experienced a final flowering in the latter days of the American empire. Billy Joel and Bruce Springsteen were representative figures of the metropolitan rim at the moment when suburbanites became the majority of the U.S. population: they embodied the moment when the margins paradoxically became the center—an efflorescence of cultural democracy. On the other hand, both were beneficiaries of American power whose decline, which they had intimations of, has greatly accelerated in the decades since, to the point where their heirs have come of age in a very different world. Trying to make sense of this—to consider how any given moment or person is a product of change and/or continuity, and which matters more—is at the heart of what it means to engage with the past. That engagement is finally personal, a process of making meaning at the heart of history. The historian points the way. The reader makes sense of the journey. But only after the kind of sustained encounter this little study intends to provide. Bon Voyage.

PIANO MAN

FIGURE 2. Irving Berlin in 1906. The prototypical pop musician in the emerging age of sound recording, Berlin wrote dozens of hit songs, among them "Blue Skies," "God Bless America," and "White Christmas," in a career that spanned most of the twentieth century. (*Life magazine/Wikimedia Commons*)

CHAPTER 1

New York State of Mind

The Emergence of the Metropolitan Sound in Popular Music

They have whiskers like hay
And imagine Broadway
Only forty-five minutes from here
—George M. Cohan, "Forty-Five Minutes from Here" (1906)

G EORGE M. COHAN. Irving Berlin. Rudy Vallee and the Connecticut Yankees. For the student of popular music, it can be haunting to consider how people who were household names a century ago—people who wrote and/or performed strings of internationally famous hit songs stretching across decades—are now almost completely unknown except among historians. Even more recent pathbreaking figures, like Bing Crosby or Frank Sinatra, are little more than vague celebrities to those born, say, after 1970. Here in the 2020s, Bruce Springsteen and Billy Joel are still names that most people recognize, even if one adolescent recently identified Joel as "a famous country singer" for bonus points on a pop quiz question designed to test popular memory. But it's only a matter of time before Christina Aguilera and Jay-Z become obscure turn-of-another-century figures. As Elvis—Costello, that is, punk heir to the original—wrote in his puckish 1978 classic "Girls Talk," "you may not be an old-fashioned girl, but you're gonna get dated."

There's something else all these figures have in common other than perishable fame: at one time or another, they were all metropolitan

New Yorkers. None were born on the island of Manhattan—some were immigrants or the children of immigrants (Berlin; Aguilera; Joel); others migrated there from elsewhere in the United States (Vallee; Cohan; Crosby); still others came from the outer boroughs (Jay-Z; Joel and Aguilera again) or nearby suburbs (Sinatra; Springsteen). But for all of these figures, New York became the crucible of their careers—the place that fired their imaginations, the professional launch pad for their callings, the sites of their greatest triumphs, or some combination thereof.

In a way, this is hardly surprising. New York City has been the cultural capital of the United States for centuries, and a magnet for talent for even longer. But it was during the twentieth century that the axis of popular music in fact shifted outside of New York: it was in blues saturated regions of the Mississippi Delta and the Anglo-Celtic hamlets of Appalachia that became the seedbeds of contemporary popular music, something New York-based media companies were slow to recognize. The city was too important in all kinds of ways to be cut out of the loop entirely, and so it was around the time Billy Joel and Bruce Springsteen were born that record companies began to exploit such music commercially and project it globally. In the meantime, many streams fed the rivers surrounding the city, and from these sources emerged a cultural style—edgy, urbane, and, above all, integrated—that took on contours of its own. New York is to music what Washington DC is to politics: a synecdoche for the nation as a whole and yet a particular place in its own right.

It didn't start out that way. For the first two centuries of its existence, New York was not the largest city in English North America, bested by Boston in the early colonial era and by Philadelphia in the early republic. Its Anglo-Dutch roots set it apart from the more culturally homogeneous New England and racially segmented Tidewater south. The city's size and importance grew rapidly on either side of the American Revolution, however, and the completion of the Erie Canal in 1825 made it the maritime linchpin between the nation's interior to the west and Europe to the east, cementing New York's place as the most important metropolis in the western hemisphere.[1]

That importance was economic, but it was also cultural. Generally speaking, the South was too decentralized to gain critical mass as an artistic center, while New England was too puritanical to permit secular music and theater to take root.[2] But New York literally became a staging ground as young people from the hinterlands flooded into Gotham—an affectionate nickname the city adopted after the publication of Washington Irving's parody *Knickerbocker's History of New York* was published in 1809—and launched the first wave of youth cultures that have been with us ever since. A series of low-priced theaters and nightclubs catered to boisterous crowds looking for plays, dancing, and, above all, music.[3]

By the 1830s, New York City became the nation's capital for what might be considered the first authentically American popular music genre: minstrelsy. Not coincidentally, it was a deeply racist art form, one rooted in a dialectical fascination with, and denigration of, African American culture that White Americans appropriated and elaborated into a very specific set of cultural conventions that came to be known as the minstrel show, in which White performers "blacked up" their hands and faces in burnt cork and performed songs, dances, and plays.[4] The actual origins of minstrelsy are somewhat murky and contested, but historian W. T. Llamon has argued that the culture of "canalling"—in particular the construction of the Erie Canal along New York state's Hudson and Mohawk Rivers—created a climate in which largely Black and Irish laborers exchanged ideas and culture that laid the foundations of what he calls "the blackface lore cycle," from which one can draw a cultural line that extends from minstrelsy to hip-hop. Llamon identifies lower Manhattan's Catherine Market, where New Jersey Blacks and Long Island Whites would mingle, as a key nexus of this culture.[5] Wherever it originated, it's clear that minstrelsy, which was widely performed throughout the United States and abroad, became a bona fide pop music industry centered in New York, and that the composers of minstrel songs, like Stephen Foster ("Camptown Races"; "Oh! Susanna") and Dan Emmett ("Dixie"; "Blue-Tail Fly") became beloved figures who laid the foundations for what has come to be known as the American

Songbook—a canonical body of work that has been recorded, adapted, and revised countless times across time and genre.

Along with Africa, Europe was also an important source of what would become distinctively American music. All through the nineteenth century, light opera was exceptionally popular across classes and across regions, with Italian composers such as Giuseppe Verdi and Vincenzo Bellini especially beloved. In 1850, the shrewd cultural impresario P.T. Barnum sponsored a tour for opera singer Jenny Lind—"The Swedish Nightingale"—who took the nation by storm, raised large sums for charity, and was promoted with merchandise that included gloves, hats, and shawls. It was only at the end of the nineteenth century that a class-based distinction between "high" and "low" culture began to emerge, but it's one that has been increasingly effaced since the end of the twentieth.[6] Billy Joel—who has routinely folded classical music allusions and flourishes into pop songs with an African American foundation—is but one example of songwriters who would fuse them in the national musical tradition. (Joel began a 2022 concert in Greenwich, Connecticut by playing a snippet of Beethoven's 9th Symphony, which whose chords seamlessly resolved into his 1978 hit "My Life.")

It's important to remember that for most of human history, the only way to experience music was in live performance. The growth of New York's theatrical culture was an important indication of a tendency to commodify and deliver entertainment on a wider scale, as theaters became larger and tours could sprawl more widely, thanks to new communications technologies like rail and telegraph. It was in this period that it began to be possible to speak of something we have come to know as popular culture, which one of its renowned scholars, Lawrence Levine, dubbed "the folklore of industrial society."[7]

The main way music was distributed before the advent of sound recording was through sheet music, which, like so much else, was increasingly commodified in the late nineteenth century. The growth of an American middle class—one which, like Great Britain, and in contrast to much of the rest of the world, began to cluster as the edge of cities in a new ecology of suburbs[8]—was accompanied by the rise of sufficient disposable income to promote the sale of musical instruments, notably pianos, that became staples of bourgeois homes. Music publishers employed "pluggers," talented young musicians who performed songs to generate sales. Partially as a result, particular compositions began to enjoy bursts of popularity; the 1892 song "After the Ball," by composer Charles K. Harris, sold millions of copies and can be considered the first modern pop hit. Harris wrote the song in a district of midtown Manhattan known as Tin Pan Alley, reputedly named by the noise generated by songwriting musicians. It became home base for an important stream of popular music and a pillar of the city's metropolitan music scene in the decades that followed.

Tin Pan Alley was one of three legs of the pop music stool in Greater New York at the turn of the new century. The other two were the city's theater scene, and the rising impact of Black music in the form of ragtime and jazz. By the 1920s, all three had coalesced to create a vibrant musical culture that was both distinctive and highly influential.

The theater scene in New York was a varied one that included minstrel shows, burlesque, concert saloons, vaudeville, and so-called "legitimate" theater of more ambitious and expensive fare centered on Broadway. They comprised some combination of dancing, acting, comedy, and, of course, singing. At the turn of the century, the famous Irish American team of Ned Harrigan and Tony Hart laid the foundations for modern musical theater with ethnic satires that would seem dated or even offensive today but often bridged communities and informed immigrants of each other's cultures. George M. Cohan dominated Broadway theater with patriotic shows beginning with *Little Johnny Jones* (1904) that spawned a series of hits that became pop standards such as "Give My Regards to Broadway," "You're a Grand Old Flag," and the World War I anthem "Over There."

Cohan, who hailed from Rhode Island, also noticed that city life was populated by those whose daily presence was temporary. Such people were typically a subject of scorn, sometimes called "rubes" because so many of them seemed to be named Reuben. In the title song of his 1906 musical *Forty-Five Minutes from Broadway*, Cohan described the suburb of New Rochelle, in city-adjacent Westchester

County, as "the place where the real rubens dwell." The government of New Rochelle, which was itself chartered as a city in 1889, threatened to sue Cohan for slandering residents with the description that they had hay in their whiskers, and the inaccurate statement that it only had one café. Its government reversed course in 1959, when the mayor's office issued a proclamation stating that "this delightful work did so much to make New Rochelle nationally and favorably known" in honor of a television production aired in the popular *Omnibus* program hosted by British journalist Alistair Cooke.[9] New Rochelle would soon become the very emblem of suburbia as the setting for *The Dick Van Dyke Show* (1961–1966).

"Forty-Five Minutes from Broadway" was only one of a number of songs that noted those on the urban fringe. A 1908 novelty tune advised a "sunburned farmer's sunburned son" to "take plenty of shoes" if he planned to make his fortune in Gotham. The 1914 song "When He Goes to New York Town" described a pious town elder whose rectitude slackens once he reaches the city. And in the 1915 song "On the 5:15," a New Jersey commuter finds himself shut out of his house by his angry wife when he misses his train because he went and had a few drinks.[10]

Other migrants to the city were more permanent. The massive demographic event known as the Great Migration, in which millions of African Americans moved from the South to the North and from the country to the city, had a major impact on Greater New York. The city had always been the home of a significant Black population (as, for that matter, was New Rochelle, an enclave for free Blacks since the eighteenth century).[11] But this new influx of residents would have a large and durable effect on the city and its environs.

The first of a series of twentieth-century black pop musical sensations, ragtime, was kicked off by St. Louis native Scott Joplin, whose "Maple Leaf Rag" (1899) was a huge hit. Joplin relocated to New York in 1907 and did some important work there before dying and being buried, impoverished, in Queens.[12] (Billy Joel recorded an affectionate tribute to Joplin in his 1974 song "Root Beer Rag.") Ragtime, in turn, was a transitional genre in the emergence of jazz, which by the

1920s had become the dominant popular idiom in the nation's musical culture, and a symbol of American cultural vitality in the world at large.

Jazz, of course, was originally a Southern genre whose cradle was New Orleans, a city with a large Black population, a surfeit of musical instruments (in part because the city was a naval base in which martial music was important), and a rich gumbo of Mississippi Delta and Caribbean influences. But jazz spread, evolved, and blended with other musical genres rapidly in Northern cities, New York principal among them. Black migration to New York was especially pronounced in Harlem, which by the 1920s had become the capital of Black America, and an important base of operation for African American entertainers. Cab Calloway and Duke Ellington, who grew up in Baltimore and Washington DC respectively, became fixtures of Harlem's fabled Cotton Club, as did Brooklyn native Lena Horne.

Though jazz was not a major influence on Bruce Springsteen or Billy Joel, it did figure in the work of both. Springsteen's 1974 album *The Wild, the Innocent and the E Street Shuffle* bears clear jazz influences in the chordal structure of many songs and their emphasis on improvisation (in part due to the work of pianist David Sancious, who went on to have a distinguished jazz career). Joel incorporated such jazz elements into a number of songs on his 1978 album *52nd Street*—whose title refers to a cluster of mid-century jazz clubs in Manhattan—as well as *The Bridge* (1986).

For Joel and Springsteen, however, the main line of their musical genealogy comes from Tin Pan Alley. The key figure here is Irving Berlin, who over the course of a long life that stretched from 1888 to 1989 showed an extraordinary capacity for absorbing and refracting musical styles and creating a mainstream musical culture in the twentieth century. He was also able to cater an accelerating marketplace for hit songs that came and went more quickly in an age of mechanical reproduction. Berlin, born Israel Baline, immigrated to the Lower East Side of Manhattan from Russia when he was five years old. Despite lacking a formal training, he showed a musical aptitude early and got a job as a song plugger before getting hired to actually churn out his own material. His 1911 breakthrough hit, "Alexander's Rag-time Band," established a musical template that would become commonplace in the twentieth century: White—if Jewish could be considered White in 1911—artists adapting Black musical styles with a distinctive spin. Berlin's adaptive capacity was also evident in his secularized take on the ultimate Christian holiday, "White Christmas" (1942). His patriotic tune "God Bless America," like "White Christmas," was written decades before it became a standard. Berlin was mostly a songwriter, but he performed as a singer into the 1960s.[13]

For the most part, however, Tin Pan Alley artists—who also included urbane figures such as Cole Porter, Howard Arlen, and Johnny Mercer—were primarily composers. In New York and the country at large, *songs*, not records, were primary. Though sound recording dates back to the 1870s, when Thomas Edison developed it as a business tool to aid stenography, records did not really become a major factor in the music industry until well into the 1920s. There are a number of reasons for this. One is that recording quality was generally poor. Another was that the nascent radio industry, which consolidated as an entertainment medium in the 1920s, was viewed as a competitor by record companies—if radio stations played records for free, they reasoned, consumers would have no incentive to buy the song. Such concerns drove the creation of the American Society of Composers, Arrangers and Publishers (ASCAP) in 1914, which successfully organized to ensure musicians were compensated for their work, like when it was carried over the airwaves.

In terms of musical performance, the dominant vocal style for the first two decades of the twentieth century was that of "belters" like stage and screen star Al Jolson, whose ability to project his voice was considered an important part of his talent.[14] However, technology—specifically the development of the microphone—played an important role in changing this equation in the 1920s and 1930s. The emphasis now shifted from sheer vocal power to an ability to convey personality and intimacy. The first major figure to exploit such possibilities was Rudy Vallee, a native of Vermont who attended Yale before relocating to New York. Vallee was a creature of a nascent national radio culture stitched together by strings of local stations arranged into networks, on which he performed with his band, the Connecticut Yankees, culminating in his own weekly radio show on NBC, which ran from 1929 to 1939. Vallee was a so-called "crooner" whose good looks, elegant fashion, and magnetic personality were conveyed in his warm tenor voice, which was reputedly attractive to young women. But Vallee was also criticized as a lightweight whose voice could only carry live when he sang through a megaphone. As such, he was the first in a string of teen idols in American history, and the first of many who managed to extend their careers by parlaying their celebrity into film, television, and other media.

The key figure in the emergence of modern pop music is Bing Crosby. For those born in the second half of the twentieth century, Crosby could seem a dated, hopelessly bland figure (which is why some were shocked when David Bowie, who remains an embodiment of avant-garde even after his death in 2016, chose to perform an exquisite duet of "The Little Drummer Boy" and "Peace on Earth" with Crosby shortly before Crosby's own death in 1977).[15] But Crosby was really the first figure in popular music to make records that are recognizably modern, absorbing elements from contemporary jazz and filtering them into a deeply natural idiom that sounds like a spontaneous expression of everyday life rather than the self-conscious performance of the belters. "Bing heralded the end of the song-pluggers and the tyranny of sheet music—although he appeared on more sheet music covers than anyone else," his premier biographer, Gary Giddins, has written. "Neutral or detached renditions designed to boost the song gave way to individualized interpretations." Giddins illustrated the point with Jolson: "Jolson threw himself at listeners; Crosby made his listeners come to him. Jolson inspired them to cheer him; Crosby seduced them into contemplation."[16] His 1944 reading of Berlin's "White Christmas," recorded during a war when many Americans were abroad and could not return home, remains the definitive one to this day. Crosby, whose career stretched from the 1920s to the 1970s, was originally from Tacoma, Washington, and flopped when he first came to New York in 1926. But by 1931 he broke records with a ten-week stint at the city's Paramount Theater, and in the years following World War II became a superstar on radio, records, and film. At his peak, he was not simply an entertainer, but an embodiment of the nation's values as it came into its pre-eminence. "Bing was quintessentially American, cool and upbeat, never smug or superior," Giddins explains. "He looked down on no one and up to no one. In an age when other nations invested in despots, America could feel proud not only of Bing but of its pride in Bing."[17]

Crosby had a passionate fan who would ultimately supplant him: Frank Sinatra.[18] Born in 1915 to Italian immigrants in Hoboken, New Jersey, the Sinatras temporarily adopted the surname "O'Brien" as a badge of respectability—which, given the lowly status of the Irish for much of American history, is remarkable testimonial of the nation's absorptive power. Sinatra's mother, Dolly, was a driven, popular, and shrewd figure who expertly steered her son through inchoate ambitions that eventually centered on music. After winning a singing contest on a 1935 radio show, Sinatra began his ascent as a singing sideman in the big bands that dominated the 1930s and early 1940s. His breakthrough hit, "I'll Be Seeing You," was perfectly timed in 1942 to resonate with soldiers going overseas to fight World War II and turned him into a teen idol who caused riots at the same Paramount Theater that Crosby filled a few years earlier.

Sinatra was clearly the heir of Crosby, but his own contributions to popular music were tremendous. "I was a big fan of Bing's," he later told his daughter Nancy (whose 1966 hit "These Boots Were Made for Walking" remains a pop classic). "But I never wanted to sing like him, because every kid on the block was boo-boo-booing like Crosby. I wanted to be a different kind of singer."[19] In the years that followed, it became clear what this meant. Like Crosby, Sinatra cultivated a naturalistic singing style—indeed, he is widely regarded as having invented modern vocal phrasing in his seemingly off-hand slang and expressions. But while Crosby was a personification of cool, Sinatra ran hot: there was an emotional intensity to his work that his elegance would never entirely contain.

FIGURE 3. Portrait of Frank Sinatra at Liederkranz Hall, New York, 1947. With his career at its nadir around the time Billy Joel and Bruce Springsteen were born, Sinatra reinvented himself—and popular music—by pioneering the concept of releasing collections of songs on long-playing vinyl records whose whole was greater than the sum of its parts. The effect was like a set of photographs—a musical album, so to speak. *(William Gottlieb, Wikimedia Commons)*

Sinatra is an important figure in the context of Billy Joel and Bruce Springsteen's careers. For Joel, Sinatra was a bona fide musical model who shaped his songwriting aesthetics. Though Sinatra never recorded it, Joel's 1975 song "New York State of Mind" is quintessentially Sinatraesque in its theme, structure, and phrasing, anticipating Sinatra's last big hit, "New York, New York," the title song from the 1977 Martin Scorsese film originally recorded by Liza Minelli. (Sinatra's peer and friend Tony Bennett has performed "New York State of Mind" with Joel a number of times; there are multiple versions online, including one at the Frank Sinatra School of the Arts in Queens that was founded by Bennett, a Queens native.[20]) Sinatra *did* record Joel's 1977 hit "Just the Way You Are" for his 1980 album *Trilogy*—and, as was typical, stamped it in his own inimitable way with phrasing that's in marked contrast with the original. In 2007, long after he ceased making albums, Joel reunited with producer Phil Ramone to record a rare new song, "All My Life," rendered in a distinctly Sinatra mode, complete with fedora and loosened tie in the video he made for it.[21]

For Springsteen, Sinatra's influence was more broadly cultural: he was the ultimate metropolitan in being born on the wrong side of the Hudson River, imagining a life on the other side of it, and becoming a star in a way that managed to straddle both. Sinatra was also an important role model as an Italian American who could, again, successfully embody both identities without a fundamental sacrifice of either. "That's Frank Sinatra," he would remember his mother telling him. "He's from New Jersey." As his own fame crested, Springsteen more frequently invoked and honored Sinatra. He sang a cover version of a song, "Angel Eyes," widely associated with Sinatra, in 1995, was on hand to honor him at a gala for Sinatra's eightieth birthday, and attended Sinatra's funeral three years later. ("It's about time, kid," Sinatra said upon meeting him.) As Springsteen said in a 2008 tribute for the New Jersey Hall of Fame and on other occasions, "Frank Sinatra owned New Jersey, but he lent me a little piece of it along the shore." In 2021, Springsteen told interviewer Stephen Colbert that if there was only one song he could listen to for the rest of his life, it would be Sinatra's 1966 version of "Summer Wind," a German song re-written by Tin Pan Alley stalwart Johnny Mercer. Springsteen included a chapter on Sinatra in his memoir, which includes a description of a dinner party attended by Robert De Niro, Quincy Jones, Bob Dylan, and Sinatra narrated in a vein of surreal good humor.[22]

What Joel and Springsteen owe most to Sinatra—what pretty much every ambitious pop music performer in the second half of the twentieth century and beyond owe Sinatra—is the invention of the concept we now consider to be the benchmark of musical artistry: that cultural construct we know as the album. Like so much else, this was a development that resulted from technological innovation. Thomas Edison's sound recordings involved using unwieldy cylinders, replaced by the flat plates introduced by German inventor Emile Berliner. By the 1920s, records, which spun on players rotating 78 times per minute, were made from shellac. Since shellac was an oil-based product, there were shortages during World War II. During the war, Adolf Hitler simulated "live" broadcasts from multiple locations using a recording format involving magnetic tape, which would go on to have a long life as both a recording method and a playback format. The pivotal moment came in the late 1940s when Columbia Records introduced the "long-playing" or "LP" record made of vinyl. These 12-inch discs were less fragile than shellac and rotated 33 times per minute instead of the 78 rpm of 10-inch shellac discs. The LP could also hold about twenty minutes of music per side, compared with about three for a 78, which created new artistic possibilities.[23]

Among the first to realize these possibilities of this new technology was Sinatra. In the late forties, his career hit the skids, in part because his moment of teen idolatry was passing, and in part because of bad behavior—he left his wife for movie star Ava Gardner—a decision that led much of his fan base to abandon him. In this moment of personal crisis, Sinatra doubled down on his music and began taking it in new directions. Using the format of the LP, he launched a comeback by conceiving a suite of thematically related songs whose whole was greater than the sum of its parts, akin to a photographic album of pictures. In a string of records that included *In the Wee Small Hours*

(1955), a collection of songs for late at night; *Come Fly with Me* (1957), an album about travel at the dawn of jet airplanes; and *Frank Sinatra Sings for Only the Lonely* (1958) a suite of saloon songs, he pioneered what would come to be known as the concept album, embraced most famously by the Beatles in *Sgt Pepper's Lonely Hearts Club Band* (1967) and many subsequent rock acts. But it was Sinatra who first made the idea a reality.

The explosion of rock & roll in the 1950s is to popular music what the French Revolution was to European history—a stark historical dividing line. In both cases, the continuities may matter as much as the changes (one reason this particular chapter has been structured and written the way it is). But there's no question that in the minds of people at the time and ever since, rock & roll blasted through a musical ancient régime in a generational revolt that reshuffled expectations, experiences, and sounds for the rest of the century.

One important aspect of the rock revolution was the way it upended Greater New York's centrality in American musical culture. In the years on either side of the Second World War, a variety of regional genres flourished, supported by local labels—King Records in Cincinnati, Chess Records in Chicago, Sun Records in Memphis—catering to communities, particularly African American ones, that would otherwise be ignored by larger companies and radio stations. The audiences for this music were supplemented by a Baby Boom of postwar Americans with historically high levels of disposable income and leisure time to explore this ferment. These subterranean changes would surface into view when a provincial working-class White Southerner named Elvis Presley exploded into popular consciousness in 1956, becoming an interracial emblem of the American Century.[24] His rise fundamentally restructured the logic and functioning of a music industry. Though it would never entirely leave New York—the Elvis revolution only went national when he was signed to RCA Records, based in Manhattan, a transformation you can vividly experience when you contrast the sonic landscape of his Sun Records and the slick reverb of "Heartbreak Hotel"—the business would soon have competing power centers in places like Detroit (soon to be home of Berry Gordy's Motown Records) and Los Angeles (where executives Mo Ostin and Lenny Waronker turned a creaky Warner Brothers into an engine of musical and commercial innovation).[25]

Suddenly, the hinterland had become central. Read any biography of either Joel or Springsteen and it won't be long before Presley comes up as a defining figure in both men's aspirations. "I do remember doing an Elvis Presley impression when I was in the fourth grade," Joel told an interviewer in 1982. "It was the first thing I ever did in front of people."[26] Years later, Joel hired Jerry Schilling, a member of Presley's so-called mafia, as his road manager. In his memoir, Springsteen devotes a chapter of his memoir to what he calls "The Big Bang." Mindful and measured of the limits of Presley's political vision and the tragic failure to fully develop his talent, Springsteen depicts him in Promethean terms: "A 'man' did this. A 'man' searching for something new. He willed it into existence. Elvis's great act of love rocked the country and was an early echo of the coming civil rights movement . . . I don't know what his thoughts were on race. I don't know whether he thought about the broader implications of his actions. I do know this is what he did: lived a life he was driven to live and brought forth the truth that was in him and the possibilities within us. How many of us can say that?"[27]

Presley, of course, was only the leading edge of a series of performers who would influence Springsteen and Joel as they began their lives in the second half of the twentieth century. Many of those figures, a significant proportion of them African American, will be cited in the pages that follow. For the moment, it's important to note that amid these developments, the metropolitan sound that had consolidated over the course of the first half of the century continued to evolve in the shadow of the Presley Revolution and would have a major impact on Springsteen's and Joel's musical development.

Tin Pan Alley didn't disappear once rock & roll arrived. Many of its most gifted artists continued to write excellent songs for established acts like Sinatra and emerging singers of standards like Barbra Streisand and Bette Midler. But a new generation of composers, based in or near the famed Brill Building (1619 Broadway, near Times

Square) powered a hit factory for a wide variety of artists in the late 1950s and early 1960s. Significantly, most of these people were metropolitans—largely Jewish natives of the outer boroughs, typically Brooklyn, who also or later lived further out on Long Island or in the New Jersey suburbs.

Also significantly, these Brill Building metropolitans were characteristically notable for integrating a series of Black and Latin textures into pop music in songs like "Up on the Roof," "Be My Baby," and "Chain of Fools," moving these vital idioms into the pop mainstream. Jerry Leiber and Mike Stoller; Neil Sedaka and Howard Greenfield; Doc Pomus and Mort Shuman; Hal David and Burt Bachrach; Barry Mann and Cynthia Weil; Jeff Barry and Ellie Greenwich; Gerry Goffin and Carole King: these duos wrote the music and lyrics for some of the most beloved songs of the era for acts that included Presley, the Drifters, the Coasters.[28] (Springsteen's 1979 song "Where the Bands Are" is clearly an act of homage to Greenfield and Sedaka's "Where the Boys Are," a 1961 hit for pop singer Connie Francis.) A number of these figures teamed up with producer Phil Spector, whose work with so-called girl groups like the Shirelles and Ronettes made him a vastly influential figure in pop music, and one that had a particular impact on Joel and (especially) Springsteen in the Spectoresque "wall of sound" that became the sonic landscape of Born to Run. Joel's 1983 album An Innocent Man bore clear Brill Building influences in songs like "This Night" and "Leave a Tender Moment Alone," and Joel recorded King's 1963 hit "Hey Girl" for the third volume of his greatest hits collection in 1997. "The nights of listening to Lieber and Stoller, Goffin and King, Mann and Greenwich, the geniuses of early rock & roll songwriting had seeped into my bones," Springsteen recalled of his musical education. "Their craft inspired me to a respect and love for my profession that's been the cornerstone of my writing work I've done for the E Street Band and my entire life."[29]

There were other metropolitan acts of the early sixties that were also literally and figuratively close to home for Springsteen and Joel. The Bronx-based Dion DiMucci, lead singer of Dion and the Belmonts, enjoyed a string of hits in the early 1960s, among them "Runaround Sue," "The Wanderer," and the Doc Pomus/Mort Shuman smash "Teenager in Love." Joel and Springsteen joined Lou Reed and Paul Simon to perform a rendition of the song in 1987. Springsteen and his wife Patti Scialfa recorded a new song with Dion, "Angels in the Alleyways," in 2021.[30] Dion's gritty, ethnic working-class style had a distinctive New York accent, one both Springsteen and Joel would cultivate in their own work and which they regarded as an essential element of its character, whether in the punkish protagonists of Springsteen's *Born to Run* or the pugnacious characters of Joel's *Glass Houses*.

And then there was (Frankie Valli and) the Four Seasons. This Newark-based quartet, formed in the 1950s, went through a series of permutations, but gelled with songwriter Bob Gaudio and producer Bob Crewe, who reeled off a string of hits in the early 1960s, including "Sherry," "Big Girls Don't Cry," and "Walk Like a Man." Though they were New Jersey based, the Four Seasons were an even bigger influence on Joel than they were Springsteen, as evidenced by his 1983 tribute "Uptown Girl."

The Four Seasons were a quintessentially metropolitan act, but in one important sense their success with their own songs was indicative of coming change, a second chapter in the rock revolution that also originated outside Greater New York: the advent of the singer-songwriter as the basis of artistic validity in popular music. Acts like Crosby and Sinatra catalyzed a shift from the *song* to the *record*, but the distinction between the *writer* and the *performer* were presumed separate, the legitimacy of the latter not depending on the former. Beginning in the mid-1960s, this began to change, a revolution led by two very different acts: Bob Dylan and the Beatles.

As with Elvis Presley, the influence of Dylan and the Beatles is a staple of any account of both Joel's and Springsteen's backgrounds, and does not require extensive exegesis here, especially since it will be further explored in the pages that follow. The Beatles were probably a bigger influence on Joel; Dylan's influence on Springsteen—the prolix, poetic man with the acoustic guitar—was so great that in his early years he struggled a bit to assert an identity beyond it, as evidenced by the early promotional campaign that positioned him as "The New Dylan."[31]

For the moment, there are two key points about how these two acts decisively shaped the subjects of this book. From the Beatles, both Joel and Springsteen absorbed the importance of being in a band—an organic unit of musicians with a distinctive style that hung together, on the road and in the studio, over time. This is a little ironic, given that the Beatles had three songwriters and functioned loosely as a democracy, while Springsteen and Joel were the bosses of their respective outfits. But coming of age in the rock era, bands were the basic unit of currency and one seemed most natural to them. As we'll see, the people who managed their early careers actually tried to steer them away from such ensembles, but both were adamant that this is want they wanted, a desire shaped by the historically determined fact of experiencing their adolescence in the 1960s.

Dylan's impact is a little more diffuse but also more profound: he, like the Beatles, but in a more emphatic form, bequeathed to Springsteen and Joel the notion of a musical career as an (individual) organic experience of self-conscious growth. Dylan began writing songs as a folk musician, an identity he brought to the New York coffeehouse scene that made him a star. The lack of beauty in his voice became a badge of honor, a marker of authenticity—his songs were literally his own—so much so that it triggered an identity crisis in the Tin Pan Alley. But Dylan was not content to simply recreate the folk traditions he inherited and expressed; from the start it was apparent early on that his ambitions involved stretching and changing, moving in and out of genres and scrambling expectations—a proto-postmodern sensibility that has become the hallmark of our time. Sinatra also evolved over time, but this was more of an ad-hoc experience, to some degree rooted in adversity, and he (in part as a matter of his masculinity) resisted such introspection as effete. Dylan made the mind an essential instrument of musical experience, a lesson that Springsteen and Joel took to heart.

As important as these figures were, however, Bruce Springsteen and Billy Joel did not hail from an English factory town, the Great Plains, or the Mississippi Delta. They were, and are, New York metropolitans. The music that emerged from this milieu here was an essential inheritance, one they would draw upon as they made their way in the world. Now it's time to explore the more specific circumstances of their origins.

BOOM BOY

FIGURE 4. Bruce Springsteen, Freehold High School class of 1967. An indifferent student at best, Springsteen (unlike Joel) actually graduated that year. By then both were embarked on a musical vocation. (*Photofest*)

CHAPTER 2

Hard Times, Boom Years

Social Mobility and Its Discontents, 1949–1971

> The fruit of a tree shows the care it has had.
> —Sirach 27:6

THERE ARE two major factors in terms of how any given life will turn out. The first is the circumstances of one's birth, variously construed. The second is the time and place of that birth. All things considered, Bruce Springsteen and Billy Joel came into the world under propitious circumstances in terms of time as well as place. But they nevertheless faced considerable challenges.

Joel and Springsteen, who arrived within four months of each other in 1949 (the former on May 9, the latter September 23) spent their formative years on the edges of Greater New York. Springsteen's childhood unfolded in Freehold, New Jersey, where his family had been anchored for generations, and Joel was born in the Bronx and moved to Hicksville, Long Island in 1950.[1] As such, they were paradoxically at the center of the vast urban sprawl of New York in the decades following the end of World War II, where an acute urban housing shortage combined with a sudden influx of veteran's benefits made it possible for a wide range of (mostly White) families to relocate to satellite counties such as Nassau and Rockland in New York and Middlesex and Monmouth in New Jersey. Many of the towns beyond city borders had been dotted with farms (particularly potato farms) in the early 1950s, and indeed some of the earliest memories of Springsteen's childhood involve accompanying his paternal grand-father in selling refurbished radios to migrant African American agricultural workers on the rural edge in Monmouth County.[2] Now such places increasingly became sites for tract housing, notably the 750-square foot, mass-manufactured houses of developer Abraham Levitt and his sons William and Alfred, who sold them for about $7,000 apiece with as little as a 10% down payment for loans backed by the Federal Housing Agency. Moreover, the deductibility of inter-est and local tax payments could make owning cheaper than renting.

The most famous of these communities was Levittown, Long Island, but the Levitts built 17,000 homes in a cluster of adjacent Long Island communities that included Wantagh, East Meadow, and Hicks-ville; Joel spent his childhood in a Levitt house there, a few blocks away from the Levittown border.[3] (The Levitts also built homes in New Jersey and Pennsylvania.) In this huge tidal housing surge of the postwar years, Greater New York was emblematic of the nation as a whole. Of the 13 million homes built in the United States between 1948 and 1958, 11 million were suburban, and a quarter of all homes in 1960 had been built in the previous decade. A *New York Times* article from the year of Joel's birth captures the sheer momentum of the demographic transformation on Long Island: "A potato patch of 1945 may now have 500 small houses, exactly or nearly alike, marching across it in parade ground alignment ... Shopping centers have sprung up where billboards and hedges used to line the roads. Small communities that were established before the war have spread out to cover adjoining areas. Garages, filling stations, stores of all sorts, movie houses, taverns, and small industrial plants have sprung up overnight."[4]

As this breathless description of commerce suggests, the economic picture was brightening in the suburbs and beyond. When World War II ended, memories of the Great Depression were still vivid, and many feared it might yet return. But the gears of the American empire mobilized to fight a two-front war continued to churn with awesome economic force. The United States had 7% of the world's population at the time Springsteen and Joel were born, but possessed 42% of global income, produced 43% of the world's electricity, 57% of its steel, 62% of its oil, and 80% of its cars, soon to play such a large role in Springsteen's creative imagination. The caloric intake of Americans was twice that of Western Europeans. This wealth was not evenly distributed, however. In 1947, a third of U.S. homes had no running water, 40% had no flush toilets, and 60% had no central heating (a lack of heat figures prominently in multiple accounts of Springsteen's childhood, including his own).[5]

There were other worries, notably global ones. The Cold War was at its height during Joel's and Springsteen's childhoods. (Joel's 1982 album *The Nylon Curtain* fused the images of Iron Curtain and suburban domesticity that shaped his youth.) The Korean War broke out in their infancies; the Cuban Missile Crisis and American entry into the Vietnam War marked their adolescence, events Joel later telegraphically memorialized in his 1989 hit "We Didn't Start the Fire." The long shadow of the draft was cast over both boys' lives. Joel escaped with a high draft number. Springsteen initially got a deferment when his aunt steered him into community college, but upon dropping out he received his draft notice, seeking to evade enlistment by claiming he was gay, drug-addicted, and mentally ill in his paperwork at the Newark draft board. (It was actually a concussion he had sustained seven months earlier that was his ticket out.)[6] Both men would end up writing songs about a war they had managed to escape, part of a larger sense of good fortune in coming of age in their time and place and avoiding its most tragic facets.

Indeed, their world was in many ways finally one of optimism, reflected in a great demographic event of American history: the Baby Boom, a generational bulge that began in 1946 and ended in 1964. The national birthrate plummeted in the Great Depression years; it surged in the generation that followed in a way that hasn't been matched since, an affirmation of life in a time of exceptional hope. You really can't find more quintessential specimens of the Baby Boom than Springsteen and Joel. One hesitates to generalize about this—any group of 76 million people is of course going to be quite variegated in terms in all kinds of ways, and there does seem to be a distinct cleavage in terms of outlook, experience, and outcomes in those born in the decade on either side of 1955. But the dominant perception of that generation by members and outsiders alike was, in the words of one notable historian of the period, one of grand expectations. And in that regard, Springsteen and Joel were typical in their hopes, if not in their outcomes.[7]

But as for most people in all times and places, their paths were neither straight nor clear.

$$\flat$$

People the world over think of the United States as a place of social mobility, but when they do they tend to emphasize upward rather than downward mobility, which has nevertheless always been an important aspect of national experience. Our famously lenient bankruptcy laws, designed to encourage risk-taking, implicitly recognized that new business ventures are likely—more likely—to fail rather than succeed. "Everyman's alma mater, the school of hard knocks, expelled at least as many as it graduated," Scott Sandage noted in his 2005 book *Born Losers: A History of Failure in America*.[8] Even the successful often found themselves haunted; in 1840, Alexis de Tocqueville noted that "In democratic countries, however opulent a man is supposed to be, he is almost always discontented with his fortune, because he finds that he is less rich than his father was, and he fears that his sons will be less rich than himself."[9] Such fears are particularly characteristic for the sons and daughters of the twenty-first century, whose prospects—for homeownership, among other metrics of success—are decidedly less promising than they were for the Baby Boomers.

For much of the past half-century Bruce Springsteen and Billy Joel have been poster children for the American Dream. So it's important to note that their family histories have both been marked by chapters of downward mobility intertwined with impoverishment, mental illness, and broken homes across generations that seeped into their own. The point here is not to valorize the myth of the self-made man—a trope that's frequently invoked, and often exaggerated, in celebrity careers, their own included—than it is to point out that one of the ways they're typical Americans is as products of downward mobility.

We'll start with Joel. His paternal roots are in Bavaria, where his paternal great-grandfather, Julius Joel, founded a textile business that his son Karl expanded into the second-largest mail-order fabric company in Germany. Karl's son Helmut (later Howard) grew up in affluence in the decade after his birth in 1923 even in the face of the notoriously unstable German post-World War I economy. But the ascent of the Nazis to power inaugurated a time of troubles for the Jewish Joels, who moved their business from Nuremburg to Berlin (Howard was sent to school in Switzerland). Karl was denounced as "a mortal enemy of the German people and a common criminal" in *Der Stürmer*, edited by the notorious anti-Semite Julius Streicher.[10] His family was ultimately forced to sell the firm for a fraction of its actual value, and when Karl was summoned back to Berlin after the family had left to work out supposed problems with the transaction, he instead fled the country with whatever cash he had. That allowed him, his wife Meta, and Howard to emigrate to Cuba, where Howard finished his college education at the University of Havana along with classmate Fidel Castro.

The Joels eventually made their way to Manhattan, where Howard met Brooklynite Rosalind (Roz) Nyman, from a family of working-class British Jews by way of Ukraine (her father had fought against Franco in the Spanish Civil War) at a Gilbert and Sullivan production in 1942. Howard served in World War II—his battalion was part of the liberation of Dachau in 1945, and he would find himself back on the streets of his hometown Nuremberg—before returning home to marry Roz in 1946. Three years later, she bore him a son. The couple later adopted Roz's niece Judy after her mother's suicide; Billy regarded her as a sister.[11]

There's no question that Howard Joel was, to use a dated but nevertheless useful term, a gentleman in terms of his social standing. The Joels were able recover some of the family fortune after the war. A passionate and classically trained pianist, Howard nevertheless embarked on an engineering career that included Dumont (its television manufacturing division), RCA, and eventually General Electric. His work increasingly involved travel overseas, and he would ultimately divorce Roz and decamp for Vienna, leaving her with the children in 1956. Billy was seven years old.[12]

Billy Joel did not grow up in poverty. If anything, Howard Joel skewed to the high side of the neighborhood in his professional status (a more affluent, largely Jewish, neighborhood of sturdy brick houses was nearby). After his departure from the family, Howard regularly sent child support, and Roz worked odd clerical jobs. Hicksville, while lacking the sheen of North Shore Long Island towns such as Great Neck or Oyster Bay, was nevertheless regarded, however imprecisely, as middle class. (And ragingly White—97.37 percent, according to the 1990 census, though Joel's neighborhood today is heavily South and East Asian.)

All this said, Billy did not enjoy the creature comforts of his father's side of the family. Actually, it was his maternal grandfather, Philip Nyman, who served as his primary male role model, who would do things like slip cigarettes to ushers in order to gain admission at theaters. Joel was keenly attuned to the markers of what he perceived as his inferior status. "We were the only Jews, the only family without a driveway—we had a carport. People made fun of us." (Most of those carports are long gone, replaced by garages.) Roz went so far as to have Billy and Judy baptized in a local evangelical church at around the time he would have had a bar mitzvah, and he attended Catholic masses for a stretch of his adolescence, which would eventually result in the satirical "Only the Good Die Young." Above all, there was the lack of a visible father at a time and place where the mythology of the nuclear family—the slogan of the time was "togetherness"—was at its height. "We were the family that didn't have a dad," he explained.[13]

As he later realized, this was not entirely a liability. The Joels possessed one key asset of respectability in their home: a piano. Howard Joel instilled a love for the instrument in his son, who could pick out Mozart tunes by ear. Roz made sure Billy got piano lessons as early as age four, which lasted for the next twelve years, and music—a wide variety of music—became a lifelong companion. (Perhaps something genetic was at work; Howard later remarried and had a son, Alexander Joel, who would go on to be an orchestra conductor.) Piano was the locus of Joel's life from an early age, and there was no one to stand in his way. "I probably would never have been able to become a musician, certainly a rock musician, if my father had been around when I was growing up," he later concluded. "He just wouldn't have allowed it—too impractical. Whereas my mom said 'Go ahead'; she encouraged me."[14]

Joel nevertheless grew up with a chip on his shoulder, one that he would carry into adulthood. His youthful exploits as a boxer are a standard part of his biography (photos of Joel carrying boxing gloves were featured at the time *The Stranger* was released). "I used to get brutally picked on when I went to piano lessons," he explained. "I'd get these kids shouting, 'Billy, where's your tutu?' They'd knock the books out of my hands and smack me around. So I took up boxing and got pretty good at it."[15] He would eventually give it up, though a vein of pugnaciousness remained, one that did not always serve him well in his songwriting or in his dealings with the media, though it did reinforce an image of toughness that many people associate with New Yorkers, who sometimes pride themselves on not caring what other people think.

𝄞

Like Joel, Springsteen had a supportive mother. Unlike Joel, Springsteen had a father at home for his entire childhood, one who did indeed strenuously object to the wildly impractical idea of his son becoming a rock musician. Ethnically speaking, Springsteen's background is a good deal more variegated than Joel's. But his story also involves downward mobility, in this case on his mother's side.

The name Springsteen is actually Dutch, and this WASP branch of his family was a sturdy one with deep roots in New Jersey. The heirs of a certain Joosten Springsteen settled in Monmouth County in the mid-seventeenth century, and ultimately fought in the American Revolution (where at the Battle of Monmouth in 1778 George Washington saved the Continental army from disaster) and the Civil War, where Alexander Springsteen joined the Union army. Another ancestor, John Fitzgibbon, decorated for his courage at the Battle of Fredericksburg in 1862, owned a house on the very street Springsteen himself would inhabit almost a century later. As his Fitzgibbon's name suggests, the Springsteens had intermarried with the rising tides of Irish arrivals, notably a Garrity family of County Kildare. Springsteen's grandparents Frederick and Alice Springsteen lost their five-year old daughter Virginia when she was hit by a truck in 1927; their saturnine son, Douglas, would battle mental illness for much of his life. By that point, a genetic curse seems to have entered the genealogical bloodstream. As Springsteen biographer Peter Ames Carlin notes, "Both sides of Frederick and Alice's lineage came with a shadow history of fractured souls. The drinkers and the failures, the wild-eyed, the ones who crumbled into themselves until they vanished altogether. These were the relatives who lived in rooms you didn't enter. Their stories were ones that mustn't be told. They inspired the silence that both secreted and concentrated the poison in the family blood."[16]

Springsteen's maternal line was Italian, and it was the dominant strain in his psychological makeup. His grandparents, Anthony and Adelina Zerilli, were both Italian immigrants who arrived at the turn of the twentieth century. They met, married, and settled in the neighborhood of Bay Ridge Brooklyn, where Anthony mastered English, earned a law degree, and became a wealthy attorney in the 1920s. But he also played too fast and loose with his clients' money—and his marriage, which ended in divorce. Convicted of embezzlement, he was sent to prison. But before he went to Sing Sing up the Hudson River (and went broke), Anthony bought a farmhouse in Freehold, where he installed Adelina and their three daughters. Sixty years later, he and Adelina reunited and he spent his final decade in that farmhouse. Their youngest child, Adele, married World War II vet Douglas Springsteen—he was at the Battle of the Bulge—and rented an apartment on the edge of Freehold.[17]

Adele Zerilli figures prominently in every major account of Springsteen's life, and she unfailingly leaps off the page—howling at jokes at her mother's house; dancing with her son in curlers; cheering on his mediocrity at baseball games; retrieving him from scrapes that landed him at the police station. By way of comparison, Joel remembers his mother affectionately as well. But she also seems like a more fragile figure who was a source of worry—his sister remembers Roz refusing to eat; Billy watching her gazing out the window, hoping Howard would return—while Adele was clearly Springsteen's emotional pillar.[18] A peacemaker among her sisters and parents, she seemed to shake off the turmoil surrounding her childhood, and carried that sense of equilibrium into her marriage, where she demonstrated a sense of fidelity and patience Springsteen would later regard as miraculous.[19] Adele found joy in music as well as a work ethic that provided a foundation of stability amid Douglas Springsteen's stretches of unemployment and periodic rages; Springsteen later described him as suffering from schizophrenia.[20] In what may be the most loving record he ever made, Springsteen would honor her in "The Wish," with its references to lipstick, rustling skirts, and the effervescent bustle of going to work. (She was employed for many years as a legal secretary.)

But Adele was not without her challenges, and one of her biggest were her in-laws, who virtually appropriated the infant Bruce as their own. For the first five years of his life, he lived in his grandparents' decrepit house with his parents and younger sister Virginia, named for the aunt who died on her tricycle. The house was adjacent to St. Rose of Lima Church, an institution that would shape Springsteen's consciousness (it would later be condemned and paved over to make a parking lot for the church).[21]

The toddler Springsteen lived without much in the way of routine, waking and sleeping at odd hours. When his grandmother suggested that her grandson need not attend school, Adele finally put her foot down, enrolling him at St. Rose of Lima and convincing her husband to move to a cold-water duplex a few blocks away. The family made a third move a few years later to a larger half-house nearby, where the three generations were once again reunited before Springsteen's ailing grandparents' deaths, and where Adele bore Pamela, a late-in-life daughter twelve years Springsteen's junior and the apple of the family's eye, including his. (Springsteen's affectionate 1979 song "Ricky Wants a Man of Her Own," included in his 1998 miscellany album *Tracks*, appears to be based on his sister's adolescence.[22])

Douglas Springsteen helped support his family in his irregular way, holding a series of jobs that included stints at a nearby Ford factory, a local rug mill, and taxi driver, among others. His dark moods could lead to fits of angry behavior that would bring state troopers to the house. But there's no documented evidence he was physically abusive toward his family, for whom he cared in a twisted way. Springsteen summed up their relationship: "He loved me but he couldn't stand me." He would later tell stories of coming home late in a dark house, the only light his father's cigarette as he drank a six-pack of beer. Among the classics of the Springsteen canon are songs such as "Factory" and "Adam Raised a Cain," which mingle empathy and anger at paternal oppression. "They ain't gonna do to me what I watched them to do you," says the narrator of "Independence Day." Here again it appears Adele provided ballast, as he relates in plainly autobiographical "The Wish": "If Pa's eyes were windows into a world so deadly and true/You couldn't stop me from looking, but you kept me from crawlin' through." All this said, Springsteen would ultimately reassess his relationship with Douglas beginning with his more decisively affectionate "Walk Like a Man" in 1987. "I haven't been completely fair to my father in my songs, treating him as an archetype of the neglecting, domineering parent," he wrote in 2016, when he was 67 years old. "Our story is much more complicated." One legacy that was passed from father to son: bouts of depression. Springsteen reported crushing despair preventing him from getting out bed as late as 2014. But he, unlike Douglas, had medication to help him.[23]

And, of course, music. Here it's worth pausing for a moment to consider the peculiar place of suburbia as a seedbed for American Dreams, none of which was more alluring in the mid-twentieth century than media celebrity. By definition, suburbs are on the periphery. They're remote from urban centers, or enclaves like Hollywood, where star-making machinery operates. But they also provided a relatively secure base from which people like Joel and Springsteen could exercise their imaginations. Springsteen, for example, would pose before his bedroom mirror, mastering poses that he would later make his own, laying the foundation for what would become an obsessive focus on his visual presentation. As a child, Joel stumbled into the allure of performing when as a fourth-grader he began imitating Elvis Presley performing "Hound Dog," to the delight of fifth-graders. The feedback from such experiences would prove durable.[24]

Springsteen's musical passion developed more fitfully than Joel's. The epiphany of seeing Elvis Presley perform on *The Ed Sullivan Show* in 1956 is standard scripture in Springsteen literature, resulting in Adele renting him his first guitar (and wearing an Elvis Presley fan club button on the cover of *Born to Run*). But—like Elvis himself—his early stirrings toward music entered a latency period until adolescence, when he finally got obsessive about it. Unlike Joel, Springsteen was an almost entirely self-trained musician, a difference of real consequence in the course of their subsequent careers: Joel acquired a classical polish and versatility reflected in the deceptively simple yet sturdy structure of his compositions, while Springsteen was closer to a folk musician in his sensibility and the genres he would go on to explore in his later career. They were both fierce students of their craft. And they both faced the same obstacle: the American education system.

$\oint$

When it came to investing in schooling, Americans have been among the most faithful people in the world. Puritan New England, whose settlers placed such emphasis on the Bible—and making sure their children knew how to read it—was among the most literate places on the face of the earth in the seventeenth century. Horace Mann laid the foundations for a public education system in the United States supported by taxpayers in the mid-nineteenth century, and by the mid-twentieth a high school diploma became a norm in American life, particularly in metropolitan New York, whose suburbs were hot-houses of upward mobility. This schooling surge carried over into higher education: between 1946 and 1970, the number of college stu-dents quadrupled from two to eight million, by which time there were more undergraduates than farmers, the first time in history this had ever been true.[25] Much of the surging student population attended the campuses of public institutions such as the State Univer-sity of New York (SUNY, founded in 1948). Rutgers, which, while founded in the eighteenth century, became the public university of New Jersey in stages between 1945 and 1956.[26] All this said, American education has always been riddled with inequities. The United States is an anomaly among its peers in that its schools are financed with local, rather than national, taxes, leading to wide disparities in resources. One result of this irregular educational landscape was the proliferation of private schools—some religious, others more secular and elite—that balkanized the student population still further.

As in many other aspects of their early lives, Springsteen and Joel attended schools that were adequate, if little more—Joel was a prod-uct of Hicksville's public school system and Springsteen St. Rose of Lima Catholic School, and then Freehold High School, also nearby, and also classic mid-century brick. Both were regarded as poor stu-dents by themselves and others, and both mythologized their failures in their work. Springsteen would tell the story of the nun who stuffed him in a garbage can telling him that's where he belonged, and though he did earn a high school diploma in 1967, he skipped his graduation and went into Manhattan instead (much to the chagrin of his family, which threw a party for him in his absence). He would later dismiss his education by singing "we learned more from a three-minute rec-ord than we ever learned in school" in "No Surrender." Joel, who spent much of his high school years hanging out at the Parkway Green in Levittown that he would later immortalize in "Scenes from an Ital-ian Restaurant," should have graduated the same year as Springsteen. But upon learning that he would have to go to summer school, he dropped out. "I didn't give a rat's ass," he said. In a famous prophecy that would prove true for Springsteen as well, Joel said, "I'm not going to go to Columbia University. I'm going to Columbia Records."[27]

Springsteen and Joel's defiant stance against formal schooling was both out of step and yet reflected an underlying confidence that reflected their time and place. Finishing high school and going to college was considered the key to achieving middle-class respectability in suburbia. While this was not something either family could take for granted for their sons, it was nevertheless a plausible hope. Springsteen, in fact, did attend Ocean County Community College for two semesters before dropping out, and the Advanced Composition class he took there seeded some of his later writing.[28] On the other hand, at this point in the American Century, a college degree was not a prerequisite for economic security; indeed, the wages one could earn in an admittedly unglamorous job could nevertheless go a long way toward supporting a family. But neither Springsteen nor Joel had any interest in *that*, either. Instead, they actually believed they could make a living as musicians, as countless young people have incorrectly believed before and since. That they succeeded is of course partly the result of their talents. But it also reflected a prosperous society and a constellation of commercial forces that made their dream more plausible than it ever had been before, or ever would be again.

Both young men had long, complex musical apprenticeships that have been widely recounted and would be tedious to review here. By the time they were about halfway through high school, both had latched on to music as a vocation, and both showed uncommon dedication to their quest to make a life of it. They were notable, for example, in their refusal to take on any other substantial employment (Springsteen would joke that the opening run *Springsteen on Broadway* at the Walter Kerr Theater in 2017 was the first job he'd ever had that required him to show up for work daily).[29] This was possible because from an early age it was evident that they could command payment for their performances, singly or with a band, and because they were both willing to merely subsist in the name of their art. "Do

ROCK CLIMBER

FIGURE 5. Billy Joel at New York's Rockefeller Center, circa 1970. Ambitious and emotionally volatile, Joel was suicidal even as he pressed forward to make a career as a recording artist. (*Photofest*)

you know how long you can live on hundreds of dollars in 1971 or 1972 with no taxes, no dependents, and no rent?" Springsteen asked rhetorically of a time when his fortunes were at a low point. "A long, long time."[30]

The life of an aspiring musician is one of repeated rejection, and Springsteen was not the only one whose life was shadowed by depression. Joel struggled with drinking for much of his life and in 1970, broke and living with his mother, he attempted suicide by drinking furniture polish. He doesn't remember anything of what followed until he woke up in the hospital after having his stomach pumped. "I thought to myself, 'Oh great, I couldn't even do this right.'" Joel subsequently checked himself into a psychiatric hospital where he spent three weeks. He came out of the experience with a new resolve to avoid self-pity but with growing doubt whether he could really break through in the music business. But he continued to hang on, later addressing his experiences in his 1985 hit song "Only Human (Second Wind)."[31]

Musically speaking, the two were very much products of rock & roll's golden era. Springsteen and Joel had both been catalyzed by Elvis and spent their early childhoods marinated in early rock & roll. Many of their influences were African American: Chuck Berry, The Isley Brothers, Gary U.S. Bonds (Springsteen would later produce an album for him). As a fourteen-year-old, Joel managed to see James Brown at the Apollo Theater in Harlem, which he described as making "an indelible impression." Not surprisingly, he was particularly influenced by piano players such as Little Richard and Fats Domino. But their high school years corresponded with the British Invasion, and in the short run it would dominate their musical styles. As biographer Dave Marsh wrote of the local bands in Springsteen's adolescence in remarks that would apply equally well to Joel, "While it would not be fair to say that all of them sounded the same, it would be accurate to say that almost all of them tried to emulate one of the half-dozen British bands: Beatles, [Rolling] Stones, The Who, Kinks, Animals, Yardbirds." Marsh noted "this music was unschooled but utterly stylized, ground out in garages and backrooms."[32] Whether in Springsteen bands like the Castiles, Steel Mill, Earth, and Child, or Joel ensembles like the Hassles and Attila, their music—captured in ephemeral recordings amid the scramble to Make It Big—sometimes sounds like sludge emanating from heavy-metal guitars.

While the British rock of the 1960s certainly left its imprint on both men's careers—Joel would pay homage to the Beatles in his uncannily Lennonesque track "Scandinavian Skies" from *The Nylon Curtain*—such influences proved largely transient or indirect. More obvious, and nettlesome in terms of their future careers, was the next turn of the wheel, which was the advent of the singer-songwriter at the turn of the new decade, represented by figures such as James Taylor, Jackson Browne, and Carole King. Part of the challenge is that both men were in fact songwriters who admired these artists and sought to emulate them, all sharing a common musical forefather in Bob Dylan.

But Springsteen and Joel also felt a strong attachment to rock songs with band arrangements. They both had broader musical allegiances than could be easily classified in an emerging commercial marketing rubric of "folk rock." For Joel, these influences included a range of genres that included Tin Pan Alley, classical music, and protean figures like Ray Charles, a lifelong hero who inspired him to write "Just the Way You Are" and with whom he would later perform on "Baby Grand." Springsteen, for his part, had moved beyond the heavy metal of the late 1960s and was burrowing back into classic R&B while absorbing the audacious fusion of Black and Celtic sounds of landmark Van Morrison albums like *Astral Weeks* (1968), *Moondance* (1970), and *Tupelo Honey* (1971). Morrison's influence would be apparent on Springsteen's first two albums, though it ebbed after that.[33]

One of the factors driving this musical evolution was geographic: the increasing importance of nearby Asbury Park as the locus of Springsteen's occupational prospects and imagination. (And vice-versa: As Springsteen historian June Skinner Sawyers has noted, "Asbury Park is to Bruce Springsteen as Liverpool is to the Beatles and Memphis is to Elvis.")[34] Located about twenty miles east of Freehold, and about fifty miles south of Manhattan, Asbury Park had been founded as an abstemious beach town for Methodists in 1870, but evolved into a carnival resort destination for New Yorkers and Philadelphians seeking not necessarily wholesome pleasures, explored with glee by the young Stephen Crane, who began his writing career there. Plagued by racial tensions—the Ku Klux Klan was a significant presence in the 1920s and beyond—Asbury began a long, slow economic decline in the wake of the Great Depression as organized crime became a factor and the city became a cut-rate day-trip destination less respectable than alternatives like Coney Island or Atlantic City (which were also suffering). A weeklong stretch of rioting in 1970, which Springsteen watched from a water tower, sealed the perception of Asbury as a typical example of urban blight it would retain for the rest of the century.[35]

Which, ironically, made it attractive to Springsteen. Cheap rents made Asbury and the surrounding areas affordable for aspiring musicians. The city's significant Black population—about forty percent by the 1970s—gave it a critical mass of Black players, some of whom, like the emerging jazz prodigy David Sancious and saxophonist Clarence Clemons, rubbed shoulders with Springsteen at the Upstage, a club that attracted serious local musicians.[36]

From this musical scene evolved a style that came to be known as "the Shore Sound."[37] It had a strong rhythm-and-blues foundation, overlaid with horns. Early practitioners included the Young Rascals, best known for their hits "Good Lovin'" (1966), "Groovin'" (1967), and "People Gotta to Be Free" (1969), as well Looking Glass, whose hit "Brandy (You're a Fine Girl)" topped the *Billboard* pop chart for one week in 1972. Other acts included Mink DeVille, which peaked in the early 1980s, and the Gaslight Anthem, a twenty-first century band that continues to perform. One exemplar of the Jersey Shore sound closely associated with Springsteen is Southside Johnny and the Asbury Jukes, formed in 1975 and led by his friend and collaborator Steve van Zandt—another largely Italian figure with a Dutch name suggestive of New Jersey's ethnic palimpsest. Even then, the Jersey Shore sound was relatively conservative, and the audience for it largely White. "We were anachronistic," Van Zandt later explained. "Retro."[38] In the short term, the Shore sound didn't catch on beyond its immediate environs, and what was once a truly interracial set of collaborations in the late 1960s dwindled to the point where Clemons was the only member of what evolved into the E Street Band by the mid-1970s. But the Asbury Park musical scene was the anvil on which Springsteen forged his style by 1972.

By this point, the most pressing issue for Joel and Springsteen was getting a purchase in an industry with high barriers for entry once you got beyond the local audiences that had sustained them. By the time they would have been college graduates, both had largely finished an intensive primary musical education, but were largely lost on how to make it in the music business. In their professional innocence, they both made serious managerial mistakes that would haunt them from years. They would also try to change their fortunes by via a change of locale, heading toward the antipodes of greater New York: the massive cultural magnet of California.

Springsteen went first. Actually, Douglas and Adele went first. To the surprise of his son and chagrin of his wife, Doug announced he was going to California in 1969, come what may, whoever else would come along. Young Pam joined them, but seventeen-year-old Virginia, married with a young child—Springsteen depicted her difficult circumstances in "The River," but her union proved durable—stayed behind, as did Bruce himself. The other three Springsteens hit the road with little sense of exactly where they were headed, like latter-day Okies. According to family lore, they made it to the coast in three days, and pulled into a gas station near San Francisco, where Adele asked the attendant, "Where do people like us live?" He answered, "You live on the peninsula," and so it was they landed in San Mateo, where they spent the next thirty years.[39]

For Bruce's generation, California was less a refuge from the Dust Bowl-like penury than it was a Beach Boys fantasy, a land of good weather, good times, and abundant opportunity. Like Joel, Springsteen straddled the counterculture and its skeptics, embracing its spirit (though eschewing drugs) while keeping one boot planted in an older antiauthoritarian youth culture closer to juvenile delinquent than flower child. "I was a faux hippie (free love was all right), but the counterculture stood by definition in opposition to the conservative blue-collar experience I had. I was caught between those two camps," he later explained.[40] The flip side of this observation is that he bridged those camps, and in so doing built an audience. Its ambit was widening—his band Child had built a following that extended as far south as Richmond, Virginia, and passed up an opportunity to play at what turned out to be Woodstock Musical Festival because it had another booking[41]—but his goal was always to go national. So it was that the manager of his various bands at the time, Tinker West, a California-émigré who owned a surfboard factory on the edge of Asbury Park, encouraged Springsteen and his compatriots to go to the west coast in 1970. Not much came of that trip beyond visiting his family; Steel Mill did manage to play at the fabled Bill Graham's Fillmore West, and cut a demo for Graham's label. But that's as close as it came to stardom. California proved to have a durable place in

Springsteen's imagination; he returned there many times, lived there for a while in the 1990s, and wrote a variety of songs that were set there. Though he finally sank his own family's roots not far from where he was born in affluent Colt's Neck, adjacent to Freehold, California has functioned as a kind of foil for him his entire adult life.

The upshot of Springsteen's first California trip (he took another the following year) was a new sense of dedication to his craft. "I had only one talent," he said of his self-appraisal at the time. "I was not a natural genius. I would have to use every ounce of what was in me—my cunning, my musical skills, my showmanship, my intellect, my heart, my willingness, night after night, to push myself harder, to work with more intensity than the next guy just to survive untended in the world I lived in." This assessment led a resolution—one he called "one of the smartest decisions of my young life"—that from now on he would be, to coin a term, the boss in any ensemble in which he played, notably the Bruce Springsteen Band.[42] The immediate result was another stretch of relative isolation and privation in and around Asbury Park as he kept his "day" job playing gigs while developing his skills as a songwriter on his own. But it ultimately led Tinker West, with whom he remained friendly, to broker an introduction to the Wes Farrell Pocketful of Tunes publishing company in Manhattan. It was there that Springsteen met the team of Jim Crecetos and Mike Appel, in November of 1971, which really marks the start of his recording career.

The sequence of events that followed are legendary among those with even a cursory knowledge of Springsteen's career. An ingenuous Springsteen signing a contract on the hood of a car in a dark parking lot;[43] Appel's demand that the legendary talent scout John Hammond audition Springsteen in New York, and Hammond's astonishment by what he heard; Springsteen's signing by Columbia president Clive Davis; Springsteen's early struggles and spectacular success, only to be consumed by three years of legal struggles with Appel after which Springsteen emerged with his artistry and integrity intact: the narrative by now has taken on the contours of a fable. Springsteen, who helped craft this legend of triumph over adversity, has in recent decades sought to temper it, and indeed by all accounts he and Appel remain friendly.[44] The narrative line that matters for our purposes is that of a small-town boy whose growing desire to succeed in a wider world led to a richer (though not necessarily happier) understanding of both.

Joel has a parallel story. His Mike Appel figure is Artie Ripp. Clive Davis, who liked "the extremely colorful" Ripp, nevertheless referred to him as "the stereotypical music biz character."[45] Like Appel, who had co-written the 1971 hit "Doesn't Somebody Want to Be Wanted" for the Partridge Family, Ripp, a native of Queens, was a singer, songwriter, and producer on the fringes of the Brill Building crowd who founded a record label, Kama Sutra, that enjoyed modest success. Joel had begun to think that his most promising path future might be as a songwriter for other people, but was persuaded by manager Irving Mazur that he would have to perform his own music if he had any hopes of sustaining a career. Mazur passed on a tape of Joel performing to Woodstock promoter Michael Lang, who in turn played it for Ripp, who was based in Los Angeles at the time. Ripp liked what he heard and signed Joel to one of his enterprises, Family Productions.

Ripp proceeded to produce Joel's first album, *Cold Spring Harbor*, recorded in July of 1971 and released that November. It's a spare, piano-based record whose simplicity did indeed fall into the singer-songwriter genre. A couple of its songs, notably "She's Got a Way" and "Everybody Loves You Now," were standouts. The latter in particular, whose sly quality edges toward the tawdry, also shows a penchant for local color: "Ah, they all want your white body / And they await your reply / Ah, but between you and me and the Staten Island ferry / So do I." (The narrator notes the woman in question never comes to Cold Spring Harbor, a favorite Joel haunt.)[46] For the most part, however, these were straightforward love songs, including a paean to his sister in "Why Judy Why," by a performer more focused on pop craftsmanship than fashioning a broader artistic statement, geographic or otherwise.

Cold Spring Harbor had a feel of amateurism to it, though the musicianship was certainly adequate. Unfortunately, Ripp inadvertently mixed the album at a higher speed than intended, making Joel's voice sound high to the point of parody. That fact, and the poorly supported tour that followed, wrecked its commercial fortunes, though "Everybody Loves You Now" and "She's Got a Way" appeared on Joel's 1981 live album *Songs in the Attic*, with the latter becoming a bona fide hit single in 1982. As with Springsteen, Joel looks back on this difficult chapter in his career with some magnanimity: "After all the people in the industry who passed on me, Artie Ripp was the guy who wanted me to be an artist. Nobody else heard it, nobody else wanted to sign me, nobody else was making a deal. He heard something."[47]

But in 1972, Joel feared that his career had hit the shoals, and that he was handcuffed to a bad deal. Its royalty payouts for Ripp and Lang were, to put it mildly, generous: by the time Joel had managed to wrangle free of it in the 1980s, Ripp had been paid an estimated $20 million, Lang about half that. Joel decided to flee to Los Angeles, improbably hoping to escape the notice of Ripp, who was now ensconced in the Hampton Bays, a pricey enclave on eastern Long Island. (As with Springsteen, Joel's flight plan was complicated by the fact that he lacked a driver's license.) It was also complicated by the fact that Joel was in a relationship with a woman who had been married, with a son, to his closest friend. She later became Joel's wife and manager. He got a gig at a bar on Wilshire Boulevard called the Executive Room under the name Bill Martin—his middle name—an experience that became legendary in its own right as later mythologized in his signature song, "Piano Man."

As with Springsteen, the story from here quickens. Joel's mentors, however selfish or misguided, did end up steering him into the big time. Ripp's own distribution arrangement with Gulf + Western, which he described as "a platinum coffin with diamond studs," led him to wriggle free of a company with a declining interest in the music business. Through a series of legal and corporate machinations, he and Lang managed to have Atlantic Records and Columbia Records—more specifically company presidents Ahmet Ertegun and Clive Davis—competing with each other to sign Joel to a contract. Joel, who respected Atlantic's storied reputation as a tastemaker but leaned toward Columbia's more burnished history as a pop label, was very aware of his peer from the other side of Manhattan. "Bruce and I signed with Columbia at the same time, and there were a lot of parallels early on," he remembered. "This was important to us."[48] Joel signed with Columbia, fortunate to find himself under the wing of A&R (artist and repertoire) chief Charles Koppelman, who proved committed to building his career after Davis departed.

So it was that Billy Joel and Bruce Springsteen, born four months apart in 1949, ended up releasing their major label debut albums on the same label within ten months of each other in 1973. The facts of their origins, geographic and otherwise, were of lasting significance, even if Joel decamped for a longer stretch to California—he would remain there until 1976—than Springsteen did. Their grappling with their place in the world, in multiple senses of that term, was just beginning.

HAZY PROSPECT

FIGURE 6. Billy Joel on tour to support *Cold Spring Harbor* in Europe, September 1972. Joel's first album was poorly recorded and supported. A contract with Columbia Records offered the prospect of stability, but it would be years before he broke through into stardom. (*Rob Mieremet/Wikimedia Commons*)

CHAPTER 3

Points of Departure

Finding Their Way, 1972–1974

ONE OF THE most important aspects of young adulthood—the very term, while not contradictory, bristles with the tension that makes the experience memorable—involves a reckoning with one's recent past. Children tend to accept their circumstances, especially geographic ones, as given, in large measure because they have little say in such matters. But part of what it means to grow up involves necessarily finite choices about how one will live, and that includes active consideration of *where* one has been and where one wants to go. Such questions are of particular importance to artists of all kinds, who typically draw on such experiences as the basis of their work.

Billy Joel and Bruce Springsteen certainly did. And their similarities in experience are indeed reflected in their early work. But in this phase of their careers, they tended to move in opposite directions. Springsteen was resolutely local in the settings of his songs, focused on Greater New York. Joel, by contrast, was more adventurous. His songs showed a continental range, and his musical vocabulary drew on a variety of genres. Springsteen demonstrated some musical variety as well, though he generally stayed within established (if at times reshuffled) grooves in the rock & roll idiom as they took root in coastal New Jersey. As we'll see, in some ways they switched places over time in their stance toward their native ground, and the contrast described here between local boy and wanderer was not hard and fast. But the general tendencies are clear enough.

There are ironies in where and how they got their footing: in Philadelphia.[1] Radio station WMMR, in particular disc jockey Ed Sciaky, were key in giving both crucial radio airplay that generated a rippling buzz. Both had begun to attract followings with unreleased recordings of live songs—Springsteen with stemwinders like "Thundercrack," a staple of his live shows; Joel with the more meditative "Captain Jack"—that got radio airplay long before they were available for purchase ("Thundercrack" didn't actually surface on a commonly available commercial recording until 1998, when it was part of the omnibus collection *Tracks*). Budding rock stars had long built audiences with hit records that landed on the pop chart—"singles," in the parlance of the time—but this was not really the way either Joel and Springsteen sought to make their mark. Since the late 1960s, the musical culture and marketplace of rock & roll was organized around the 33 1/3 rotations-per-minute vinyl record: the album. While Frank Sinatra pioneered the form, it was the Beatles who essentially institutionalized it as a rock format (there weren't even singles released to accompany the quintessential rock album of the 1970s, *Led Zeppelin IV* in 1971). For Springsteen and Joel, it was a foregone conclusion that the opening statements of their careers would take the form of albums. Yes, there would be singles: Springsteen's first, "Blinded by the Light," went nowhere in 1973 (though a cover version by Manfred Mann's Earth Band three years later would be his only number one song on the *Billboard* chart, albeit as a writer); Joel's "Piano Man" would reach the bottom half of the Top 40 in 1974. But it was the albums—the collective implicit statement made by a suite of songs—that mattered. Like the movements of a symphony, their songs varied in mood and content. But the wholes were understood to be greater than the sum of their parts. And it's in that spirit that they are being evaluated here, specifically in their sense of place.

𝄞

Like Bruce Springsteen, Billy Joel spent much of 1972 in limbo. The failure of *Cold Spring Harbor* in the months after its release in November of 1971 threw his career in doubt (again), and while the jockeying between Atlantic and Columbia Records reflected well on his future prospects, it took months for the various contractual issues to be sorted out. Like Springsteen, Joel was rattled in May of 1973 by the exit of Columbia president Clive Davis, who championed both of their careers. But both received reassurances and got to work on their respective records. In Joel's case, that meant reporting to Devonshire Sound studios in North Hollywood.

Columbia chose Michael Stewart, a veteran folk musician, to produce Joel's album—an album which in effect would be a reset, a de facto debut. Though Stewart was relatively inexperienced behind the control panel (he had only produced one previous album, for his brother, John Stewart), he had deep roots among country-influenced Los Angeles session players. These included the highly esteemed guitarist Larry Carlton and drummer Ron Tutt, a seasoned veteran whose credits included highly influential country/folk figures like Emmylou Harris, Graham Parsons, and Jerry Garcia. Such choices reflected a larger strategy to position Joel in the acoustically minded singer-songwriter vein dominated by early 1970s figures such as Cat Stevens, Joni Mitchell, and of course, Elton John—his primary point of comparison, and a pianist with whom he shared the bill on a series of future tours.[2] As we'll see, a similar mentality underlay Columbia's approach to Springsteen, and he chafed at it, as did Joel. But Joel, Stewart, and arranger Michael Omartian (well on his way to storied status in the industry), were able to craft a record notable for its tremendous sense of range—geographic and otherwise.

The resulting album, *Piano Man*, has long enjoyed a cherished place in the Joel canon among his fans. What's not typically recognized— and what bears some closer examination here—are the remarkable ambitions that animate this record. Considered as a set, the songs of *Piano Man* amount to a notably textured statement, an effort to articulate a truly national musical vision while simultaneously anchoring it in his local milieu and sensibility. Like another ambitious New York metropolitan, Walt Whitman, Joel strives to be both universal and local at the same time.

That's evident—actually, when considered from this perspective, it's downright striking—from the second *Piano Man* begins. The first track of the album, "Travelin' Prayer," opens with Tutt's snare drum (he's using brushes) to create a sound of steady motion, like a train engine moving down some tracks. It's augmented by Larry Russell's walking bass, which goes for eight measures before Joel's piano— sharp, staccato chords—punctuate the rhythm. When his voice enters the mix thirty seconds later, it's rapid, even hurried, and the momentum of the song intensifies after the first verse, when the piano moves from isolated chords to a steady rhythmic presence. And then something surprising happens: a banjo enters the mix. (Not just any banjo: it's played by Eric Weissberg, whose hit version of the 1954 Arthur "Guitar Boogie" Smith song, "Dueling Banjos," was featured in the 1972 film *Deliverance*, whose main riff became a musical meme in the 1970s and well beyond.)[3] The song barrels toward a break, at which point Joel plays a honky-tonk solo, followed by a spirited fiddle. The piece ends with a fifty second coda featuring a twangy mouth harp.

In other words, what we have here is pure—well, it's probably a mistake to call any American music pure—bluegrass. That this is more than a dilettantish gesture is suggested by the fact that bluegrass legend Earl Scruggs recorded a cover version in 1974 of "Travelin' Prayer" that chugs along even faster than Joel's. In her 1999 album *The Grass is Blue*, Appalachian darling Dolly Parton belted out her own cover, which was nominated for a Grammy in 2001. There is something genuinely precocious in the twenty-four-year-old Joel's ability to so credibly capture a musical genre so far outside his immediate geographic frame of reference and yet have it embraced by those with genuine connections to that musical terrain. But part of what it means to have a New York legacy involves a cosmopolitan capacity to reproduce a variety of authentic cuisines, musical and otherwise.

That's not the only reason "Travelin' Prayer" opens *Piano Man* on an unexpected note. Songs of wanderers on the road are staples of the western musical tradition, but their protagonists are usually male. In a reversal of standard convention, the main character here is female, and the narrator anxiously hoping for her return—"Hey Lord, would ya look out for her tonight" / And make sure that she's gonna be alright"—is male. (In yet another piece of imaginative embellishment, the decidedly secular Joel uses off-handedly religious language.) This narrative gender twist is nevertheless seamlessly embedded in a sense of tradition; as critic Ken Bielen notes, Joel's "prayer is reminiscent of the traditional Irish blessing in that he asks things to go easy for her on her journey back home."[4] Growing up in Irish-heavy Long Island may have been a factor here.

Having staked out this roots-music opening, the album pivots to its title track. "Piano Man" is by now such a familiar pop song, and so closely associated with Joel, that it can be hard to hear anything novel about it. As Chuck Klosterman noted in a 2002 profile of Joel, "Drunk people will sing 'Piano Man' for as long as there are karaoke bars, so he shall live forever."[5] Joel himself does not hold the song in high regard—"I don't think it's that great a melody"—and dismisses its lyrics as a set of limericks.[6] Famed producer Jerry Wexler was also unimpressed when Joel played it for him at his Atlantic Records audition, asserting that it sounded like a knock-off of Jerry Jeff Walker's "Mr. Bojangles," and that Joel's piano playing was too busy. (This was not be the last time a music industry insider was critical of Joel's work, though the label still would have signed him had he not chosen Columbia.[7]) But considered in its pop culture moment, "Piano Man" is quite unusual: a composition that blends the melancholy mood of a saloon song, a folky, harmonica-driven pop tune, and a waltz—"one of a handful of Top 40 songs in that meter during the rock & roll era," according to Joel biographer Hank Bardowitz.[8]

This dance of the disenchanted also depicts a quintessentially metropolitan experience. As is well known, "Piano Man" is an autobiographical song performed by a man referred to as "Bill" in the lyrics, which in fact is how people who know Joel refer to him.[9] It grew out of his experience in a six-month 1972 gig at the Executive Room, a bar in the semi-suburban Wilshire Park section of Los Angeles (the bar was torn down in 1978; today the area is known as Koreatown). The song's cast of characters—John the bartender; Paul the real estate novelist; Davy the sailor; and the politically minded waitress who was Joel's wife Elizabeth—are strivers who can be found on the periphery, figurative if not literal, of a city. While they're universal enough to be encountered in rural America (though they'd be likely to leave) or in the swanky heart of the metropolis (if they could afford it, or be allowed in), they are essentially characters of a middle ground. All of them nurse ambitions—even Davy, who's still in the Navy, will only *probably* be there for life—that are unrealized. Actually, their very hopes are a source of oppression, as they are acutely aware of the gap between who they are and who they want to be. "Bill, I believe this is killing me," John tells him, explaining that he may be tending bar but he's *really* an actor. It is both a sad statement of where they are, and a validation that they are nevertheless experiencing a kind of transcendental excellence, when they literally pay Bill tribute in the form of tips and ask, "Man, what are you doing here?"

The subtle but clever trick of the song is that any listener who actually hears "Piano Man" knows that "Bill" has left the Executive Room behind—if not because they're familiar with what might be termed the legend of Billy Joel, then because they're listening to a song whose very existence represents the triumph of the American Dream, a triumph all the more satisfying because it so credibly depicts sorrow and failure. It is perhaps this, more than anything else, that has made "Piano Man" such a beloved document of the late twentieth century pop music canon, where it is likely to remain as a specimen, long after the American Dream is conclusively regarded as dead.

If "Piano Man" grounds *Piano Man* in a metropolitan space (albeit not a New York metropolitan space), much of the rest of the album follows "Travelin' Prayer" in staking out continental terrain, whether in music, lyrics, or both. The third track on the album, "Ain't No Crime," is a gospel-tinged homily on the aftermath of a bender, but warning against too moralistic an approach in reproaching oneself or allowing others to reproach you ("everybody gets that way sometime"). It's one of a number of songs—"Tomorrow is Today," from *Cold Spring Harbor* is another—where Joel's debt to Ray Charles is unmistakable. In both cases, it's also unmistakably derivative, though

"Ain't No Crime" is more convincing in channeling the echoes of the rural South. Joel's vocal also evokes that of Englishman Joe Cocker, another devotee of gospel and soul music who had a successful commercial career spanning the 1960s to the 1980s. (The two appeared together in a 1971 concert in Puerto Rico, and Joel enjoyed mimicking Cocker, reputedly trading backstage impersonations with John Belushi, whose Cocker impression was famous, when Joel appeared on *Saturday Night Live* in 1978.[10])

Indeed, *Piano Man* can be characterized as a musical suite of the open road. "You're My Home" is another travelogue, this one a fairly straightforward, guitar-based, country-rock song of the kind that dominated the airwaves in the early 1970s. It was one of a number of tracks based on that first road trip to California with Elizabeth, to whom the impecunious Joel gifted the song as a Valentine's Day offering. "You're My Home" is reminiscent of the 1968 Simon & Garfunkel hit "America" in its evocation of continental travel (Pennsylvania, Indiana, California: "Home is just another word for you"), and its affection for the country rivals that of the woman to whom the song is addressed. Another song from that road trip, "Worse Comes to Worst," is a reggae workout—Joel returned to that idiom for "You're Only Human"—that refers to a visit he and Elizabeth made to her sister to New Mexico.[11] "Stop in Nevada," a relatively rare piece third-person storytelling in Joel's work, describes a woman fleeing a loveless marriage to make a new start in California. Indeed, the only song on the album that truly seems untethered to a particular place is "If I Only Had the Words to Tell You," a mournful ballad of the kind that dominated *Cold Spring Harbor.*

Despite all this range, there are two songs that anchor *Piano Man* to the suburbs generally, and Long Island in particular: "The Ballad of Billy the Kid" and "Captain Jack." Each was strategically situated on what was once the key real estate on the 33 1/3 vinyl album—the former at the end of side one, and the latter at the end of side two. "Billy the Kid" is notable for its musical ambition; "Captain Jack" for its social critique. Their outsized presence on the album has led *Piano*

Man to be remembered, for all its ethnomusicological sprawl, as a document of Greater New York.

"The Ballad of Billy the Kid" is essentially a musical western (Springsteen wrote one of his own 36 years later with "Outlaw Pete"). This west is of an avowedly mythic sort evoked in movies like *The Magnificent Seven* (1960) and long-running TV series of the time like *Bonanza* and (especially) *Gunsmoke,* which dominated the airwaves in Joel's youth. As is abundantly clear to anyone familiar with the actual story, "The Ballad of Billy the Kid" makes no effort at factual accuracy; it has its main character born in Wheeling, West Virginia, when the real Billy (born Henry McCarty) was a native Gothamite. The lyrics refer to "east and west of the Rio Grande," which doesn't really make sense, given that it runs in that direction—a more logical referent is north and south of that river. The real Billy the Kid committed most of his crimes in Arizona and New Mexico, but Joel has him roaming from Utah to Oklahoma, probably to enhance his continental ambit—and, in all likelihood, because it scans better as a lyric. The real Billy the Kid was famously killed by Pat Garrett, but this Billy is tried, convicted, and sentenced to an execution witnessed by an admiring crowd.

Joel seems downright determined to serve up a familiar (some would say stereotypical) character who traveled light, traveled alone, and in death became a legend. He described "The Ballad of Billy the Kid" as a "nonsense song" in a videotaped 1977 interview before going on to deliver a mini lesson from the piano of the kind that he would later perform on the lecture circuit showing how it was musically constructed from his influences.[12] In a 2006 review of a Joel live show where the song was performed, writer Laura Sinagra dismissed it as "a bombastic throwaway," and even Joel biographer Hank Bardowitz described it as "somewhat jejune"—which is certainly true considered solely as a matter of lyrics and by those unenchanted by the nevertheless durable mythology of the western.[13] Springsteen's similarly cinematic "Outlaw Pete," by contrast, is a highly complex rewiring of that mythology that both valorizes and subverts it, concluding what is essentially a short story from the point of view of an indigenous woman.

The real charm of "The Ballad of Billy the Kid" rests more in its music than its lyrics. Here too Joel engages in a willful embrace of stereotype: after a series of rising notes on strings, we hear percussion evoke the clippety-clop of horses' hooves and a poky four-note phrase redolent of cowboy movies. But the remarkably evocative string arrangement that drives much of the song reveals deeper influences: the soaring major chords in the strings and sonorous horns of Aaron Copeland (who wrote a ballet, *Billy the Kid*, for choreographer Lincoln Kirstein in 1938), the scores of Ennio Morricone (who composed the music for Clint Eastwood's trilogy of Spaghetti westerns), and those of Hollywood legend Elmer Bernstein (Joel has described "The Ballad of Billy the Kid" as "kind of an homage to him.").[14] To translate into academese: "The Ballad of Billy the Kid" is a highly overdetermined and densely intertextual set of playful signifiers designed to deconstruct and reinscribe the signs of a highly specific cultural discourse. But from the standpoint of progressive ideology, Joel's obvious affection for his material puts him on the wrong side of history: he fails to sufficiently problematize that which he depicts.

As with "Piano Man," much of the song's appeal rests on its clever wink beyond its immediate frame. The final verse of the song incongruously describes a boy from Oyster Bay, Long Island with a six pack in his hand. Most listeners assume Joel, who lived for a time in Oyster Bay, is referring to himself here, though he later claimed he was referring to a local bartender.[15] The larger point—probably an instinctive but nevertheless palpable one—was to integrate Joel's experience on the urban fringe with that of a shared national culture. In the liner-note commentary included with *Songs in the Attic*, which contains a live version of the song, Joel describes "The Ballad of Billy the Kid" as "cowboy movie impressionism" crossed with "pure East Coast suburban romanticism."

It's worth pausing for a moment to note the moment of the song's release. In 1973, the United States was wracked by a failed war in Vietnam, an energy crisis, and the tawdry drama of Watergate. The appeal of national mythology was at a low ebb. Joel has never really been seen as a political artist—Springsteen also tried to sidestep politics in his early work—but viewed from the angle under discussion here, *Piano Man* is a perhaps surprising piece of Americana. Which may explain why the album gradually became one of Joel's most beloved works. It may also explain why a largely liberal musical intelligentsia has often regarded him with disdain over his willfully, even obnoxiously, conservative in his musical politics, even if his ability to move in and out of various genres suggests an incipient postmodernism.

Such theorizing notwithstanding, *Piano Man* ends with a piece of populistic social criticism in "Captain Jack," one of the most searing—even vicious—portrayals of suburban ennui this side of John Cheever. It was a crowd favorite from the start; originally recorded live as part of a promotion for WMMR in Philadelphia, "Captain Jack" began getting regular radio requests, which is how it came to the attention of executives at Columbia. A 2012 reader's poll in *Rolling Stone* named it the fifth most popular song in the Joel canon.[16]

Joel later explained he wrote the song in 1971 while living in a Long Island apartment that looked out on a housing project where teenagers were buying heroin from a dealer named Captain Jack.[17] This is surprising in two ways: first, that the "Jack" in question is not Jack Daniels, a referent more likely to come to mind for most listeners; and second, that the song's inspiration was so downscale, given that it's a critique of what might be regarded as bourgeois affluenza (though rich boys have been buying drugs on the "wrong" side of town as long as there have been addicts). But whatever the depiction of class, the force of its portrayal of chemical dependency is unmistakable.

In literally faint irony, the song fades in and out with a churchy organ, conferring a sense of religious solemnity on its tawdry tale of a lost soul. The narrator enters in a voice of wan enervation: "Saturday night and you're still hanging around," he sings in the second person to a suburbanite from a "one-horse town" whose depression leads him to wish he could disappear into a hole in the ground. But the narrator offers no compassion for his subject, mocking the mockery of his snide smile when he makes forays into Greenwich Village to voyeuristically gaze on junkies and drag queens ("it's like some pornographic magazine"). Vacations, new cars, a cutting-edge stereo, fashionable

English couture: none can clothe his malaise or the vulgarity signified by nose-picking and masturbation. Not even finding his father dead in the family swimming pool can cut through his solipsism ("And you guess you won't be going back to school anymore"). The severity of this portrait can be usefully contrasted with Frank Ocean's 2013 song "Rich Kids," a similarly scabrous—and more racially inflected—portrait somewhat softened by the use of the pronoun "we" to implicate the narrator in what he describes. One could legitimately say "Captain Jack" is truly heartless.

What complicates this picture is the rousing chorus of "Captain Jack." The languid verses periodically give way by a sudden rising of voice and melody, carried along by an implacable guitar line that surges like a ship plowing through waves, while sharp staccato chords on that organ chug forcefully toward a predetermined destination. "Captain Jack will get you by tonight," the singer shouts over a massive wall of noise, "and take you to your special island." There's something downright thrilling about it. (It's worth noting here that Joel, who has struggled with alcoholism over the course of his life, seems to write about it with notable intimacy here.) One is reminded of critic Greil Marcus's analysis of the Velvet Underground's 1967 song "Heroin": he asserts that a truly effective antidrug song has to risk creating addicts by portraying addiction with sufficient appeal and credibility to give its message force. Such a messenger "does not sing about, he sings *as*." It takes one to know one.[18] Self-loathing is never far from Joel's savagery.

"Captain Jack" thus ends *Piano Man* with Joel surveying native ground. But the contempt of his portrait may help explain why he spent three years on the other side of the country. Joel ultimately made his peace with, and found his home on, Long Island. But for the moment, he was gazing back from afar, and not impressed by what he saw.

Indeed, in the years to come he maintained his distance, literally and figuratively. Joel followed the release of *Piano Man* in November of 1973 by heading out on tour in February of 1974, where he played major New York venues that ranged from hip Max's Kansas City to Lincoln Center's Avery Fisher Hall. John Rockwell of the *New York*

Times praised his virtuosity and versatility, noting the "overt theatricality" in Joel's songs, as well as a tendency to "court the bombastic." But the success of his shows notwithstanding, Joel was back in Los Angeles at Devonshire Studios in May, getting to work on his second album with a set of session players. Stewart was again behind the controls.[19]

Joel was under some duress. Promising debut albums create pressure for a follow-up, and in those days it was not uncommon for pop artists to release two albums within a year, as indeed both Joel and Springsteen did in 1973–1974. "This is why people talk about the sophomore slump," Joel later remembered. "You spend your youth building up material, crafting that bildungsroman that tells your story, and then, in the middle of abruptly finding success and crashing Holiday Inns, of being a bandleader and wondering when the checks will arrive, you have a couple of months to write ten or twelve heartfelt songs. By the way, the songs about how much the road sucks have already been done, and nobody wants to hear them."[20] (The notable exception would be Jackson Browne's *Running on Empty*, released in 1977.)

This sour, cynical air pervades Joel's second album, *Streetlife Serenade*, released in October of 1974. Joel himself considers it his weakest record—"I have a very low regard for that album"[21]—and the fact that it consists of ten short songs, two of them instrumental, suggests he was indeed struggling to fill it. But two of its pieces, "Streetlife Serenader" and "Los Angelenos," appeared in more robust versions on *Songs from the Attic* seven years later.

Streetlife Serenade is indeed a document of Joel's Los Angeles years. But Joel's Los Angeles has a distinctly suburban air. The album's cover painting, by the distinguished artist Brian Hagiwara, who worked on covers for artists ranging from Luther Vandross to Willie Nelson, is closer to a neighborhood street than an urban square. "I did the painting based on a photo I took in old San Pedro, CA," Hagiwara remembered about forty years later, noting that Joel asked for something that evoked the work of Edward Hopper.[22] The deracinated quality of the image speaks to a state of mind where suburbia is less a place than a largely soulless way of life.

Such a view is evident in the songs of *Streetlife Serenade*. They're most explicit on "The Great Suburban Showdown," an amusing, if dour, account of a young man's (airplane) trip home to visit his parents. "The streets all look the same, and I'll have to play the game," he laments. "We'll all sit around on kitchen chairs / With the TV on and the neighbors there." Dad mows the crabgrass; he and mom host a barbeque. "I know it should be fun, but I think I should have packed my gun," he says in a moment of gallows humor. Another suburban portrait, "Weekend Song," is narrated from the point of view of a cranky commuter. "Pick me up at the station," he tells his partner, looking for what will apparently be an alcohol-fueled respite. "Seven years for the same corporation and I ain't got nothin' to show." "Streetlife Serenader," whose setting seems to straddle an urban/suburban line, is nominally more sympathetic, even sentimental, toward its characters, but there's an implicit contempt in the way he describes them as "shoppin' center heroes" still living in the Eisenhower era.

That contempt is more explicit when it comes to the urbanites of "Los Angelenos." Joel describes them as hedonistic expatriates luxuriating at beaches, on mountains, and in canyons. "No one has to feel / like a refugee," he intones, noting their penchant for "going into garages for exotic massages." Los Angeles is in fact a sprawling and diverse metropolis a good deal more complex and interesting than what amounts to the Woody Allen view of Los Angeles Joel offers here.

He's not entirely misanthropic. "Last of the Big Spenders," yet another blues number in a Ray Charles mode, has some charm (the currency in question is time, not money) and "Souvenir" is a brief, melancholy meditation on evanescence. "Roberta" is apparently a sympathetic portrait of a man in love with a prostitute—Joel reportedly told a SiriusXM radio audience that he one had a crush on such a woman whom he tried to talk out of that line of work[23]—though he seems less sympathetic than pathetic.

Yet for all this cynicism, *Streetlife Serenade* does not come off as an especially dark or unpleasant record. The main reason for this is a preponderance of brightness in the music. Though not as expansive as *Piano Man*, Joel continued to stretch his horizons. Some of this was a matter of instrumentation (like many rock musicians at the time, he finally took the plunge by introducing synthesizers into his vernacular), as well as some experimentation with style. Joel shows off his impressive chops in the instrumental pieces: the first, "Root Beer Rag," is a ragtime piece with a band arrangement—there was a vogue for Scott Joplin following the release of *The Sting* in 1973, whose theme song, his 1902 hit "The Entertainer," topped the charts in 1974. The other is a light, jazz-inflected piece, "The Mexican Connection," which concludes the album. Much of *Streetlife Serenade* features proficient, if unremarkable, 1970s rock that goes down easy a half-century later.

The best song on the album, "The Entertainer," epitomizes this musical paradox. The lyrics offer a grim portrait of a would-be star trying to make it in the music business—rapacious agencies, unfeeling record company executives, fickle fans—and Joel's penchant for lapsing into vulgarity ("I've learned to dance with a hand in my pants"). But the music of "The Entertainer" is marvelous: a sprightly, almost manic, synthesizer riff somehow evocative of troubadours, and an arrangement that includes strings, woods, and horns. The song was the album's only single, managing to poke the bottom of the *Billboard* Top 40 at #34 in 1974.

Streetlife Serenade stalled, even reversed, the momentum that Joel had generated with *Piano Man*. The album sold poorly—ominously, more poorly than *Piano Man*—and was dismissed in a high-profile *Rolling Stone* review by Stephen Holden. "Billy Joel's pop schmaltz occupies a stylistic no man's land where musical and lyric truisms borrowed from disparate sources are forced together," Holden wrote. "Joel's keyboard abilities notwithstanding, he has nothing to say as a writer at present."[24]

The release of *Streetlife Serenade* was followed by a brief tour, one that included a show at Rutgers University where he invited Bruce Springsteen to join him for a version of "Twist and Shout," a staple of Springsteen's live shows.[25] Columbia, disappointed by the album, was nevertheless pressuring him to get back in the studio. But Joel needed to regroup and figure out where he was going—which, as it turned out, was back home.

§

When it came to a sense of place, Bruce Springsteen was an entirely different story than Billy Joel. While Joel was determined to range far afield (even if he kept an eye on his roots), Springsteen was resolutely local. And while Joel looked upon his native ground with an ironic or cynical eye, Springsteen was unabashedly exuberant in celebrating the Jersey shore in the face of its dilapidation. His debut album, *Greetings from Asbury Park, NJ*, delivered to listeners a postcard from a provincial paradise.

He did so in the face of substantial opposition. Amid chatter of Springsteen as "The New Dylan," Columbia sought to position him as the next generation bard of the Greenwich Village coffeehouse. "The main reason I put [that title on] first album was because they were pushing for this big New York thing," he told the British music magazine *Melody Maker* in November 1975, as his career was taking off there. "I said, 'Wait, you guys are nuts or something? I'm from Asbury Park, New Jersey. Can you dig it? NEW JERSEY.'"[26] Springsteen also sought to evade Columbia policy that every debut album must have an image of the artist of the cover—a maxim forcefully endorsed by manager Mike Appel—by instead insisting on what has become its iconic image of an old-fashioned postcard illustrated with beach and boardwalk scenes inserted in the lettering. But Columbia art director John Berg sided with Springsteen. "This is absolutely what we're going to do," he said, forever branding Springsteen's music with a strong sense of place (and leading some to believe that Asbury Park was actually his hometown). In a visual wink, his mug appears on the back cover framed as if it's a postage stamp.[27]

Springsteen was less successful in getting his way with the album's sonic contours, which turned out provincial in a way he didn't intend. Appel and John Hammond held fast to their view—in part because it was the only one they'd really heard at that point—of Springsteen as a rising folk rocker. Springsteen himself wanted something closer to the Shore Sound with a full band. Columbia president Clive Davis agreed that he should be more than a folkie, and the result was a compromise—what Springsteen later called "primarily an acoustic record with a rhythm section." The first person Springsteen played it for was his keyboard player, Danny Federici, who liked it but who wondered, given his bandmate's axe-wielding skills, "Where's the guitar?" To save money, the album was recorded on a shoestring budget at the somewhat cut-rate 914 Sound Studios in suburban Rockland County (named for the area code of its location at the time), with the relatively inexperienced Appel and partner Jim Crecetos as producers—and it shows.[28] While nowhere near as disastrous as Artie Ripp's work on Joel's *Cold Spring Harbor*, *Greetings* does not quite sound ready for prime time by the prevailing standards of the record business at the time of its release in January of 1973.

Springsteen was able to compensate with sheer charm, coupled with a hazy sense of place. If Joel on *Piano Man* was a musical adventurer, the core appeal of *Greetings* lay in its lyrics, which are indeed Dylanesque in their wordplay. Some of the songs don't even have choruses; they're poetic recitals set to music. The opening track, "Blinded by the Light"—"madman drummers bummers and Indians in the summer with a teenage diplomat / In the dumps with the mumps as the adolescent pumps his way into his hat"—was written with the aid of a rhyming dictionary. (Legendary critic Lester Bangs, assessing the song and album for *Rolling Stone* in 1973, was impressed: "It's really bracing as hell because it's obvious that B.S. don't give a shit. He slingshoots his random rivets at you and you can catch as many as you want or let 'em all clatter right off the wall."[29]) "Most of the songs were twisted autobiographies," Springsteen recalled from the perspective of almost a half-century later. They "found their seed in people, places, hangouts, and incidents I'd seen and things I'd lived. I wrote impressionistically and changed names to protect the guilty."[30]

Indeed, for all his insistence on explicitly situating *Greetings* as a document of greater Asbury Park, there's little in the way of specific referents in what amounts to a musical watercolor. The scenes Spring-steen describes—the exultant boy finding the key to the universe in the engine of an old parked car; the interstate biker whose tires stroke the pavement in "The Angel"; the lost vet wandering town in "Lost in the Flood" (the one dark song on the album)—describe scenes that seem local, but archetypal. Springsteen's sole imagistic gesture toward the heartland, "Mary Queen of Arkansas," is grating in its mawkishness.

The one song on *Greetings* that does, however obliquely, seem to be grounded on the Jersey shore is a late addition, one which, along with "Blinded by the Light," was coaxed out of Springsteen by Davis, who felt that the album lacked hit material.[31] This is "Spirit in the Night." Yet even here the locale in question remains a subject of speculation. A narrative of romantic abandon unfolds on Greasy Lake, a fictive name for what appears to be a composite of two locations—one of which is indeed, as the song says, off Route 88 of the Garden State Parkway, and the other at the intersection of Routes 88 and Route 9 in Lakewood, New Jersey, southeast of Asbury Park. There are also those who claim Greasy Lake was actually Lake Topanemus Pond in his birthplace (now known as Freehold Pond).[32] While one could argue that such ambiguities undermine Springsteen's stated goal of giving *Greetings* an unmistakable sense of place, he's clearly inter-ested in universalizing particulars in an instinctively Whitmanic manner.

There is one locale, however, in sharp relief: Manhattan. Exhibit A is the uptown of "Does this Bus Stop at 82nd St.?" where a breezy nar-rator begins, "Hey bus driver, keep the change / bless your children, give them names," proceeding to identify destinations that include Broadway and Harlem (the song is reputedly based on a trip Springs-teen took to visit a paramour in Spanish Harlem).[33] He also cites the *Daily News*, where the latest development appears to be "the dope's that there's still hope." However, the ironic effect of this figure's sheer insouciance is to cast doubt that he's a native New Yorker: any regu-lar bus rider would likely know better than to distract or annoy a driver or attract attention to himself in a space where quiet interiority is typically at a premium. It's easier to be charmed by such figures at a distance—where, it should be said, they should be irresistible to anyone with a heart.

Springsteen swerves downtown for one of the true gems on the record, "For You." Here he addresses an ex-partner in a moment of crisis in the aftermath of what appears to have been a tempestuous relationship marked by emotional power struggles. There are references to a "Chelsea suicide" and Bellevue Hospital, location of a famed psychiatric treatment center, where "they're waiting for you with their oxygen masks," but these may be metaphorical rather than literal. Despite the somber mood suggested by such language, and the singer's evident anger over the end of the relationship—"You didn't even give me time to cover my tracks / You said, 'Here's your mirror and your ball of jacks'"—the mood of "For You" is nevertheless buoyant, even triumphant, in his loving celebration of her resilience. "Your strength is devastating in the face of all these odds," he tells her. And even though he describes her life as "one long emergency," he nevertheless draws on her strength: "your cloud line urges me / and my electric surges free."

Greetings closes with one more urban track, "It's So Hard to Be a Saint in the City." This is the song that riveted Appel's interest in Springsteen, and also impressed John Hammond during Springsteen's audition ("I heard immediately he was a born poet," he later wrote.)[34] "Saint" is yet another celebration in adolescent rebel mode: "The devil appeared to me like Jesus through the steam in the street / showing me a hand even the cops couldn't beat." But it lacks the specificity of the other city songs of the album, notwithstanding references to the "sages of the subway" who "sit just like the living dead." Taken as a whole, however, *Greetings from Asbury Park, NJ* is a decisive statement by an enraptured young man savoring his seedy metropolitan home.

It didn't make much of an impact beyond there. *Greetings* did attract some critical attention, notably the first serious piece of journalism by Peter Knobler and Greg Mitchell for the rock magazine *Crawdaddy* in March of 1973. "There hasn't been an album like this in ages," they wrote. "There are individual lines worth entire records."[35] But *Greetings* sold a mere 23,000 copies—"a flop by record company standards, but a smash by mine," Springsteen reported. He also saw some real money for the first time in his life, even if most of it went toward the cost of making the record. Now he went back to earning money on the road (thirty-five dollars a week after expenses, to be exact). "I was twenty-three and I was making a living playing music! Friend, there's a reason they don't call it 'working,' it's called PLAYING," he later wrote.[36] He wasn't always this happy, however; a series of shows as the opening act for the big-time group Chicago, whose members treated him well, nevertheless convinced Springsteen of the need to perform on his own terms, however modestly. There were record company woes as well; Davis's exit from Columbia cost Springsteen a major supporter when he really needed one.

He also faced looming competition at Columbia from another local boy. "Bruce's star had been eclipsed by the just-signed Billy Joel, whose piano-based melodicism leaned much more mainstream than the New Jersey street poet could ever be," Springsteen biographer Peter Ames Carlin reported in his well-regarded 2014 biography *Bruce*. "What's more, Joel had come to the company through the just-elevated A&R chief Charles Koppelman, who had sworn to make him a success. And if the time and investment that required came at the expense of another young artist, well, welcome to the record industry."[37]

Still for all this precariousness, the conventional wisdom remained that success in the music business took time, and Springsteen had enough good will with the label to make another album. He was more ready to go than Joel was, having compiled a mountain of material with which to work.

But he was going to work with that material in a different way. "*Greetings* was primarily an acoustic record with a rhythm section. That was fine for the first time out, but I had made my living primarily as a rock musician," he wrote in 1998. "Now I wanted to continue the lyrical content of the first album, but to add in the physicality my music always had coming through the clubs. For this record, I was determined to call on my songwriting ability and my bar band experience."[38] The shore now colored the sound no less than the lyrics.

Springsteen had long been an inveterate movie-watcher, and as many observers have noted, there is a distinctly cinematic quality to much of his work. In particular, he was arrested by *The Wild and the Innocent,* a 1959 Audie Murphy Western about a pair of frontier teenagers who come to the big city.[39] (There's a festive carnival scene about halfway through the movie that loosely resembles that of Asbury Park's boardwalk in its heyday.) Springsteen had not given a formal name to the band he had been leading between 1972 and 1974, but it was unofficially known as the E Street Band, named after the address where keyboard player David Sancious lived with his mother just south of Asbury Park, and where the band sometimes rehearsed—and where, as the increasingly important saxophonist Clarence Clemons later remembered in his colorful memoir, the band was often forced to wait outside for Sancious. "This band has spent so much fucking time on this fucking street, we should call it the E Street Band," he quotes Springsteen as saying.[40] These verbal pieces coalesced into *The Wild, the Innocent, and the E Street Shuffle,* recorded in stints between touring from May to September and released in November of 1973. To cut costs, the record was again made in suburban Blauvelt at 914 Sound Studios with the band making two-hour commutes between Rockland County and the Jersey Shore.[41]

Even a casual listener can hear that *E Street* is a very different record than *Greetings.* It's a true rock album featuring a cohesive set of musicians whose collaboration had been honed through touring. This is apparent at the outset in the opening track, "The E Street Shuffle," with its funky, brassy arrangement based on the 1963 hit "Monkey Time" by Major Lance.[42] The prolix, impressionistic lyrics were still there, but the songs were more complex with more robust choruses—and longer. The album consists of seven tracks, three of which clock in at over seven minutes. Springsteen described "Kitty's Back," which comes straight from the Van Morrison playbook, as "a remnant of the jazz-tinged rock I played with a few of my earlier bands." Such pieces were "arranged to leave the band and the audience exhausted and

SHORE ENOUGH

FIGURE 7. Springsteen with the core of what became the E Street Band—Vini Lopez and Danny Federici to his left; Garry Tallent and Clarence Clemons to his right—at the time of *Greetings from Asbury Park*. Marketed as a singer-songwriter, Springsteen always saw himself as the leader of a rock & roll band. *(Photofest)*

gasping for breath. Just when you thought the song was over, you'd be surprised by another section, taking the music higher."[43] The best-known example of such a song was "Rosalita (Come Out Tonight)," an autobiographical rave-up about a girl whose parents disapprove of the penniless narrator, culminating in his triumphant announcement that he's signed a contract with a record company. Yet it's clear that Springsteen's ambitions were not simply to show off his performance chops on a record that could never fully capture the spontaneity of a live show in any case. For example, fan favorites like "Thundercrack," and "The Fever" didn't make it onto the album because they didn't figure into his larger ambitions for the record.[44]

Springsteen was subsequently quite clear about what those ambitions were: to document a life that might be termed Jerseyside metropolitan. He was aware that his adopted hometown had lost some of its former glory. "I'd lived in Asbury Park for the last three years," he explained. "I watched the town suffer some pretty serious race rioting and slowly begin to close down. The Upstage Club, where I met most of the members of the E Street Band, had shut its doors. The board-walk was still operating, but the crowds were sparse. Many of the usual summer vacationers were now passing Asbury Park by for less troubled locations further south along the coast." He later continued: "The cast of characters came vaguely from Asbury Park at the turn of the decade. I wanted to describe a neighborhood, a way of life, and I wanted to invent a dance with no exact steps. It was just a dance you did every day and night to get by."[45]

Notwithstanding his concerns, the new record, like *Greetings*, was an enraptured celebration of his habitat. "Sparks fly on E Street when the boy prophets walk it handsome and hot," are the first words he utters in the title track. Even unwelcome developments—"My tires were slashed and I almost crashed but the Lord had mercy / My machine she's a dud, I'm stuck in the mud somewhere in the swamps of Jersey"—cannot dispel the joyful mood of "Rosalita" (or the album at large). As with *Greetings*, characters with names like Jack the Rab-bit, Weak Knees Willie, Sloppy Sue, and Big Bones Billy inhabit these songs as if they're characters in a cheerful Charles Bukowski poem. "Wild Billy's Circus Story," which closes the first side of the album, is a darkly affectionate memoir of a circus that periodically came through Freehold when he was a kid.[46]

And as with *Greetings*, *E Street* features forays to Gotham, no less seedy than Asbury Park—these were the years the city was back on its heels—but on a much larger scale. "'Incident on 57th Street' and 'New York City Serenade' were my romantic stories of New York City, a place that had been my getaway from small-town New Jersey since I was sixteen," Springsteen said.[47] The former, an elaborate short story about a small-time punk named Spanish Johnny and his girlfriend Puerto Rican Jane, is shameless in its unbridled romanticism and, like "Does this Bus Stop at 82nd St?", seems more like the work of an outsider than a true urban denizen. The same can be true of "New York City Serenade," a ten-minute survey of the city landscape: "It's midnight in Manhattan, this is no time to get cute / It's a mad dog's promenade / So walk tall, or baby don't walk at all." The piece ends with a tribute to a junk man, one of a series of trades once plied by Douglas Springsteen.

"Bruce Springsteen does not know the city well," Dave Marsh observes in his generally effusive 1979 biography *Born to Run*. "Geographically," Marsh notes, he is "as far from Latin New York as he is from Leonard Bernstein."[48] But as Marsh and others have long understood, this is largely beside the point, in that Springsteen's New York, like Bernstein's *West Side Story*, is largely a mythic one imagined from a hazy familiarity in a liminal zone. Such an approach is sometimes viewed as problematic, and rightly so, particularly given the exploitative history of racial appropriation in popular music. But it can also be reductive and misguided to dismiss it entirely: from Shakespeare to Lin-Manuel Miranda, the best art is borrowed and filtered.

There is one significant way, however, in which *E Street* departs from the lyrical sensibility of *Greetings*: a sense of restlessness in paradise. For all its raucous pleasure, "Rosalita" is a song in which the narrator tells the title character that they should pick up and head to California, where apparently the guitars will sound sweeter "down San Diego way." There's no sense of a life beyond careless abandon— yet. But it looks like happily ever after will be somewhere else.

The finest song of *E Street*, perhaps not surprisingly, is the one most securely grounded in a sense of place: "Fourth of July, Asbury Park (Sandy)." It's also one that signals impending departure because that's really the only way to grow up. Springsteen has described the song as "a goodbye to my adopted hometown and the life I'd lived there before I recorded. 'Sandy' was a composite of some of the girls I'd known along the Shore. I used the boardwalk and the closing down of the town as a metaphor for the end of a summer romance and the changes I was experiencing in my own life."[49]

On the most basic level, "Fourth of July" is a love song. But it's also clear that while the narrator of the song is professing his devotion to Sandy, it's even more clear that what he's really in love with is the teeming life of Asbury Park and its environs—dubbed "Little Eden" in the opening line and lovingly evoked with references like that to Madame Marie, the fortune teller on the Boardwalk who Springsteen made world famous in this song. We survey a scene of what borders on the homoerotic, with "boys from the casino who dance with their shirts half open" and "boys in high heels" whose "skins are so white," along with more conventional figures like wizards who play on pinball way (an allusion to The Who's 1969 song "Pinball Wizard").

Yet the very affection with which the narrator describes such figures suggests a degree of detachment from them: he can see them so clearly, and fondly, because he has a consciousness of something else by which to measure them. This becomes clear in a remarkably evocative middle verse in which the character gets trapped on an amusement park ride when his shirt gets caught on it: "Didn't think I'd ever get off." His diction is telling: while words like "tilt," "drag," and "caught," are rendered in a voice of wistful sheepishness, there is a strong undercurrent of entrapment in them, matched by a gathering resolution to break free. "For me this boardwalk life's through," he tells Sandy. "You oughta quit this scene, too."[50]

It won't be easy, because the scene evoked by the song's chorus is so gorgeous. Danny Federici plays an accordion, Sancious offers starry notes on an electric piano, and an angelic choir of voices echoes Springsteen's. (Those voices are actually overdubs of Israeli Suki Lahav, the wife of sound engineer Louis Lahav; she later played violin for "Jungleland" on *Born to Run*).[51] Repeated three times over the course of the song, the chorus has a distinctly old-world feel that would have charmed Springsteen's Zerilli ancestors. The best music is grounded in a time and place, but also finds a way to transcend them, an ambition Springsteen clearly sensed in the way he fiddled with place names on these records. With "Fourth of July, Asbury Park (Sandy)," he hit the sweetest of spots in one of the most beautiful, and place-centered, songs in his body of work.

Unlike Joel's sophomore effort, Springsteen's E Street did sell better than *Greetings*. But not by much. And while he continued to have champions at Columbia, Walter Yetnikoff, president of CBS, the parent company of Columbia, was not sold on him. "The kid's not selling any records for us!" he yelled at Peter Philbin, a publicist who was a staunch Springsteen supporter. "Fuck you!" Philbin instinctively—and, under the circumstances, perhaps unwisely—replied. "Don't you know what this kid's gonna *be*?" Philbin managed to keep his job, and Springsteen managed to hang on at the label. By a thread.[52]

There were signs of life for Springsteen beyond 52nd Street. Critical reception for the new album was strong; Robert Hilburn of the *Los Angeles Times,* one of a number of national observers beginning to pay attention to Springsteen, put *E Street* on his ten best list of the year. Five years later, it was memorably celebrated by critic Ariel Swartley in a chapter-length essay she wrote on the one album she would take to a desert island. But as Dave Marsh noted in 1979, "In terms of influence, rock critics have never been as significant in their field as reviewers of drama, film or 'serious' music, partly because the audience for rock is barely literate."[53] The exception that proved the rule is the most famous review in the history of pop music criticism: Jon Landau's review of a Springsteen show for Boston's *Real Paper* from 1974, in which he famously declared, I saw rock and roll future and its name is Bruce Springsteen." Landau was the record review editor of *Rolling Stone;* though this piece was published in a local arts publication, it caught the attention of Columbia executives, who took out a full-page review promoting Springsteen.[54] It would be the beginning of a decisive relationship.

For the moment, the important figures determining Springsteen's fate were disc jockeys like Ed Sciaky—Kid Leo in Cleveland was another—who convinced their bosses to simulcast Springsteen shows when he came to town. They helped build word-of-mouth in their enthusiasm and in getting his songs on the airwaves. By August of 1974, *E Street* had sold about 100,000 copies, half of them in greater Philadelphia.[55]

Of course, the most important agent of Springsteen's destiny was Springsteen himself. Much of what these people were responding to—much of what his growing legion of fans was responding to—were his legendary live performances, whose length and intensity were unique even by the Wagnerian standards of rock concerts, though part of his appeal is the way in which he eschewed rock star theatrics in favor of emotional directness. Springsteen was building a following the way one did in those days: touring relentlessly to support records. (Now it's pretty much the other way around.) The question was whether it would be enough.

$$\oint$$

By 1975, Billy Joel and Bruce Springsteen had reached critical junctures in their careers. Both had made a vocation of music from a young age, and over the course of a decade both had a lot to show for it: they had evolved into professional songwriters and performers who played big-time venues. Both had landed a recording contract with the same label. Each had made two albums for that label, and each had enjoyed a modicum of success. But neither had broken through to a mass audience, and both had high-profile doubters who were skeptical they ever would.

Of the two, Joel was probably in the stronger position. *Piano Man* peaked at 25 on the *Billboard* chart and *Streetlife Serenade* reached 35 (*Greetings* hit 60 and *E Street* 59, respectively). *Piano Man* sold steadily, certified gold for sales of a half-million in its first year and platinum (a million copies sold) by 1978. Joel had a bona fide hit single with "Piano Man," something Springsteen didn't achieve. Joel also got some positive media attention: *Cashbox* named him "Best New Male Vocalist for 1973" and *Stereo Review* awarded *Piano Man* album of the year. There is also evidence Joel was regarded as the more promising of the two at Columbia. Dave Marsh describes a promoter at the company encouraging a Houston radio station to drop Springsteen in favor of Joel, and Peter Ames Carlin cites anecdotal reports that record shop owners were being compelled to trade copies of *Greetings* and *E Street* in favor of *Piano Man*.[56] Over the long haul, Joel may well have seemed the better bet.

On the other hand, Springsteen had momentum. Many of the critics he had on his side were skeptical of Joel; the tough-minded Robert Christgau, who gave *Greetings* a B+ and *E Street* an A-, graded Joel's two efforts as a pair of Cs, describing him as "one of those eternal teenagers who doesn't know how to shut up" and "the Irving Berlin of narcissistic alienation."[57] Joel's sales were trending down; Springsteen's were trending up.

But his back was also to the wall. In the aftermath of the Philbin/Yetnikoff shouting match, Columbia decided to advance Springsteen enough money for a single. "We gave him the assignment of making a good record," Bruce Lundvall, Davis's successor at Columbia, said. "If it turned out to be good, the company forked over the money to produce the rest of the album."[58] Springsteen knew: This Was It.

Joel was getting more encouragement than Springsteen, but not of a kind he found helpful. Columbia was still thinking of him as a singer/songwriter in the early 1970s mold and making plans for him that didn't feel right. Like Springsteen, he was nearly broke—most of the money both men earned went to band overhead and recording—and like Springsteen, he saw his live shows as the wellspring of his recordings.[59] He concluded he needed to change direction when he made his next album.

For both men, the solution involved taking a second look at their native turf.

SAX APPEAL

FIGURE 8. Bruce Springsteen and Clarence Clemons onstage at the time of *Born to Run*. The bond between the two became legendary, but the tensions could be almost as potent as their affection. *(Photofest)*

CHAPTER 4

Arrivals

Movin' Out—and Back, 1975–1977

> Camerado, I give you my hand!
> I give you my love more precious than money,
> I give you myself before preaching or law;
> Will you give me yourself? Will you come travel with me?
> Shall we stick by each other as long as we live?
>
> —Walt Whitman (who began his life on Long
> Island and finished it in New Jersey),
> "Song of the Open Road" (1856)

THE LIVES OF Bruce Springsteen and Billy Joel proceeded in remarkably parallel fashion in the mid-1970s. Both were as fiercely committed to their careers as ever, and both had reason to believe their best days were ahead of them. But both believed changes were necessary, and though they were sometimes difficult to make, they went forth confidently.

Some of these changes involved personnel decisions. For Springsteen, that meant firing his longtime drummer, the aptly named Vini "Mad Dog" Lopez, whose antics and musicianship Springsteen found wanting. The E Street band underwent other permutations, losing pianist David Sancious (and Ernest "Boom" Carter, the drummer who performed on "Born to Run"; both joined a jazz ensemble). But it gained two seasoned players in Roy Bittan and Max Weinberg to fill those gaps. Both were relative outsiders, but Bittan was from Queens and Weinberg South Orange, so they too were metropolitans (Springsteen described Bittan as "a bundle of drive, neurosis, and wily suburban street smarts."[1]) He also formed a close bond with critic/producer Jon Landau, who steered his music in a different direction—and, gradually, away from manager/producer Mike Appel, though a divorce there was still a couple years away. Joel, too, underwent a shakeup, placing his financial affairs in the hands of his wife Elizabeth, who proved forcefully deft in running his career. Joel also waged and won struggles over who he would work with and where, temporarily taking on the role of producer for himself. The result of these moves helped turn both men into superstars whose futures in the music business would henceforth not be in doubt.

Joel and Springsteen also reconsidered where they were literally as well as figuratively. Joel decided to come back to New York, a geographical relocation that was accompanied by a psychic one. The resulting album, *Turnstiles*, may be the best album he ever made— best in the sense of the consistent quality and cohesion of its songs *as* an album. Perhaps not coincidentally, it's also an album thematically centered on the city and state of New York. *Turnstiles* was not a commercial success, but it was strong enough on its merits to sustain him for one more return to the well, which became *The Stranger*, the smash album that shot him into the stratosphere from its metropolitan launchpad.

Springsteen's center of gravity was also greater New York in his own breakthrough album, *Born to Run*. But a dramatic change had taken place in the stance he had taken toward it on *Greetings from Asbury Park, NJ*, and *The Wild, the Innocent, and the E Street Shuffle*. With those records, the region had been a playground. Now, however, it was a prison from which "we gotta get out while we're young," as he conveyed on the album's title track. This new sense of desperation shaped Springsteen's music in the coming years, giving his work a sense of intensity that has been associated with him ever since.

So it was that the two men remained in a similar place—but facing in different directions.

$

To get back to New York, Joel's path crossed, as it did a number of times in the course of his career, that of Elton John. John, who like Joel was a relatively rare piano-playing rock leading man, was at his artistic and commercial peak in the mid-1970s. In 1974, he went to Boulder County, Colorado, to record the first of three albums at Caribou studios, a recently built facility owned by producer Jimmy Guercio, best known for his work with jazz-influenced acts Blood, Sweat, and Tears, and Chicago. (John's first album to come from there, *Caribou,* was named for the studio; it was followed there in 1975 by what many regard as his best work, *Captain Fantastic and the Brown Dirt Cowboy.*) In addition to his production duties, Guercio was also a talent manager, and Joel, who had parted ways with what had become his ad-hoc manager Jon Troy, took Columbia's advice in signing with Caribou Management. In early 1976, Guercio set Joel up at Caribou, and recruited bassist Dee Murray and drummer Nigel Olssen from John's band, with Guercio himself as producer. But Joel was unhappy with what was happening. "I was already sick of being called 'the American Elton John,'" he remembered. "It was just not the right company for me at all." Joel took the somewhat risky step of firing Guercio, leaving Caribou, and turning his affairs over to Elizabeth, who was inexperienced (and presumably cost-effective) but who quickly learned the ropes.[2]

Joel then made another difficult decision. George Martin, the great Beatles producer, offered to work with him. But Martin believed that Joel should make an album with studio musicians, by which point he had decided this was no longer something he was willing to do.[3] He instead decided to make his next album with his touring players, whose sound had been honed on the road by playing with him over a period of many years. As Springsteen once said, in a sentiment with which Joel would surely have agreed, "You're not looking for the best players. You're looking for the *right* players who click into something unique."[4] The core of Billy Joel Band, as it came to be known, consisted of a set of Long Islanders—Liberty DeVitto on drums, Douglas Stegmeyer on bass, Richie Cannata on winds—who remained with him through most of the 1970s and 1980s. (Joel went through a series of guitarists in these years, including Russell Javors, David Brown, and Hiram Bullock.)

Joel made another unorthodox call: he recorded the album at a studio on Long Island. The change of venue was more than a musical decision. By 1975, he decided he had enough of Los Angeles. "I got very defensive about New York at one point," he told John Rockwell of the *New York Times* in 1978. "When I was in LA, there was all this anti-New York sentiment, especially among ex-New Yorkers—they are the worst."[5] (Joel seems to overlook the degree to which he himself had taken a critical stance toward his native turf on his first two records.) It was time to come home.

He did so at a notable moment. In 1975, New York City was lurching toward financial collapse, on the very brink of insolvency when President Gerald Ford initially denied federal aid—prompting the famous New York *Daily News* headline FORD TO CITY: DROP DEAD—before changing course and signing off on a congressional bailout. This was the age of movies like *Dog Day Afternoon* (1975) and *Taxi Driver* (1976), which depicted the city as a fevered, decaying metropolis. The sense of malaise radiated outward to the suburbs, which, while to some degree insulated from the city's woes—one reason for the existence of suburbia in the first place—was still part of an aging Rust Belt that ran from New England into the Midwest, regions losing ground to a Sun Belt that stretched from the Southeast through Texas and into California. Taxes, crime, inflation, unemployment: it is an era known to historians as the Age of Limits.[6] Joel was of course aware that New York was, in his words, "going down the tubes," and decided this was precisely the reason to return: "I'm going back to see this. It looks like the place to be, to write about."[7]

Joel's imaginative turn to New York began before he left LA, which is where he wrote "Miami 2017." Title notwithstanding, the song is really about New York City, depicting a post-apocalyptic moment from a perspective of 42 years later, the city's figurative ruin transfigured into an actual one. It starts with the sound of distant sirens. "I've seen the lights go out on Broadway / I've seen the Empire state laid low," the narrator begins meditatively, noting that life goes on beyond the Palisades that form the west wall of the Hudson River. But once the bridges connecting Brooklyn to Manhattan get blown up, the song revs up with a muscular guitar riff, and the pace accelerates, as does the imagery: burning churches, collapsing buildings, striking workers, refugees rescued by naval vessels. The paroxysm of destruction comes to its climax as the city literally disintegrates: "They blew the Bronx away / And sank Manhattan out at sea." (Brooklyn and Queens—which is to say Long Island—apparently survives.) These events, the narrator explains, happened many years earlier, before the refugees decamped to Florida, and the Mafia took over Mexico.

As with "The Ballad of Billy the Kid," narrative logic is not really the point of "Miami 2017." The former was a celebration of national mythology; the latter is an anthem of local resilience. "There are not many who remember," the narrator concludes as the song returns to its quiet opening mode. "They say a handful still survive / To tell the world about / The way the lights went out / And keep the memory alive." The song is a tribute to New York toughness.

"Miami 2017" is the track with which *Turnstiles* ends. But the album begins with "Say Goodbye to Hollywood," Joel's swan song to his temporary home. In it he pays tribute to his erstwhile manager Jon Troy ("He won't be my fast gun anymore") and expresses apprehension over his departure ("Moving on is a chance you take every time"). Stylistically, however, the song is grounded in the sounds of New York. "Hollywood" is a work of homage to the Bronx-native producer Phil Spector and his onetime muse Ronnie Spector, lead singer of the Ronettes, an early 1960s girl group best known for "Be My Baby," which "Hollywood" resembles in its reverb, strings, and castanets.

"I heard Ronnie in my head as I wrote the lyrics!" Joel later said. He was pleased when Spector recorded her own version of the song in 1977, backed by Springsteen's E Street Band (Springsteen himself played guitar on that recording; more on this below).[8]

Joel's affection for New York is not limited to the city, or, for that matter, Long Island. The second track on *Turnstiles*, "Summer, Highland Falls," is also autobiographical, and one of his most beloved songs. He wrote it in the summer of 1975, when Elizabeth rented the couple a house in the Hudson River town about 50 miles north of Manhattan, adjacent to the United States Military Academy at West Point. Their abode was part of an estate formerly owned by J.P. Morgan, overlooking the river, not far from the densely clustered, somewhat ramshackle downtown.[9] Highland Falls makes no direct appearance in the song, but its rolling rhythm does evoke an aquatic summer idyll. (Joel cites the influence of Bach in its arpeggiated notes.) The putative subject of "Summer, Highland Falls" is Joel's manic-depressive state of mind—"it's always sadness or euphoria"— which he attributed to his change of venue as well as his marital difficulties at the time.[10] But its measured composition and delivery gives the song a reflective beauty that suggests an achieved, if temporary, equilibrium.

Two other songs from *Turnstiles* speak to Joel's reorientation from west to east. The first, "I've Loved These Days," is in effect his real farewell to Los Angeles, one that unlike "Say Goodbye to Hollywood," looks back rather than ahead. A probably exaggerated elegy to a life of unsustainable luxury ("a string of pearls, a foreign car"), it evokes the pursuit of the Good Life that enchanted Joel—nice weather, palm trees, spectacular views—when he came to California in 1972.[11] Its fondness contrasts sharply with the biting satire of "Los Angelenos."

The other homecoming song, a composition that has been incorporated into the American Songbook, is "New York State of Mind." There are conflicting accounts of its provenance. Joel told biographer Fred Schruers that the inspiration came before his resettlement back east, when he and Elizabeth were driving across the Newburgh-

Beacon Bridge in the mid-Hudson Valley amid its autumnal splendor. But Joel has also said its source is in the very Greyhound bus he describes in the song, which he wrote immediately upon finishing his trip.[12] "New York State of Mind" fuses the bluesiness of Ray Charles with the pop elegance of Frank Sinatra in what may be the most heartfelt valentine the Empire State has ever received, with the possible exception of Jay-Z and Alicia Keyes's "Empire State of Mind." Its urbanity is balanced by a light class consciousness, suggested by the proletarian Greyhound, that gives the piece pleasing weight: "I seen all the movie stars and their fancy cars and their limousines . . . But I know what I'm needing and I don't want to waste more time." In its classical elegance, "New York State of Mind" is entirely outside the rock tradition, and, as they had with "Travelin' Prayer," outsiders seized on it. Barbra Streisand immediately recorded a cover version for her 1977 album *Superman* ("My mom looked at me with a fresh set of eyes—finally a *real* singer had picked up on one of her son's efforts," Joel reported), and subsequent versions were recorded by Tony Bennett, Shirley Bassey, and Mel Tormé, among others.[13]

Strictly speaking, *Turnstiles* is not a concept album—it is not uniformly thematic the way, say, Sinatra's *In the Wee Small Hours* is—and includes tracks that do not speak directly to New York as a state of mind or place. "All You Wanna Do Is Dance" is another one of Joel's forays into reggae, which was enjoying a vogue in pop music amid the success of Bob Marley and the Wailers in the U.S. and Eric Clapton's hit cover of Marley's "I Shot the Sheriff" in 1974. It's notable in this context that the singer of the song chides its female character, who wonders why the Beatles won't get back together or why there's nothing she wants to listen to on the radio. "You can stand by your blue suede shoes," he tells her. "But the party is over and I'm getting tired of waiting for you." The steel drums featured in the song appear to be synthetic, a designation that may apply to the song as a whole, one that remains a minor entry in Joel's body of work, though its theme of nostalgia became more important and nuanced in *An Innocent Man*.

There are three tracks on *Turnstiles* that open side two and blend together: "James" and "Prelude/Angry Young Man." Like "All You

Wanna Do Is Dance," the narrators spanning them strike notes of forbearance shading into condescension. "James, we were always friends," begins the ballad, where the principal instrument is the mellotron and the protagonist is a composite figure of people from Joel's youth.[14] The narrator delivers advice—"Do what's good for you, or you're not good for anybody"—that would form the core logic for his hit "My Life" a couple years later, and reflects the "Me Decade" ethos satirized by Tom Wolfe in the famous essay published in *New York* magazine shortly after *Turnstiles* was released.[15] Though issued as a single, "James" was not a hit and is not among Joel's most played or cited songs.

What follows, however, *is* a fan favorite. The instrumental "Prelude" exhibits Joel's piano chops at their most rigorous in a piece of pure progressive rock. "Prog," as it was sometimes known at the time, was much derided among critics, though it was extremely popular with white male rock fans (the two facts not unrelated). This is a piece of virtuosic red meat that bands from Kansas to Yes might envy. "Prelude" segues into the shuffling, caffeinated narration of "Angry Young Man," which only adds insult to injury for a rock intelligentsia predisposed to dislike him: "I once believed in causes too / Had my pointless point of view / And life went on no matter who was wrong or right." (The soaring synthesizer solo that follows seems to banish abstract meditations into irrelevance.) Joel has never been more explicit in his cultural conservatism than he is here. Those inclined to agree have seen him as wise; those not, smug. If "New York State of Mind" became part of Joel's pop legacy, "Prelude/Angry Young Man" kept him anchored in the rock world that was for the moment his most important and loyal constituency.

As with *Streetlife Serenade, Turnstiles* was visually stitched together by its cover, this one designed by the very John Berg who greenlighted Springsteen's *Greetings from Asbury Park, NJ*. It features a photograph of Joel in the Astor Place subway station surrounded by a cast of characters clearly meant to stand for figures in the album's songs: A sober man with his arms full of books, a tourist with a travel bag, a flapperish woman in a gown with a stole, etc. Notably stylish, it effectively conveys Joel's message of New York as a staging ground for personal dramas that resonate outward and upward.

But *Turnstiles* was not considered a success. Joel's critics grudgingly acknowledged his musicianship while savaging him for mediocrity. "As Joel's craft improves," Robert Christgau wrote in the *Village Voice*, "he becomes more obnoxious."[16] (As with many rock critics, especially the epigrammatic Christgau, such pronouncements are treated as self-evident.) A more serious problem was the lack of sales: *Turnstiles* performed even more poorly than *Streetlife Serenade* did on the *Billboard* chart, reaching only 122. "Say Goodbye to Hollywood" and "Summer, Highland Falls" tanked as singles. The implicit endorsement of a figure like Streisand may have mattered in suggesting that Joel was a talent that Columbia should not finally give up on. But this was hardly obvious from an accounting perspective.

The figure who really seemed to have saved him at this critical juncture was Elizabeth. She managed to cultivate CBS president Walter Yetnikoff—nicknamed "the Wolf"—who, as we've already seen with Springsteen, could be a very tough customer. There was some speculation at the time that there was more to their relationship than business, which both Joel and Yetnikoff subsequently denied. (Yetnikoff, who was never modest about his sexual prowess, makes no mention of it in his memoir.) In any case, Elizabeth convinced Yetnikoff to see Joel live, and he came away convinced that "there's something going on here." Elizabeth negotiated a new deal for Joel in which Yetnikoff helped him renegotiate the Artie Ripp deal, gave him back his publishing rights, and set him up for another record. Meanwhile, a buzz was building on college and mainstream FM radio stations, the disdain of the rock press establishment notwithstanding. Though, by conventional metrics, Joel was failing, in fact he was on the cusp of historic success. But he would have to go back to the well one more time.[17]

$$\oint$$

When it came to making it in the music industry, Bruce Springsteen had been a half-step behind Joel in the early 1970s. But in 1975, he leapfrogged over him with his breakthrough album *Born to Run*. Joel caught up, at least in terms of sales, before too long. But this moment belonged to Springsteen.

The story of *Born to Run* is such a familiar part of Springsteen mythology—first documented by Dave Marsh in his book of the same name, and in a series of accounts since—that it seems superfluous to recount it in any detail here. The agony of making the record (Springsteen drove himself and those around him crazy in his fanatic attention to detail); the enormous buzz that crested in his legendary Bottom Line shows in Greenwich Village in August; the simultaneous cover stories in *Time* and *Newsweek* in October and the backlash that followed; his first overseas tour in Europe that fall; the nasty lawsuit he had with Mike Appel that stalled his career in 1976–77: they're all part of what might be termed the Springsteen Legend, in which an anointed seeker slays a series of dragons, some of them internal, in the course of achieving his destiny. To his credit, Springsteen soft-pedals some of this in his memoir, to the point of citing the account of Appel's version of their conflict, in which he himself admits "I worked hard for the Oscar."[18] Our primary lens in reviewing this history will be its relevance insofar as it involves the psychic, musical, and geographic landscape of his work.

As we've seen, Springsteen's treatment of his native turf was largely rhapsodic on his first two albums. But as he began work on his third one, there were signs he was growing restive. "Jersey's a dumpy joint," he told the writer of a British music publication in early 1975. "I mean, it's okay, it's home. But every place is a dump."[19] As is often the case, it appears that some of this dissatisfaction was psychological; certainly, Springsteen was feeling pressure and fearing failure. There was also a developmental factor at work. British novelist Nick Hornby's memorable description of the album's opening song, "Thunder Road"— "the sharp fear that comes on in late youth"[20]—dominates this new phase in Springsteen's career.

One should also consider the broader historical context that informed Springsteen's understanding of the world he inhabited as he began work on the album. The same national pall that suffused

Piano Man songs like "Captain Jack"—Vietnam, Watergate, energy shortages—was still present. "People were contemplating a country that was finite, where resources and life had limits. Slowly the dread I managed to keep out of 'Rosalita' squeezed its way into the people of *Born to Run*,"[21] he said. This sense of limits was national, but as Joel's experience in writing "Miami 2017" indicated, it was especially acute in metropolitan New York. That song was fatalistic in its depiction of decline. But Springsteen was groping toward a more systematic revitalization of the American Dream that he could express musically in a local as well as national way.

The process began with the title song. He had been assigned the task of coming up with a hit single as a condition for getting a green light to make an album, and he went about the work of songwriting with a new intensity, devoting six months to a task that had previously took a matter of days, even hours.[22] He was living by himself in a rented house in West Long Branch, adjacent to Asbury Park, and giving himself a tutorial in the rock music of the early 1960s. "At night I'd switch off the lights and drift away with Roy Orbison, Phil Spector or Duane Eddy lullabying me to dreamland," he remembered. (The famous guitar riff of "Born to Run" was directly inspired by Eddy.) "Those records now spoke to me in a way most late-sixties and early-seventies rock music failed to." The challenge was to integrate the best of the old in ways that addressed contemporary realities: resonance without clichés. "Lyrically, I was entrenched in classic rock and roll images, and I wanted to find a way to use those images without their feeling anachronistic."[23]

One effect of this experience was a desire to discipline his sound, a move that prompted a shift in his musical geography away from the Jersey shore. "These were well-crafted, inspired recordings," he said of those early 1960s hits, many of them emanating from the Brill Building. "There was little self-indulgence in them. They didn't waste your time with sprawling guitar solos or endless monolithic drumming. There was opera and a lush grandness, but there was also restraint."[24] This meant eschewing the raucous improvisational solos that dominated *The Wild, the Innocent and the E Street Shuffle*, and the

Shore Sound generally, though the process was gradual and the free-wheeling spirit of those early records remained a core component of Springsteen's live act for decades to come.

The important point here is that Springsteen was thinking less in terms of writing *songs* than making *records*, and less about capturing a local scene than transcending it. "It was the first piece of music I wrote and conceived as a studio production," he said of "Born to Run." Here the influence of Phil Spector proved crucial, even more than it was for Joel. Though "Born to Run" is not the obvious work of homage that "Say Goodbye to Hollywood" is, the song's sonic topography featured a wall of sound in which layers and layers of instruments, not all of them clearly discernible to the naked ear, generated a perception of mass and speed akin to a well-tuned engine.

It was a painstaking process. In the summer of 1974, Springsteen played a recording of "Born to Run" for Columbia president Bruce Lundvall. "You just made a hit record," Lundvall told him, clearing the way a full album.[25] Yet Springsteen was not satisfied with "Born to Run," and spent months to come tinkering with it.

He was helped in this regard by Jon Landau, who had become Springsteen's friend and advisor, and who began taking on the role of producer and bringing a new emphasis on sonic polish to Springsteen's sensibility. One of the most important things he did was convince Springsteen to leave behind the professional provincialism of Sound Shore studios in Blauvelt and make the album at the Record Plant, a major Manhattan facility. He also convinced Springsteen to work with young engineer Jimmy Iovine, then at the dawn of a storied career that included founding his own record label, Interscope Records. Ever so gradually, a set of songs were chiseled and slotted. Steve Van Zandt showed up and made a key contribution in arranging the horns, Jersey shore style, for the album's second track, "Tenth Avenue Freezeout," a brassy depiction of Asbury Park.

Van Zandt liked *Born to Run*. But he also recognized that something was changing. "As impressed as I was, I thought the middle section was too complex," he said of the title track in terms of its likely success as a pop record.[26] In years to come, Van Zandt expressed disappointment about Springsteen's subsequent musical direction, which moved further away from the Shore Sound, though he remained a steadfast friend and collaborator. Van Zandt was among those bemused by Springsteen's perfectionism on *Born to Run*; others got increasingly impatient, then angry. When Springsteen famously threw an early pressing of the album into a hotel pool in the presence of shocked band members, a desperate Mike Appel disingenuously agreed with Springsteen that the project was a failure. "Let's scrap the whole thing. I mean, obviously, just *f-ck* it." It was during the tense subsequent car ride home on the New Jersey Turnpike with Appel, his brother, and Springsteen's girlfriend Karen Darvin that Springsteen began to laugh, his dam of reluctance finally breaking. "I was born, grew old, and died making that album," he told *Playboy* in 1976.[27]

Throughout this period, however, a wave was building. The album's cover, an image of Springsteen and Clarence Clemons palpably savoring each other's company, was shot by photographer Eric Meola and supervised by the seemingly omnipresent John Berg. It is now considered a classic of design—and an important statement of racial integration at a time when rock & roll was resegregating. (The generally genial Clemons nevertheless later noted tartly to Boston Red Sox slugger David Ortiz that he's on the back cover, not the front.[28]) Lundvall authorized $250,000 in advance publicity for the album, and radio stations were playing "Born to Run" in advance of its official release as a single. In Philadelphia, Washington DC, and Boston, *Born to Run* sold more advance copies than any album in history. The E Street Band had done live shows throughout the making of the album and commenced a tour that broke Springsteen nationally as well as internationally. A few weeks later, the dual *Newsweek* and *Time* stories—the former more a process story about the record industry; the latter a more impassioned celebration of Springsteen's work by critic and future Martin Scorsese screenwriter Jay Cocks—turned him into a national phenomenon.[29]

Given all the noise and the obsessiveness that went into its construction, the truly remarkable thing about *Born to Run* is just how fresh it sounded—and still sounds a half-century later. This freshness is all the more remarkable when one considers the essential conservatism of Springsteen's vision. (Ironically, he was at the vanguard of American culture in his instinct to look back—more on this in Chapter 6.) "*Born to Run* makes no stylistic breakthroughs, as the fundamental Elvis Presley and Beatles recordings had done," Dave Marsh, Springsteen's biographer and friend, noted in his 1979 bio. "But it does represent the culmination of twenty years of rock & roll, and when it was released in October of 1975 it was the strongest possible testimony to the continued vitality of that tradition."[30]

The paradox here is that the effort to articulate a credibly hopeful affirmation of national mythology is made against a backdrop of doubt and fear. "Dread—the sense that things might not work out, that the moral high ground had been swept out from underneath us, that the dream we had of ourselves had somehow been tainted and the future would forever be uninsured—was in the air," Springsteen said in a memoir that is not coincidentally titled *Born to Run*.[31] Note, however, that *tainted* is not the same thing as *spoiled*, and that an uncertain future is not necessarily a bleak one. A strong sense of contingency hovers over *Born to Run*—which is one of the things that makes it exciting.

That's because things can go, and do go, either way on an album whose every song focuses on the key theme of escape. This, Springsteen told *Washington Post* writer Eve Zibart in 1978, "was the idea of rock 'n' roll in the beginning," citing Chuck Berry and Bob Dylan as exemplars in their different ways.[32] The idea recurs repeatedly on *Born to Run*: "I'm pulling out of here to win" in "Thunder Road"; "We gotta get out while we're young," in "Born to Run"; "You run sad and free until all you can see is the night" in "Night."

The question is where the characters of *Born to Run* were escaping—or not escaping—*from*. Figuratively speaking, a desire to flee a psychic state of unhappiness is broad, even universal. But in terms of actual settings of particular songs, the answer is pretty clear: a series of points between Asbury Park and Manhattan—"from the shoreline to the city," in the words of "Tenth Avenue Freezeout." While not numerous, the album does make a number of specific references to local settings, ranging from "Highway 9" in "Born to Run," a multi-lane thoroughfare that runs through the Monmouth County of both Freehold and Asbury Park; to the Circuit, a loop of Ocean and Kingsley Avenues in Asbury Park that gets mentioned in "Night"; to the Harlem of "Jungleland," a song whose protagonist drives over the "Jersey state line," though strictly speaking it isn't possible to get between New York City and New Jersey unless you take a bridge or tunnel (the latter of which figures as a key plot point in "Meeting Across the River").

What's even more clear, however, is that Springsteen is trying harder than ever to universalize his settings and characters. But you can't really do this effectively without some sense of specificity, which he accomplishes by etching distinctly urban and hinterland scenes in the eight songs that comprise the album. The opening of "Thunder Road" is one of the most evocative in the history of rock & roll, with its yearning harmonica, bright piano chords, and hopeful first lines: "The screen door slams / Mary's dress waves / Like a vision she dances across the porch while the radio plays." Such a scenario could unfold just about anywhere, but the overall imagery is far more pastoral than urban. Similarly, as it very title suggests, "Backstreets" is a story of two lives on the margins, people who catch "rides to the outskirts" and sleep "in that old abandoned beach house." We hear of locales like Duke Street or Stockton's Wing, which gives songs like these a sense of particularity (like the "giant Exxon sign that brings this fair city light" in "Jungleland"), but they seem imaginary, or, at any rate, not associated with a particular place. As with *Greetings*, the city locations seem more familiar, as in the settings of "Meeting Across the River" (one surmises that the meeting will take place in Manhattan via the Holland Tunnel) and the Harlem of "Jungleland." But here too such referents are sparse.

There are glimpses of the old Springsteen on *Born to Run*. It's not hard to imagine "Tenth Avenue Freezeout," which its insouciant spirit and punchy brass, showing up on *The Wild, the Innocent and the E Street Shuffle*, and indeed the song remains a staple of Springsteen's live shows, which he typically deploys when he wants to evoke or sustain a boisterous mood. That's why it's surprising, when one scrutinizes the lyrics, how claustrophobic they are: "I've got my back to the wall"; "I'm on my own / And I can't go home." Similarly, "Jungleland" is a ten-minute rock opera that one could plausibly compare with "Incident on 57th Street" or "New York City Serenade." But it has none of the light-hearted or improvisational feel of those two earlier songs, and indeed was sweated over within an inch of its life in the studio, a composition whose grandeur comes from its meticulousness rather than captured spontaneity.

The dramatic tension of *Born to Run* derives in part from varying outcomes that are uncertain at best—these are the hopeful songs—and others of defeat. A listener can feel sanguine about the realistic but nevertheless inspiring protagonists of "Thunder Road" and "Born to Run," who are counting on lovers to pull them through. (Peter Knobler, an early champion of Springsteen who got a preview of the song at Springsteen's Long Branch house, was intrigued to note a poster of Peter Pan leading Wendy out a window over Springsteen's bed, which both suggests enchantment as well as disillusionment in the choice of its female character.[33]) On the other hand, the unreliable—in more ways than one—protagonist of "Meeting Across the River" does not inspire confidence when he asserts "tonight's gonna be everything that I said," even as we may hope he's right amid jazz trumpeter Randy Brecker's solos. More fatalistic is the narrator of "She's the One," still in the grip of a femme fatale with whom, he muses to himself, he bonded "back when her love could save you from the bitterness."

In those cases where we actually know the outcome, it's tragic. "Backstreets" begins in the aftermath of a shattered love affair, so hard for its narrator to accept: "Remember all those movies, Terry, we'd go see / Trying to walk like the heroes we thought we had to be." His bitterness at Terry's betrayal is conveyed in his voice even more than his words as he realizes "we're just like the rest," a pair of losers wandering backstreets.

Springsteen endows the story of these very ordinary people with a musical splendor carried largely by Bittan's piano. It might seem ridiculously over the top (as it surely does for Springsteen skeptics), but the song is rendered with such unselfconscious conviction that it tends to overpower casual cynicism. "Backstreets" requires a similar suspension of disbelief in its dramatic tale of the Magic Rat—here's its Federici's organ that underlines a dream of glory—who goes down in a hail of bullets, leaving behind poets whose survival becomes a badge of dishonor.

The larger point of the album is, to borrow the title of a 1965 Animals song Springsteen often performed, "We Gotta Get Out of This Place." At the very moment Billy Joel decided to come home and was writing songs about the way it gave him succor, Springsteen was describing his homeland as "death trap." As Louis Masur has observed of the album, "Every song on *Born to Run* includes the word "night."[34] Springsteen's impulse toward flight did not abate in the coming years. Indeed, rage and anxiety fueled much of his next three albums, as suggested by the very title of the next one: *Darkness on the Edge of Town*.

The irony is that such fears notwithstanding, *Born to Run* catapulted Springsteen to a level of success that secured his place in the history of rock & roll. But there was an irony within that irony: Mike Appel's overweening desire to secure his own future with Springsteen with a contract renewal precipitated a legal brawl that suspended Springsteen's recording career and brought the E Street Band to the cusp of dissolution. At a time when revenue had almost completely dried up, the recording session for Ronnie Spector's version of Joel's "Say Goodbye to Hollywood" generated an infusion of cash that tided Springsteen and the band over until a loan for $100,000 from Frank Barsalona of the Premier Talent booking agency kept him afloat while he worked toward a settlement with Appel.[35] Springsteen was ultimately able to resume recording and performing, and recovered his lost momentum. But that incident only seems to have intensified the shadows that haunted his imagination—and his determination to leave New Jersey behind.

§

In the fall of 1975, Bruce Springsteen became a rock star. In the fall of 1977, Billy Joel became a pop star.

The difference was subtle, but was also significant, especially for Joel, who chafed at the lack of seriousness with which he was regarded by critics. But there was no denying the scale of his success with *The Stranger*, which went on to sell over 10 million copies, achieving Diamond status from the Recording Industry Association of America. It became the bestselling album in the history of Columbia Records— until it was displaced eight years later by Springsteen's *Born in the U.S.A.*[36]

Joel began work on *The Stranger* in 1977. At that point, Springsteen was wrangling with Appel, but Joel had put his own management struggles behind him (temporarily, as it turned out). There were nevertheless remaining parallels in the ways the two men were dealing with the challenges of their still unrealized promise. Like Springsteen, Joel placed much faith in touring and working with his band, commencing a shoestring tour in the aftermath of *Turnstiles*. Yetnikoff's positive impression of Joel's live show allowed Elizabeth to coax support from him that the company had previously denied, just as Columbia had done with Springsteen in financing *Born to Run*.

Elizabeth was also instrumental in brokering a partnership between Joel and what might be termed the Jon Landau figure in his life: Phil Ramone. As Landau did for Springsteen, Ramone was a producer who entered Joel's career after it was underway but was able to capture magic no one previously had. The difference is that Ramone was an older and far more experienced producer than Landau. Born in 1934, he was a musical prodigy who began his career as a Julliard-trained violinist. He co-founded the A&R Recording studio in 1959 and proceeded to work with an array of musicians that included

Quincy Jones, Liza Minelli, and a bevy of rock stars. In 1975, Ramone was the producer of Paul Simon's *Still Crazy After All These Years*, which took the Album of the Year honors at that year's Grammy Awards. George Martin wanted Joel to work with studio musicians, but Ramone was eager to work with Joel's band.

Unlike *Streetlife Serenade*, Joel went into the studio with a batch of material he had been developing already. And unlike *Born the Run*, the process went quickly and smoothly. "We did songs in five takes rather than fifteen," he remembered, adding that Ramone "was one of the guys. We'd throw around ideas, kick the songs around, try them different ways."[37] A good example was the title track of *The Stranger*. Joel had written a minute-long intro and outro with a piano background, but couldn't decide what instrument should accompany it. As he explained in a tribute to Ramone after his death, he whistled it to the producer to show what he meant. "And he looks at me and he goes, 'You just did it.' I hadn't even considered that. I'm not the greatest whistler in the world, but he said that's what should be on the recording. And I listened back and I went, 'Holy shit, he's right.'"[38] This whistling melody also becomes a two-minute coda at the end of the album, creating a musical throughline that stitches it together.

Ramone was also an instrumental figure in helping Joel realize his breakthrough song. He had written "Just the Way You Are," but was unhappy with it—though not as unhappy as his bandmates, who hated it. "Liberty threw his sticks at me and said, 'I'm not a damn cocktail lounge drummer,'" Joel told James Lipton in a 1999 episode of *Inside the Actor's Studio*. It was Ramone who suggested that Joel tweak the song's cha-cha rhythm by replacing it with a backward samba beat. When that didn't work in changing his mind, he pulled Phoebe Snow, a singer with whom Ramone produced and who happened to be nearby, into the studio with her friend Linda Ronstadt. The two were adamant Joel should include the song on the album. "That's one of the greatest songs I've ever heard," he recalls Ronstadt saying. "You don't want to put it on the album? Are you nuts? That's a hit record."[39] She was right, of course. She may have also been

MOVIN' UP

FIGURE 9. Billy Joel at the time of *The Stranger*. The album would sell over ten million copies and spawn four hit singles, smashing doubts about his commercial viability. *(Wikimedia Commons)*

articulating a gender difference regarding the song that characterized its subsequent life.

As with *Born to Run*, a positive buzz surrounded the recording of *The Stranger*. "That just sort of went click," Yetnikoff recalled of hearing the title track for the first time. "It hit me right away, you know—this guy's got it—it's a done deal."[40] The album was released in September of 1977, with "Just the Way You Are" cresting at #3 in January of 1978. It was followed by "Anthony's Song (Movin' Out)," "Only the Good Die Young" and "She's Always a Woman," making Joel a staple of the airwaves for most of 1978. For the next fifteen years, he would be a veritable hit machine. *The Stranger* peaked at #2—unable to dislodge the monstrously successful *Saturday Night Fever* soundtrack—but at the 1978 Grammy Awards, it won album of the year, while "Just the Way You Are" was Song of the Year.

The Stranger is not as decisively a New York record as *Turnstiles* is. There are only a couple tracks that are clearly set in the metropolitan area; most are love songs illustrating facets of the title's theme (reinforced by an image of Joel on a bed facing a commedia dell'arte mask). But those songs have an outsized presence and echo on the record, and the back cover, which depicts Joel and the band—along with Ramone, wearing a New York Yankees jersey—was shot at Guido's, an Italian restaurant in the Hell's Kitchen neighborhood on the West Side of Manhattan.[41] Even those unfamiliar with Joel's previous musical history immediately saw him as a New Yorker of the white ethnic variety that had long since spilled over into the suburbs.

And from the start, they heard him as one. The album kicks off with "Anthony's Song (Movin' Out)," which bridges city and suburb. After its memorable piano/electric guitar riff, we meet the title character. He was part of a scenario Joel imagined of a Long Island grocery-store worker with dreams of making it big. "At the time I just pictured some lady yelling out of a house, 'Anthony! Anthony!'" he explained. (Whether or not he consciously remembered it, Joel was almost certainly recalling a famous Prince spaghetti advertisement that ran on network television between 1969 and 1982.)[42] "I was thinking about a kid who's been living at home and getting a lot of pressure from his family to go his own way. He isn't buying into the whole upward mobility thing."[43] So it is that we have a chorus of "If that's movin' up, I'm movin' out." The setting of the second verse shifts to Sullivan Street in Soho, where police officer Sergeant O'Leary moonlights as a bartender at an Italian restaurant, foolishly exerting himself for the sake of a Cadillac he "can't drive with a broken back."[44] We shouldn't take the line literally, but rather a characteristic form of New York-style working-class exaggeration, punctuated by the sound of a revving and screeching motorcycle at the end.

Thematically speaking, "Movin' Out" resembles "The Great Suburban Showdown" its sardonic portrayal of suburban life ("Who needs a house in Hackensack?"—a rare Joel venture across Manhattan into Jersey). But while that song had a more affluent overlay involving transcontinental air travel, this one is rendered in a more sharply working-class ethnic patois ("Mama Leone left a note on the door, she said 'Sonny, move out to the country'"). Though it only reached the bottom half of the Top Twenty at the time of its release,

"Movin' Out" is a song strongly associated with Joel, as attested to the fact that it became the title of Twyla Tharp's 2002 musical based on his work. It has been a mainstay of FM classic rock stations for decades.

The other deeply New York track on *The Stranger*, also a signature song of sorts, is "Scenes from an Italian Restaurant." "Scenes" has been described as Joel's "Jungleland," and it's not hard to see why: like the Springsteen track, it's an epic rock narrative.[45] (Such songs were in vogue in the late 1970s; one thinks of Meat Loaf's 1977 classic "Paradise by the Dashboard Light," in which he was backed by pianist Roy Bittan and drummer Max Weinberg of the E Street Band.) But Joel has made clear that his immediate inspiration was the 1969 Beatles album *Abbey Road*, whose second side featured a string of songs that flowed into each other.[46]

"Scenes" has three separate melodic sections: The first, which frames the piece on either side, is what Joel called "The Italian Restaurant Song"—clearly, that cuisine looms large in Joel's imagination. (The inspiration for this setting has been contested over the years, but Joel told the Long Island newspaper *Newsday* in 2015 that it's a composite of Fontana di Trevi on West 57th Street, across from Carnegie Hall, and Il Cortine in Little Italy.)[47] Here two old friends meet at a table in the street, the narrator savoring the company of his companion. The key piece of orchestration here is the presence of the inveterate session man Dominic Cortese, whose accordion-playing gives the song an Old-World Italianate flavor comparable to what Springsteen does on "Fourth of July, Asbury Park (Sandy)."

From here we move to a faster-paced middle section—Joel first dubbed it "Things Are OK in Oyster Bay," the Long Island town where he was living at the time—in which the narrator catches his companion up on recent events in his life, which include a new job and a new wife with an implication that he has attained a modicum of upward mobility. He then invites his companion to remember hanging out at the (West) Village Green in Joel's native Hicksville, which in fact is little more than a copse of trees in a park behind a strip mall on Route 106. But in the mythicized setting of the song, you can put a dime in a jukebox to hear a song about New Orleans, at which point the music suddenly changes turns into a lovely Dixieland jazz arrangement before transitioning to the third, and longest section of the song.[48]

Which brings us to what Joel explained was actually the origin of the piece, "The Ballad of Brenda and Eddie," which he dubbed "the meat and potatoes course" of the sonic meal. It tells the story of high school sweethearts, the king and queen of the prom, who ruled from their roost at the Parkway Diner (location indeterminate). The main action of the piece takes place in the summer of 1975—the length of Brenda and Eddie's marriage, which they celebrated by buying a pair of paintings from Sears; there was one down the road from the Village Green on Route 106. Brenda and Eddie mistakenly believe they can return to the Village Green, though of course, as he explains, you can't, really. "We all know people who peaked a little too early," Joel explained of such characters.[49]

The song unfolds so effortlessly, and yet so intricately, at the hands of this dinner-table raconteur that listeners who have heard it hundreds of times may not pause to consider what it actually means. Joel seems to have weighed the question from the outset. "Am I being preachy? Am I putting someone down?" he wondered at the time he wrote it.[50] The answer in some minds may well be yes: that vein of condescension that sometimes surfaces in Joel's work is discernible here, that of the urban sophisticate looking down at the hometown rubes whose notion of class is a couple of paintings from Sears. Joel seemed to think that adding the opening and closing section would take that edge off of it.

But an alternate reading of the song is available in one of the early lines of the Brenda and Eddie saga. Noting that neither one of them— or anyone else in the narrator's youth—knew they could want more out of life than high school glory days, he also notes, "Surely Brenda and Eddie would always find a way to survive." That "surely" can be interpreted to actually raise doubt, but seems to underline the larger theme of Brenda and Eddie's resilience. "That's all I heard about Brenda and Eddie / Can't tell you more than I told you already," he concludes. But it seems safe to guess they did indeed survive. One is reminded of John Mellencamp's 1982 hit "Jack and Diane": "Life goes on, long after the thrill of living is gone." Unlike Springsteen, Joel does not seem to be at his best when he tells tales in the third person; his warmth and empathy are most apparent when he addresses a loved one directly. But whatever "Scenes from an Italian Restaurant" may lack in compassion, it is nevertheless a vivid and compelling piece of storytelling.

One other song that seems worth mentioning in a metropolitan context is "Only the Good Die Young," the third single from *The Stranger,* which, like "Movin' Out," wasn't a big hit at the time, but has become one of the more durable songs in the Joel catalog. There's no specific reference to Greater New York in the lyrics, but the track is a pitch-perfect satire of the kind of working-class Irish Catholicism that flourished in places like Long Island with its references to confirmation dresses, gold crosses, and heavy heapings of guilt. The song is autobiographical, based on Joel's lust for a certain Virginia Callahan when he was in high school. The original version of "Only the Good Die Young" was recorded in a reggae rhythm, which once again aggravated DeVitto (he threw his drumsticks at Joel this time as well). "'Ugh, I frigging hate reggae!,'" Joel later remembered him saying. "'The closest you've ever been to Jamaica is when you changed trains in Queens.' So I said, 'Yeah, what's your solution?' And he played that opening fill and went into this kind of shuffle." Springsteen, a cradle Catholic with a long history of writing anti-Catholic songs, beginning with "If I Was the Priest" in his audition for John Hammond, in which the mother of Jesus is a prostitute at the Holy Grail Saloon, joined Joel onstage in 2009 to perform "Only the Good Die Young" at the Rock & Roll Hall of Fame 25th anniversary concert. Springsteen traded lines and verses with Joel and hopped on his piano, clearly enjoying the moment.[51]

The Stranger has a couple of other fan favorites that extend beyond the contours of the main line of argument of this book but which are worth noting in passing. The fourth single from the album, "She's Always a Woman," remains a radio mainstay. "Vienna," an evocation of his father's world and a call for relaxation and reflection, is one of two songs—"Summer, Highland Falls" is the other—that he has called his favorites, and is particularly prized among his more ardent fans.[52] The closing two tracks, "Get it Right the First Time," and "Everybody Has a Dream" (in which Joel once again channels Ray Charles, and in which he is backed by Phoebe Snow) are competent but not especially memorable efforts. But they end the album pleasantly enough and do nothing to tarnish what most fans consider his best work.

Billy Joel had arrived. And Bruce Springsteen was in flight.

FIGURE 10. Promotional advertisement for a (recorded) broadcast of a live Bruce Springsteen show, WMMS-Cleveland, 1978. Though not the pop star he would later become, Springsteen had taken his place among the leading rock acts on FM radio in the late 1970s. *(David Helton/WMMS, Wikimedia Commons)*

CHAPTER 5

Through Glass, Darkly

Years of Growth and Uncertainty, 1978–1982

BY THE END of the 1970s, Bruce Springsteen and Billy Joel had attained a level of success that was pretty much all anyone in their line of work could ever hope to achieve. They had hit records, toured the world, and while neither was really rich—they had ploughed most of their earnings into making the records on which they staked their reputations—they both lived relatively luxuriously and traveled in celebrity circles. The two were also adults by the standards of their society, though neither had achieved some key benchmarks of maturity. When they turned thirty in 1979, Springsteen was still single (and was beginning to suspect that this suggested something was wrong with him);[1] Joel, who had married relatively young at 24, was headed for a divorce. Neither had children. Nor were they really settled, various real estate deals notwithstanding, though both considered Greater New York home, with Joel spending a good deal of time on Long Island and Springsteen in coastal New Jersey.

Both men, however, had moved beyond the preoccupations of youth—in particular, those involving a sense of place. Springsteen, as we've seen, depicted his home ground as a playground, until it became a trap from which to escape. Joel, by contrast, left home, though the work that resulted from his flight to Los Angeles was largely defined against a background of (if not opposition to) his suburban Long Island childhood. By 1978, however, when Joel released 52nd Street and

Springsteen *Darkness on the Edge of Town*, neither artist was as preoccupied by home, broadly construed, as they had been—Springsteen self-consciously etched a national vision on his musical canvas, while Joel made forays into jazz and Latin music in an effort to widen his horizons. As such, we have reached a turning point in this story: neither man was as definitively metropolitan in the way they had been at the beginning of their careers. That said, their previous histories continued to define them in the collective imagination, and both returned periodically to Greater New York in the coming decades, reconnecting to their roots as a matter of inspiration, solidarity, or personal preference. Cosmopolitans in spirit, they were nevertheless metropolitans at heart.

$$\text{\textflat}$$

Billy Joel did not pause in the aftermath of his success with *The Stranger*. He toured with the band in support of the record, and in mid-1978 returned to producer Phil Ramone's A&R studio to make his next album. Like Springsteen, Joel was now thinking of in terms of records rather than songs, and thinking in terms of band arrangements from the outset. Ramone, whose professional experience and musical frame of reference were wider than Joel's, appears to have influenced him to experiment with more challenging compositions. "We were channeling all this jazz stuff, even though we weren't jazz musicians by any means," he remembered. "We were rock & roll guys. But I always felt like an adult when we attempted jazz."[2]

The name of the emerging album—*52nd Street*—reflected Joel's new musical orientation as well as a badge of his geographic heritage. The Midtown Manhattan locale was the address of CBS Records headquarters; from the 1930s until the 1950s it was also known as "Swing Street," noted for its profusion of jazz clubs. The brief title track, which is the final song on the album and which functions as a kind of coda, sums up what Joel was attempting: "If we shift the rhythm into overdrive / we could generate a lot of heat." To achieve this end, the core of Joel's band was augmented by what the liner notes call "The Lords of 52nd Street," which includes a bevy of cele-brated jazz players, notably trumpeter Freddie Hubbard and vibes/marimba player Mike Mainieri. As a number of observers have noted, Joel was making the album around the time Steely Dan released its landmark 1977 album *Aja*—on balance a more complex record from a band that also managed to achieve a pop bounce with hit singles like "Peg"—and it may have been an indirect influence on Joel, perhaps in way comparable to Beatles, Beach Boys, and Bob Dylan engaged in friendly rivalry in the mid-1960s.

None of this is immediately apparent from the start of 52nd *Street*, however, which opens with three songs that quickly became fairly conventional pop hits and remain staples of Joel's repertoire. The first, a sneering diatribe against egotism, is "Big Shot," powered by the electric guitar of Steve Khan (who played on *Aja* and Steely Dan's subsequent 1980 album *Gaucho*). Like Carly Simon's 1972 hit "You're So Vain," there has been considerable speculation about who "Big Shot" is about. After many years, Simon confirmed "You're So Vain" was partially Warren Beatty,[3] but Joel has given conflicting answers about his song, telling an audience at Florida State University in 1996 that he wrote it about himself, and Howard Stern's radio show in 2010 that he imagined the song as about Bianca Jagger, sung from Mick's point of view.[4] "Big Shot" is followed by the similarly truculent "My Life," which reasserts the themes of "Movin' Out" from a first-person point of view. And "Honesty" is a ballad of the "Just the Way You Are" variety.

52nd *Street* starts to get more interesting in the next three songs on the album. The writing of "Zanzibar" began, as usual, with the music. But Joel liked the name of the island archipelago off the coast of East Africa as a title. When he asked Ramone whether he liked the idea, the producer—who probably knew Café Zanzibar, which featured Cab Calloway in the 1940s—said it reminded him of a sports bar, prompting Joel to write lyrics about Mohammed Ali and baseball star Pete Rose (who he calls "a credit to the game," which is ironic given that Rose was later barred from the Major League Baseball for wager-ing on games in which he was a manager and player).[5] "Zanzibar" is among the most sophisticated pieces of music Joel has ever written, and Hubbard's trumpet solo is a standout. Less original, but still compelling, "Stiletto" is one of Joel's femme fatale songs—elements of which were apparent on She's Always a Woman," and which reappeared two years later in "All for Leyna"—that features Richie Cannata's saxophone playing.

The third piece in this trio, "Rosalinda's Eyes," is an interesting song in the Joel canon because in it a number of different points intersect in Joel's history, geographic and otherwise. It's told from the point of view of a musician in a Puerto Rican band frustrated by small-time gigs like weddings ("hardly anyone has seen how good I am"). He's sustained by his love Rosalinda and images of "crazy Latin dancing in Herald Square" while imagining a better life in Havana. This psychic blend of New York and Cuba reflects Joel's family history, and indeed the song is a bit of an odd transposition in that it's his father's family, not that of his mother Rosalind, that lived on island. Joel has explained that the song is narrated from his father's point of view, imagining the what he might have said to the woman who became his wife.[6] As with "Zanzibar, the song features a Latin arrangement graced by Mainieri's marimba. In 1979, Joel performed at a Cuban music festival organized by CBS, but his refusal to be filmed for a video of the event, one possibly prompted by Elizabeth Weber's hard-nosed managerial tactics, cost him some goodwill.[7]

The ensuing two tracks on 52nd Street sound a lot like . . . Bruce Springsteen. The brassy "Half a Mile Away" is an R&B rave-up backed by muscular horns reminiscent of Springsteen's style in The Wild the Innocent and the E Street Shuffle. "Until the Night" is a kind of Righteous Brothers song—in fact Bill Medley of that duo went on to record his own version in 1980—with a sax break by Cannata that's easy to imagine coming from Clarence Clemons. These pieces lack the ambition of the preceding ones, and did not catch on as hits the way "Big Shot," "My Life," and "Honesty" did. But the two songs, along with the title track, round out the last third of what most observers continue to consider one of Joel's better efforts. Certainly, it was a successful album in the moment, winning the 1979 Grammy

TEAM PLAYERS

FIGURE 11. The core of the Billy Joel Band—Liberty DeVitto, Doug Stegmeyer, Billy Joel, Richie Cannata—circa 1978. Like Springsteen, Joel always saw himself as a band leader, though his ensembles were more variable—and more volatile—than the E Street Band. *(Photofest)*

award for Album of the Year. Having caught a tailwind with *The Stranger,* Joel enjoyed a string of hits and continued doing so into the new decade.

Springsteen was in a different position. Unlike Joel, who released an album each year between 1976 and 1978, Springsteen's career was suspended by his legal dispute with Mike Appel, which meant that three years passed between the release of *Born to Run* in 1975 and his next album, *Darkness on the Edge of Town* in 1978—a much longer interregnum than is common for successful acts today. Springsteen's situation also contrasted with Joel's in that he did not enjoy a string of hits. Indeed, the singles from *Darkness* ("Prove It All Night," "Badlands," and "The Promised Land") went nowhere. Initial sales of the album were also subpar. The situation improved when Springsteen began to touring support it, beefing up previously weak appeal in parts of the country the like the South that so far had not shown what might be termed Springsteenmania for his live shows. He also received some adoring press from the likes of Dave Marsh, who wrote a cover story on Springsteen for *Rolling Stone*. Eventually, *Darkness* was seen as one of Springsteen's most important records, in part because it signaled a shift in his musical style and imaginative vision.[8]

At the core of that shift was yet another contrast with Joel: while Joel was moving in the direction of musical complexity, Springsteen was stripping his music down to its rock essence. Gone are the horn sections from the first three albums; Clemons, who figured so prominently as a visual as well as an aural icon, is reduced to brief solos on "Badlands," "The Promised Land," and "Prove It All Night." (The artwork for the cover is similarly sparse, the cover featuring a white t-shirt and leather-jacketed Springsteen against a set of blinds, the text produced on a typewriter with a faded ribbon.) Springsteen's signature organ/piano doubling is still prominent, but *Darkness* is a more guitar-driven record, with the hard metallic solos that Springsteen largely eschewed on his earlier records. The effect is spartan, even severe. "Out went anything that smacked of frivolity or nostalgia," he explained in his memoir, citing the influence of punk rock in acts like Elvis Costello, the Sex Pistols, and the Clash. "In '78 I felt a distant kinship to these groups, to the class-consciousness, the anger. They hardened my resolve."[9]

Springsteen *had* written and even recorded songs in the old style, but systematically tossed them aside. One, "Fire," written with Elvis Presley in mind before he died, became a top ten hit for the Pointer Sisters in 1979. (Another song from the period, "Because the Night," was co-written with rising punk star Patti Smith, who also took it to the top ten.) Such rejection of his musical heritage chagrined Steve Van Zandt, as Springsteen tilted away from his influence and toward producer Jon Landau, who encouraged his artistic ambitions. "It's *easy* to be personal," Van Zandt later said. "It's *easy* to be original. Pink Floyd is easy. 'Louie Louie' is hard. *Sgt Pepper's*—yeah, great. But 'Gloria'? Harder. Give me those three chords and make 'em work?

That is the ultimate rock & roll craft/art/inspiration/motivation. That's the whole thing!" Springsteen's response: "That's my buddy, you know. He's very particular about the things he likes."[10] A number of the discarded tracks from the *Darkness* sessions were resurrected in 2010 for *The Promise*, a collection of outtakes from these years that includes the title track, a song that seems to allude to Springsteen's legal troubles (one reason why he decided not to use it).[11] In its relative warmth and fuller arrangements—like the lovely fiddle playing in "Racing in the Street" by longtime Jackson Browne strings player David Lindley—*The Promise* offers a fascinating view of a road not taken, especially given how differently *Darkness* turned out. And not always for the better: there are times when Springsteen seems to strain for significance; his caterwauling vocals on "Something in the Night," for example, can be a bit much. At least one normally sympathetic critic, Jim Miller of *Newsweek*, was surprised that *Darkness* "is as bad as it is," repelled by what he regarded as its lugubrious, repetitive imagery of cars, deserts, and biblical archetypes in songs like "Adam Raised a Cain" and "The Promised Land."[12]

The one domain that does get expansive treatment on *Darkness* is geography: clearly, we're not (only) in Asbury Park anymore. The album opens with "Badlands," a title that is metaphorical but nevertheless evokes the wide horizons of the Dakotas. The first lines of "The Promised Land" refer to "a rattlesnake speedway in the Utah desert," which is inaccurate since that highway is actually located in Nevada, but nevertheless clearly intentional in evoking a western landscape. Such imagery is evoked by the photographs of Eric Meola, who shot the *Born to Run* cover, from a desert trip he, Springsteen, and Van Zandt took in 1977, which has since been absorbed into the lore surrounding the album.[13] There is an Asbury Park reference to Kingsley Avenue in "Something in the Night," but it's one that really flies under the radar (it's no boardwalk, so to speak). As is his wont, Springsteen aims to be evocative rather than specific. A song like "Racing in the Street," one of his true masterpieces, could take place anywhere—in *The Promise* version, the lyrics refer to "northeast states" while the *Darkness* version changes this to a more generic "northeast state"—though the drag-racing culture the song describes is often associated with California.

The irony here is that the *psychic* geography of the album is quite tight, even claustrophobic. "After *Born to Run*, I wanted to write about life in the close confines of the small towns I grew up in," Springsteen reflected in the essay he wrote about *Darkness*.[14] Some of those confines are quite literal, as in "Candy's Room," where "strangers from the city" unsuccessfully compete with the narrator for the affection of the title character, whose sultriness is evoked by glissandos on Bittan's piano that rise like wisps of smoke. (This is another track in marked contrast to its variation, "Candy's Boy," that appears on *The Promise*.) Such claustrophobia is evident again in "Adam Raised a Cain," the first of what might be termed a series of semi-autobiographical "father" songs Springsteen wrote about his relationship with Douglas. "Daddy worked his whole life for nothing but the pain / Now he walks these empty rooms looking for something to blame," the narrator snarls. Those rooms may be empty, but seem they offer no way out. In "Factory," another song based on his father's experience— Douglas Springsteen's work history included a stint at a local rug factory[15]—the workplace is again a steel cage: "Factory takes his hearing, factory gives him life." If *Born to Run* represented a bid for escape, on *Darkness* Springsteen pauses to look back at what he left behind. "For my parents' lives I was determined to be the enlightened, compassionate voice of reason and revenge," he later explained, adding "The piece of me that lived in working-class neighborhoods of my hometown was an essential and permanent part of who I was. No one you have been and no place you have been ever leaves you. The new parts of you simply jump in the car and go along for the rest of the ride."[16]

Make no mistake: getting out was still as important to the characters of *Darkness* as it was to those of *Born to Run*. Now, though, the obstacles seem greater, both internal and external. The protagonist of "Badlands" may believe in the promised land, but does so amid enervating doubt ("sometimes I feel so weak I just want to explode") and in the face of failure ("let the broken hearts stand as the price you gotta pay"). Other characters, like those of "Something in the Night" and "Streets of Fire," seem lost; still others, like those of "Prove it All Night" or "Racing in the Street" proceed with grim or patient determination. The dominant overall mood, captured in the title track that concludes the album, is fierceness in the face uncertainty: "Tonight I'll be on that hill 'cause I can't stop / I'll be on that hill everything that I've got."

Darkness is one of the more uneven records in Springsteen's body of work. Some of these songs sound labored, but others have stood the test of time, given pride of place in his repertoire. "The songs from *Darkness on the Edge of Town* remain at the core of our live performances today and are perhaps the purest distillation of what I wanted my rock 'n' roll music to be about," he said from the perspective of four decades later.[17] In years to follow Springsteen resumed his journey of distillation—much of it even darker than *Darkness*. But in his next record he veered back toward his musical home.

Meanwhile, it was Joel who now took a turn toward simplicity—with different aims and different results. Like Springsteen, he had taken note of punk rock and professed to admire some of it. But he was also inclined to see much of it as little more than a retread of 1960s garage bands of the kind he and Springsteen had been members when they were young. Springsteen made little attempt to replicate a punk sound directly, but tried to channel its aggressive spirit on *Darkness*, where some of his protagonists could express anger with the best of Johnny Rotten or Joe Strummer. Joel, by contrast, seemed to react defensively, conscious that at this point in his career he was best known as a balladeer. He decided to mimic the punk sound—and sounded snide doing it. It was in this phase of his career that the chip on his shoulder was most apparent. His 1980 album *Glass Houses*—the cover depicts him about to through a rock through the plate glass window of his home on Cove Neck, adjacent to Oyster Bay—was among his most popular, but also the most costly in terms projecting an image of gratuitous bellicosity.[18]

Unlike *52nd Street,* in which he wore his cosmopolitanism on his sleeve, *Glass Houses* shows Joel staking out the persona of a street-smart New Yorker. The album opens to the sound of breaking glass, followed by the opening track, "You May Be Right," which landed in the top ten in the spring of 1980. "I walked through Bedford Stuy alone," his narrator asserts, referring to what was once a dangerous neighborhood in Brooklyn. "I may be crazy," he bellows to his paramour, "but a lunatic may be what you're looking for." In "Close to the Borderline," we're told "The bums drop dead and the dogs go mad / In packs on the West Side," accompanied by a bluesy guitar riff. The lonely protagonist of "I Don't Want to be Alone Anymore" follows unwelcome instructions to show up in a suit and tie at the Plaza Hotel as the price he pays for an uneasy reconciliation with his companion.

The dominant musical style of *Glass Houses* is hard rock, featuring the electric guitar of David Brown, who replaced the generally more elegant stylings of Steve Khan on *52nd Street*. Notably, Joel doesn't even play piano on "You May Be Right." There's a small synthesizer part on "Sometimes a Fantasy," Joel's reverb-heavy celebration of phone sex, but the song is driven by Brown's metallic chords and ends with a fast-fingered solo. The attitude may be punk, but the sound is retro.

That's especially true of the signature song on the album, and Joel's first number one hit, "It's Still Rock & Roll to Me." Here again, there's no piano, the song driven by a rockabilly guitar riff and Joel's sneering vocal. "Everybody's talkin' 'bout the new sound but it's still rock & roll to me," he complains in the chorus. The bridge virtually baits his critics: "There's a new band in town / but you can't get the sound / from a story in a magazine / aimed at your average teen." Those critics took the bait. A *Rolling Stone* critics poll named "It's Still Rock & Roll to Me" as the worst song ever written on the subject. "Yes, Mr. Joel has written some memorable melodies," the formerly restrained John Rockwell of the *Times* wrote in his review of a string of Joel shows at Madison Square Garden during his *Glass Houses* tour. "But no, this listener can't stand him, not on the radio and especially in person. He's the sort of popular artist who makes elitism not just defensible but necessary."[19] Reviewing the album for *Rolling Stone*, Paul Nelson wrote that "Billy Joel writes smooth and cunning melodies, and what many of his defenders say is true: his material's catchy. But then, so's the flu."[20] Even the usually mild-mannered satirist Al Yankovic weighed in with "It's Still Billy Joel to Me," which he performed on an accordion instead of a guitar ("what's the matter with the songs he's singin' / Can't you tell that they're pretty lame"). Joel was left to fulminate all the way to the bank.

The only other song of note on *Glass Houses*—the only one with any real charm—is "Don't Ask Me Why," which followed "You May Be Right" and "It's Still Rock & Roll to Me" in reaching the top twenty. Conjuring Paul McCartney at his catchiest, the song has a light Latin beat, castanets, and a ballroom piano solo that consists of fifteen overdubbed keyboards. More typical in terms of the album's mood is "All for Leyna," another of Joel's femme fatale songs with its jagged guitar and piano chords. This one is told from the point of view of an adolescent boy marinating in self-contempt. It's the kind of progressive rock song a band like Styx or Foreigner (led by Joel's friend and future producer, Mick Jones) would have been pleased to record—bands rock critics loved to hate. Unlike *52nd Street*, the songs of *Glass Houses* that didn't get much attention (like "Sleeping with the Television On" and "Through the Long Night") were competent but largely forgettable. Joel rightly considers the ballad "C'Est Toi (You Were the One)" among his weakest work.[21]

The Stranger, 52nd Street, and Glass Houses generated a continuous stream of hits from 1977 into 1980, and Joel sustained that momentum in 1981 by releasing a live album of older material, *Songs in the Attic,* that gave "She's Got a Way" (from *Cold Spring Harbor*) and "Say Goodbye to Hollywood" (from *Turnstiles*) a new lease on life on the pop charts going into 1982. While Springsteen struggled to find his voice and maintain his integrity, Joel had become a commercial juggernaut.

But behind the scenes, Joel's life and career were in turmoil. The collapse of his marriage to Elizabeth Weber lay at the intersection of the two, as she was his manager. At one point she had brought her brother Frank into Joel's financial affairs, a development that created further complications when he sided with Joel over his sister, whom he later sued. Joel eventually broke with Frank, and his finances would not really be on a stable footing until the 1990s.[22] Over two and a half years lapsed between the release of *Glass Houses* and his next album—an interval about as long as that between *Born to Run* and *Darkness on the Edge of Town* in 1975–1978. One reason for this was a motorcycle accident Joel sustained on Long Island where he damaged his wrist and thumb.[23] When he finally did resurface in the fall of 1982, the resulting album was his magnum opus: a work of reckoning with his suburban heritage.

$$\phi$$

In 1980, while Billy Joel was winding down, Bruce Springsteen was winding up. *Darkness on the Edge of Town* was a downbeat album with a muted reception, but the ensuing tour raised his profile (and, it appears, his spirits). He went into the Hit Factory, a famous Manhattan studio in March of 1979 with a bevy of material he tested on tour, like "Sherry Darling," a comically boisterous account of an exasperated man stuck in a traffic in Midtown Manhattan while taking his aggravating girlfriend's mother to a weekly appointment at an unemployment agency. ("She can take the subway back to the ghetto tonight," he threatens, with a cheering chorus in the background.[24]) Now he wanted to find a way to blend, rather than separate, components of his psyche. "Rock & roll has always been this joy, this certain happiness that is in its way the most beautiful thing in life," he told *Los Angeles Times* critic Robert Hilburn at the time. "But rock is also about hardness and coldness and being alone. With *Darkness*, it was hard for me to make those things co-exist. How could a happy song like 'Sherry Darling' co-exist with 'Darkness on the Edge of Town?' I wasn't ready for some reason within myself to feel those things. It was too confusing, too paradoxical. But I finally got to the place where I realized life had paradoxes, a lot of them, and you've got to live with them."[25]

The result of this effort was *The River*, the most emotionally full, rich, and resonant album of Springsteen's career. As had always been the case, he had a batch of songs he recorded and winnowed. The first track he recorded and discarded, "Roulette," depicting a family fleeing their home, was written in the wake of the Three Mile Island nuclear disaster in 1979. But this time, the album grew rather than shrank: after handing in the album to Columbia, he decided *The River* should be a double album, and spent over $1 million in the studio ("Oy vey," CBS chief Walter Yetnikoff responded upon learning this. "Can't you just give me a nice one-record with two or three hit singles?") But as Springsteen later explained, "I wanted something that could only come from my voice, that was informed by the internal and external geography of my experience. The single album of *The River* I'd just turned in didn't quite get us there, so back into the studio we went."[26]

Sonically speaking, *The River* did indeed harken back to his roots, picking up the road not taken with *The Promise*. "I wanted to create songs that would sound good played by a bar band," he later explained. "To me, basically, that's what we remained. All the years I'd been performing, I'd start with something that sounded like it came out of the garage. In the past, these were the kinds of songs that fell by the wayside when we went into the studio to record. For *The River*, I wanted to make sure this part of what I did didn't get lost."[27]

Actually achieving this effect meant changing the way he made his records, tilting away from the polished sheen that had marked Jon Landau's methods (not only on *Born to Run*, but especially in his work with Jackson Browne on the 1976 album *The Pretender*) and more toward a slightly muddier sound favored by Van Zandt (whose presence on this album is more apparent than any other, which included roles as backup vocalist in songs like "Out in the Street"). "Most studios, in those days, were completely padded to give the engineer the utmost control over each individual instrument," Springsteen said. "The Eagles, Linda Ronstadt, and many other groups had a lot of success with this sound, and it had its merits, but it just didn't suit our East Coast sensibilities." The goal was now was "instruments bleeding into one another and a voice sounding like it was fighting out from the middle of a brawling house party"—which is exactly what "Sherry

Darling" sounds like.[28] It's a step back toward the Shore Sound of his Asbury Park youth.

There was another, more subtle shift on *The River*, which might be described in terms of its psychic geography. Springsteen has always described himself as an autobiographical songwriter, even if he often rearranged any number of external details in describing an internal state. And in a lot of ways, that remained true. But from here on out, he seems more committed to capture the lives of *other* people at least as much as his own. And the particular people he had in mind—the particular world he sought to recreate—was the parochial world from which he had been born. At the center of that world was his family, who became a synecdoche for the white working class as a whole. As fans of his music know, Douglas Springsteen loomed large in this regard. "He never said much about my music, except that his favorite songs were about him," Springsteen told the audience in his acceptance speech when he was inducted to the Rock and Roll Hall of Fame in 1999. "And that was enough, you know? Anyway, I put on his clothes [Springsteen is speaking literally as well as figuratively here] and went to work. It was the way I honored him."[29]

This family-Freehold-America axis is especially clear in the title track of *The River*, which he wrote for his sister Ginny. Springsteen had been listening carefully to country music since the *Darkness on the Edge of Town* sessions—an important indicator of a creeping fatalism edging into his work—and found himself in a hotel room singing Hank Williams's 1949 recording "My Bucket's Got a Hole in It," a light-heartedly mournful song about a man unable to drink his sorrows away. Williams's line "I looked down in the sea" morphed into going down to the river. From there, he crafted a story about his sister and brother-in-law's marriage. (The female character's name is Mary, clearly alluding to that of "Thunder Road" and thus giving an implicitly tragic ending to that hopeful story.) Ginny got pregnant at age 18, at which point she married the child's father, Mickey Shave, who went to work in construction in New Jersey. But a crash in the industry left him without a job in the late 1970s, and the young family struggled, events described in the song. Springsteen debuted "The River" at the Musicians United for Safe Energy (MUSE) concerts at Madison Square Garden in 1979. "That's my life," she told her brother backstage. "That's still the best review I ever got," he reported in his memoir. "My beautiful sister, tough and unbowed, K-Mart employee, wife and mother of three, holding fast and living the life I ran away from with everything I had." (The marriage survives to this day; the couple has three children and a passel of grandchildren.)[30]

Springsteen may have been running away, but he was also looking back. This is evident in "Independence Day," an elegiac farewell song in which a son leaves his father. He can be brutally frank—"they ain't gonna do to me what I watched them do to you"—even as he shows a kind of paternal affection for his dad ("Papa go to bed now, it's getting late"). What's also interesting here is the son's recognition that both men are subject to forces larger than themselves and that the young too will grow old: "Soon everything we've known will be swept away."

Indeed, an air of willful anachronism hovers over *The River*. The headline from Paul Nelson's effusive review in *Rolling Stone*—"Let Us Now Praise Famous Men"—captures the album's spirit.[31] That headline alludes to the famous 1941 book by James Agee, with photographs by Walker Evans, whose title in turn refers to the Book of Sirach: "Let us now sing the praises of famous men, our ancestors in their generations / The Lord apportioned to them great glory, his majesty from the beginning."[32] *Let Us Now Praise Famous Men* is a classic work of the documentary impulse of the 1930s, exploring the lives of three southern tenant families in a quest to endow the lives of ordinary people with a sense of democratic dignity that reflects the best spirit of the age.[33] Part of what makes the book so evocative is the way in which it is a work of present-tense journalism (albeit of an unorthodox sort in its novelistic approach) while at the same time evoking a spirit of timelessness. As Nelson notes, Springsteen tries to do the same thing: "Because he realizes that most of our todays are the tragicomic sum of a series of scattered yesterdays that had once hoped to become better tomorrows, he can fuse past and present, desire and destiny, laughter and longing, and have death or glory emerge as just another story."[34] The final lines here allude to a song by the Clash, whose recent *London Calling* was a point of comparison.

We can see this dynamic operating in a number of songs on *The River*. One obvious example is "Out in the Street," a celebration of working-class consciousness. "I work five days a week girl, loading crates down on the dock," the narrator says. "I take my hard-earned money, and meet my girl down on the block." It's here that he—they—achieve a sense of freedom: "When I'm out in the street / In the crowd I feel at home." The song is presumably contemporary, but as Springsteen probably knew, longshoremen, so vividly evoked in the 1954 movie *On the Waterfront*, were a vanishing breed in the early eighties, especially on the East Coast, as declines in union power and technological innovation undermined the profession.

The process works in the other way, too. In the context of its time, "I Wanna Marry You" sounds almost comically dated, not only in its old-fashioned idiom—using the term "little girl" was questionable in a post-feminist age—but in its dreamy, organ-driven melody that sounds like something from Bobby Vinton, the Polish/Lithuanian pop star of the fifties who had sentimental hits like "Mr. Lonely" and "Blue Velvet" (memorably turned into an ode to dread in the 1986 film of the same name by David Lynch). But the lyrics describe a single mother of two struggling to get by and a narrator who tells her of his father, who went to his grave with a broken heart, believing true love was a lie. In this context, aspiring for romance is a risky thing, and yet this character suspects that even the most worldly of women may still yearn for it, however imperfect its source. "To say I'll make your dreams come true would be wrong," he admits to her. But maybe, he asserts, "I could help bring them along."

This pattern plays out even in clearly comic songs like "Cadillac Ranch," a tribute to the open-air museum in Amarillo, Texas. Again, in the 1980s, Cadillacs had become something of a relic in an age of expensive gas and Japanese imports, and yet this character clings fast: "Buddy when I die throw my body in the back / Take me to the junkyard in my Cadillac." Springsteen describes "Ramrod," a paean to drag racing, as "one of the saddest songs I've ever written."[35]

Nowhere is Springsteen's penchant for paradoxical compression more evident than in his first big hit, "Hungry Heart," which peaked at number five on the *Billboard* chart in December of 1980. (Springsteen had written the song for the Ramones—he went through a bit of a phase imitating that Queens-based band in 1979, most notably in outtake "Livin' on the Edge of the World," some of whose lyrics reappeared three years later in "Open All Night"—but Landau convinced him to keep it.) "Hungry Heart" has an almost relentlessly cheerful melody, sustained by a Federici's glockenspiel and the backing vocals of Mark Volman and Howard Kaylan of the Turtles, best known for their 1968 hit "Happy Together." But there's a melancholy overlay to the tune—it was inspired by the Four Seasons 1964 hit "Dawn (Go Away)"—and the lyrics begin by describing a man who makes a spontaneous decision to abandon his family: "I took a wrong turn and I just kept goin." Yet his concluding assertion—"Don't make no difference what nobody says / Ain't nobody likes to be alone"—speaks to a truth that Nelson aptly describes as "simple but sturdy."[36] In the words of another track, "two hearts are better than one."

What really stands out here—the thing that makes *The River* a true turning point in Springsteen's career—is his growing power of empathy. (It's really the area where he outshines Joel, who tends to condescend to characters when he strays too far from his own experience.) "Point Blank" is a ballad about a man who's still in the throes of grief about a woman who has left him. He's angry, but he's nevertheless compassionate as he considers the struggles that she's had. She's someone who did what she was supposed to in her life, but what the unnamed "they" asked for was unfair: "You didn't have to live that life." The album ends with "Wreck on the Highway," inspired by the powerful 1938 Roy Acuff song of the same name. Acuff's tune takes an accusatory tone toward indifference to human tragedy: "When whiskey and blood run together / Did you hear anybody pray?" But Springsteen's character is more haunted as he imagines a state trooper knocking on the door of a girlfriend or young wife. He goes home to his own beloved with a new appreciation for the preciousness and fragility of life.

Commercially speaking, *The River* was Springsteen's breakthrough album. It was his first to top the *Billboard* album chart, and sold 1.5 million copies by Christmas.[37] It attracted the attention of no less august a figure than John Lennon, who shared the top ten with Springsteen with his comeback hit "(Just Like) Starting Over" in December of 1980. On the day he died Lennon called "Hungry Heart" his favorite song on the radio.[38] There was no longer any doubt: Springsteen had arrived, and had taken his place among the leading rock artists of his time.

It was all the more striking, then, that Springsteen followed *The River* with the least commercially accessible record of his career.

To a great degree, this was the result of personal circumstances: when he returned from a national as well as international tour to support that album at the end of 1981, Springsteen once again found himself facing demons that had been nagging him before he had begun working on *The River*. He ended a relationship of four years, restlessly looked at real estate, and spent nights driving obsessively around Freehold. "Mine was a pathetic and quasi-religious compulsion," he later recalled. "On my visits to my hometown, I would never leave the confines of my car. That would've ruined it. My car was my sealed time capsule from whose bucket seats I could experience the little town that had its crushing boot on my neck in whatever mental time, space, or moment I chose." On a drive west in the fall of 1981, he had a mental breakdown in an unnamed town. When he arrived in Los Angeles, where he had just bought a house, he called Landau, who set him up with a psychotherapist, and indeed would be treated for depression for decades to come.[39] (Joel has also struggled with depression, at times destructively resorting to alcohol to treat it, and as we've seen, he himself was in a dark moment in his life at this juncture of 1981–1982.)

This psychic journey was accompanied by an intellectual one as well. A series of explorations began to converge: the fiction of Flan-

nery O'Connor; the folk music of Woody Guthrie; songs by Mississippi Delta bluesmen John Lee Hooker and Robert Johnson; a reprint
edition of Allan Nevins and Henry Steele Commanger's 1942 classic
A Pocket History of the United States; director Terence Malick's 1973
film *Badlands*. Springsteen began writing a series of "black bedtime
stories."[40] In January of 1982 he recorded a series of demos on a cas-
sette tape, thinking he would bring this material to the band to record. And some of those songs did in fact form the germ of *Born in the
USA*, including the title track. But after lots of experimenting, Springsteen decided to release ten songs from those demos pretty much as
he originally recorded them—songs that sounded like they could
have easily been written and recorded in the early 1930s rather than
the early 1980s. The album, *Nebraska*, was released in September of
1982.

At first glance, *Nebraska* seems like *Darkness on the Edge of Town* in
that it has a broad continental sweep in its locales. This is most obvious in the case of the title track, a retelling of the notorious Charles
Starkweather murders of 1957–1958, when the nineteen-year-old
Starkweather, traveling with his fourteen-year-old girlfriend, Caril
Ann Fugate, went on an eleven-person shooting spree before he was
captured, tried, convicted, and sentenced to death. (A fictionalized
version of this story is told in Malick's *Badlands*.) Springsteen's version, which ranges across Nebraska and Wyoming, is rendered in flat,
first-person narration; when asked why he did it, Springsteen's Starkweather replies the language of unsparing Catholic existentialism:
"Well sir I guess there's just a meanness in this world."[41] (Little wonder that Landau worried about his friend's emotional state and helped
get him into therapy.) The setting of "Highway Patrolman," which
tells the story of two brothers, one a cop and the other criminal,
moves from Ohio to Michigan to the Canadian border. As is often the
case in Springsteen songs, other venues are clearly intended to be
more archetypal. The haunting "Reason to Believe"—its seemingly
hopeful title betrayed by bewilderment that people *do* believe—has
verses set in a highway ditch, a shotgun shack, and a church congrega-
tion by a riverside. While there are clearly autobiographical echoes

"My Father's House," this tragic tale of unrealized reconciliation functions at least as well as a Christian allegory than it does a narrative account of a bad dream.

Given these facts and the widening aperture of Springsteen's geographic vision, it's notable, even ironic, that more than half the songs on *Nebraska* have fairly specific New Jersey referents—indeed it may be the most explicit such album in his canon. Admittedly, some of these are a little far afield; "Atlantic City" does not appear to be a typical locale in Springsteen's ambit, and the song is a fictive rendering of criminal activity that seems to come straight from the headlines that followed that city's legalization of commercial gambling in 1977 (the opening lines refer to "the Chicken Man," nickname of Philip Testa, who led an organized crime family before his murder in 1981). "State Trooper," in which a man ominously tells a police officer that "I've got a clear conscience about what I've done," takes place somewhere on the New Jersey Turnpike. "Johnny 99," the tragic story of a man who asks to be executed after having a breakdown and killing a man, is triggered by the closing of the Ford Motor plant closure in Mahwah, right up against the New York border, in 1980. The only thing resembling an upbeat song on the album, "Open All Night," refers to the "early North Jersey industrial skyline," a kind of liminal zone between suburb and city reminiscent of F. Scott Fitzgerald's Valley of Ashes in *The Great Gatsby*.

Other tracks are literally and figuratively closer to home. "The songs on *Nebraska* are connected to my childhood more than any other record I'd made," Springsteen has said.[42] This unveiled directness seems palpable in "Mansion on the Hill," in which seems to refer to his grandfather's house as well as the hidden injuries of class as the boy narrator and his sister hide in the cornfields while a party goes on beyond "those gates of hardened steel."[43] The concluding verse situates the song in Linden Town, an archaic name for Linden, in northern Jersey. Another song told from a child's point of view is the heartbreaking "Used Cars," which brims with empathy for the father, mother ("sittin' in the backseat all alone"), salesman, and the little sister eating an ice cream cone. Yet none of this takes the edge off the narrator's angry declaration in the chorus: "Mister the day the lottery I win I ain't never gonna ride no used car again." The child speaks of a drive down "Michigan Avenue," a thoroughfare off the Garden State Parkway in Kenilworth (there are still dealerships there).

All parties involved recognized that *Nebraska* was a stark, modest effort (the cover depicts a wintry prairie highway as viewed from a dashboard; the typography is red against a black background). CBS chief Walter Yetnikoff later described his reaction as, "you made it your garage, thank you. We'll do the best we can."[44] For the first time in his career, Springsteen did not go on tour to support the album, something that did not happen again until *Western Stars* in 2019. But *Nebraska* ultimately sold a million copies, and remains a favorite among those who might otherwise be skeptical of Springsteen. "I didn't know there was music like that, that was as impactful and heavy as *Nebraska* was," Tom Morello, founder of the rap-metal band Rage Against the Machine, remembered years later.[45] Rage, as the band was sometimes known, was famous for an explicit brand of revolutionary politics not commonly associated with Springsteen (it did record a fiery version of the title track of Springsteen's 1995 album "The Ghost of Tom Joad" in 1998). Morello later joined the E Street Band as a guitarist for a series of tours in the early twenty-first century.

For the moment, Springsteen had exorcised some demons, whom he fought on his home ground. In the coming days, he picked up some of the fragments of *Nebraska*, which formed the core of his next album. It was many years before he returned as directly to his youth, and never again with the intensity he showed here. It was time for him to move on.

$$\oint$$

As their careers progressed, Billy Joel and Bruce Springsteen developed an increasingly acute historical consciousness. One dimension of this, of course, is musical: all musicians borrow from their predecessors with greater or lesser degrees of conscious appropriation. But Springsteen and Joel were unusual in the intensity with which they went about absorbing the sounds of their forefathers. In this and other ways, Springsteen was an autodidact, and a fairly systematic one at that—we've seen, for example, the way he gave himself a tutorial in rock & roll history before recording *Born to Run*. Joel had years of formal training, but his musical education was to a great degree a matter of learning by doing, and there are few people in the history of popular music more able to replicate sounds and traditions than he is, a skill derived from close observation.

Historical consciousness operates on additional planes as well. Joel has long been an avid reader (of history, among other subjects), a habit Springsteen picked up belatedly. As they grew older, their music and lyrics took on an increasingly generational cast. The Baby Boom has long been notable for its strong sense of itself, particularly in contrast with their parents, alternatively admired for their stoicism and dismissed for their stodginess. Joel and Springsteen both exhibit strong desires to depict and document ordinary American life since World War II.

However, they've done this in different ways. Springsteen tends to work from the inside out—he never makes general pronouncements, preferring to depict historical phenomena, from deindustrialization to changes in gender relations, at a granular level in the lives of ordinary people whose words and actions implicitly connect to broader national dramas. He resolutely uses the "I" pronoun when telling such richly resonant stories, and *Nebraska* represents the full crystallization of this approach. Joel, by contrast, sometimes surveys scenes from a broader canvas, whether it's invoking the wild west in "The Ballad of Billy the Kid," or situating a quotidian visit to one's parents as "The Great Suburban Showdown." Beginning in the 1980s, Joel refined this strategy, focusing on more specific frames of reference and deploying a "we" pronoun to speak in generational terms. (He also uses "you" expansively, as in "Big Shot," which straddles between outer-directed irritation and self-loathing.[46]) Such an approach is evident in *The Nylon Curtain*, released one week before *Nebraska*. Like—and with—*Nebraska*, it was considered a major statement. The two albums were reviewed together in *Time* under the headline "Against the American Grain: Bruce Springsteen and Billy Joel Risk Big and Score Big." Reviewer Jay Cocks called the albums "devastating."[47]

Joel himself certainly thought he was doing his best work. This is the material I'm most proud of, and the recording I'm most proud of," he said of *The Nylon Curtain* in a video to accompany the release of a complete set of his albums in 2011. Joel described the making of the record as a laborious process after which "I felt like I had almost died." (Springsteen used similar language in describing the making of *Born to Run*.) "There was so much recorded—different instruments, sound effects, orchestral things, percussion instruments, vocals, synthesizers. It's very rich."[48]

The two axes of history described here are abundantly evident on *The Nylon Curtain*. In musical terms, the whole album is an act of homage to the Beatles in general and John Lennon in particular. As we've seen, Lennon virtually passed a baton to Springsteen when he died, but Joel was really the true inheritor of the two, something he himself found surprising. "I felt a genuine sadness that John was gone, that there were never going to be any other John Lennon recordings. The Beatles were over; we'd all accepted that. But as much as I had loved them and as easy as it was for me to idolize Paul McCartney, I had never realized how much John Lennon meant to me, how much he and Paul were the irreplaceable sweet and sour. It was only later that I realized I was channeling John in a lot of the vocals on that album."[49]

Actually, it's remarkable just how many John Lennons appear on *The Nylon Curtain*. The biting, cynical, early-Beatles Lennon, with the hard-driving rhythm guitar of "Money (That's What I Want)" is evident in "A Room of Our Own." The experimental mid-sixties Lennon of "Strawberry Fields Forever" and "I Am the Walrus" is unmistakable in "Surprises" and Scandinavian Skies," complete with baroque touches and sound effects. The sinewy late-Beatles Lennon of "I'm So Tired" is palpable in "Laura," which transcends mere imitation in its vivid depiction of an exhausting woman who is apparently modeled on his mother, Roz.[50] (These and other songs gain considerable punch from Liberty DeVitto's drumming.) The post-Beatles

Lennon had written a similarly anguished "Mother," but the most of the referents here reflect Beatle-scale ambitions. "I wanted to write a real sonic masterpiece," he said. "Almost like I was trying to go for *Sgt. Pepper* kind of thing where I was playing the studio as a kind of instrument."[51] In that regard, the album's "A Day in the Life"—it's suite of melodies stitched together—is the seven-minute epic "Goodnight Saigon," with its stark sections, spooky percussion, and helicopter sounds.[52]

Which brings us to consider *The Nylon Curtain* as a generational statement about the Baby Boom generally and its suburban component in particular. (The sleeve photograph of the album features an overhead shot of what appears to be Levittown, with all the windows covered in yellow shade. The back cover shows Joel drinking a cup of coffee while reading the *New York Times* in what is clearly a suburban home.) "It had to do with the suburbs, with a certain degradation of our lives as everything went synthetic," he said of his decision to give the album its name. "By contrast to the Iron Curtain, a dominant image in Americans' heads from the forties until the fall of its key physical feature, the Berlin Wall, the nylon curtain is not a clear image. It wavers, it's hazy." And yet it has an evident tidiness to it, reflected in the orderly image houses in sunset, modeled on a paperback book cover.[53]

The sunniness of some of its melodies notwithstanding, the overall portrait of the nation that Joel offers, like that of Springsteen in *Nebraska*, is dark. "Pressure" is a deeply caustic portrait of affluent anxiety rendered with jabbing synthesizer chords and a throbbing bass in a minor key. "Here you are with all your faith, and your Peter Pan advice," he sneers in the second person at those who rely on public television and *Time* magazine for their sense of reality. "You have no scars on your face, and you cannot handle pressure." "Goodnight Saigon" is Joel's effort to make a statement about the defining historical experience of his youth, the Vietnam War (which, as we will see, was also major preoccupation of Springsteen's). It's a good example of his use of the collective pronoun—"we would all go down together," he sings in the chorus on behalf of the working-class boys who, unlike himself and Springsteen, went to war. Joel's portrayal of the war is of a piece with a broader liberal discourse about the Vietnam that depicted it as a tragic mistake, typified by movies such as *The Deer Hunter* (1978) and *Platoon* (1986).

Like Springsteen, Joel was also living in the present tense, even as he connected the nation he inhabited in 1982 to earlier events. Both were both appalled by the election of Ronald Reagan in 1980—Springsteen, who called it "pretty terrifying" the next night and performed "Badlands" in an ironic tribute[54]—and both saw the rise of neoconservatism as a repudiation of the upward mobility that they had considered a birthright. "All of a sudden you weren't going to be able to inherit what your old man had," Joel said of recession of 1981–1982, the worst the nation had experienced since the Great Depression. He noted the "creeping pessimism, but also philosophical resignation, a little bit of paranoia."

These ideas are vividly expressed in the opening track of *The Nylon Curtain*, "Allentown." Originally written as "Levittown," Joel changed the venue to the eastern Pennsylvania city afflicted by the massive closures at Bethlehem Steel and takeover of Mack Truck by Renault. The song speaks of a dream betrayed, "the promises our teachers gave / If we worked hard, if we behaved." The grimness of the lyrics are hedged by the melody, "an Aaron Copeland-influenced arrangement of major sevenths that's percussive and stirring."[55] Factory whistles and the sound of compressors also give the song a distinctive air.

A similar friction characterizes the penultimate song on the album, "Surprises," which has a buoyant air but reflects the experience of his motorcycle accident and the end of his marriage. The album closes with light, even lovely, "Where's the Orchestra?" which Joel has described as one of his favorite songs. The track, which describes a man who goes to what he thinks is a musical only to find it's a straight play, is a meditation on disappointment. As with Springsteen, depression has hovered over Joel's career, and, as with Springsteen, he was in a rough spot in 1982.

Like *Nebraska*, the reception of *The Nylon Curtain* was relatively muted. But the album was more respectfully received than *Glass*

Houses. "Pressure" and "Allentown" were hits, albeit at the bottom of the top twenty. Sales were respectable, and the album reached #7 on the *Billboard* chart. But compared with his previous three albums, *The Nylon Curtain* underperformed.

Unlike previous disappointments, however, Joel was in no serious danger of losing his standing at Columbia, any more than Springsteen was with *Nebraska*. Both men had experienced hard times personally, and responded by making records that reflected their desire to pursue artistic ambition rather than commercial success. Better days were coming.

FIGURE 12. Bruce Springsteen in his *Born in the U.S.A.* heyday, circa 1984. Springsteen's visual iconography cemented his status as the bard of the white working class, something he has been associated with ever since. *(Photofest)*

CHAPTER 6

Right Time

The Stars Align, 1983–1986

BILLY JOEL AND BRUCE SPRINGSTEEN are talented people. They are also lucky people. As noted, their first stroke of luck was a matter of where and when they were born: though both faced early challenges and genuine deprivation, they came of age in a time of rising expectations and outcomes. Their other great good luck was a matter of reaching their peak of productivity and influence in the mid-1980s, which turned out to be an extraordinarily propitious time for their careers to crest, both as a matter of the prevailing ideological climate as well as the state of the music industry at the time. We will explore each in turn as a matter of understanding just how astoundingly successful they were in the 1980s, and why that success sustained their careers for decades to come.

$\oint$

There are different ways to periodize the twentieth century, but for our purposes, the middle third of that century had a very distinctive character. These were of course decades of war, economic upheaval, and social change, but the prevailing mindset of this era was a widespread belief in the efficacy of social and economic reform and a belief in the efficacy of government intervention to achieve such ends—a worldview we know as liberalism. Liberalism wasn't the only ideology available at the time; indeed, there were strong countercurrents on both its left and its right. But in the period that began with the ascension of Franklin Delano Roosevelt's New Deal in the 1930s and ended Lyndon Johnson's Great Society in the 1960s, liberalism was the prevailing common sense in American society, against which people defined themselves as they came of age. This was not only a matter of politics and economics; it was also a matter of culture, in which the dignity of ordinary people and the legitimacy of their aspirations became a default setting against which people measured themselves and each other (as opposed to, say, knowing one's place in the social order or subsuming oneself in the name of a collective cause).

Bruce Springsteen and Billy Joel were born right smack in the middle of the liberal era, and right smack in the middle of the twentieth century. In the context of this particular discussion, they were utterly unremarkable people in their attitudes and assumptions of the time, in no way more so than the disinclination of either of them to seriously engage in politics in the first half of their lives. You will look in vain when combing through accounts of their youth for sharply etched partisan identities. As Jews, the Joels were more likely to be Democrats, long the party of the ethnic working class, than Republicans, though as an engineer by profession Howard Joel may have leaned right on account of his managerial status, but he was a largely absent father in any case. (The only truly pointed public political statement Joel has ever made came when he wore a Star of David onstage in the aftermath of the notorious 2018 "Unite the Right" rally in Charlottesville.[1]) Even when Joel himself edged in the direction of politics on *The Nylon Curtain*, he avoided doing so in explicitly partisan terms. "I didn't want to get up on a soapbox and become a sociopolitical songwriter, but I wanted to talk about people going through hard times," he told biographer Fred Schruers. "My ethic about writing songs throughout that era was always to be talking about *people*, whether it's a love song, a song about a relationship, or a friend, or a barfly—it's always got to be about a particular person."[2] As noted, this isn't quite accurate; "Allentown," for example, is written with collective pronouns. But the spirit of the remark is nevertheless true enough; Joel has never been remotely as political as Bob Dylan, for example, and his work was not marked by any obvious political valence long after Springsteen himself fully embraced a partisan identity as a progressive Democrat in the twenty-first century.

Springsteen's youthful relationship to politics, racial, cultural and otherwise, is a bit more complicated. "I don't remember a political discussion ever being held," Springsteen recalled of his childhood. He does remember asking his mother the family's political affiliation, to which Adele responded, "We're Democrats, they're for the working people." This is not to say he was entirely lacking a political consciousness. "I did grow up a child of the sixties, so social conscience and political interest were bred into my cultural DNA," he explained. He also asserted, not quite convincingly, that "the subversiveness of Top 40 radio can't be overestimated." But he was nevertheless aware of its real-life limits. Given the growing prominence of race relations in mid-century it's notable that Springsteen, far more than most of his white suburban peers—and Joel—interacted with African Americans in sustained and complex relationships over the course of his youth. "We had black friends, though only rarely did we enter each other's homes," he later remembered.[3] The early E Street Band was genuinely interracial, but by 1975 Clarence Clemons was only the black member who remained. A similarly real, but finite, quality marked his engagement on other political fronts. In 1972, as a favor to a friend, Springsteen played a benefit show for Democratic presidential candidate George McGovern. He immediately, and durably, regretted it. "He was entirely apolitical," a peer remembered. "He didn't believe anything would be better or worse at the end of the day because of politicians."[4] During the 1979 MUSE concerts against nuclear power, Springsteen was conspicuously skittish about making a public statement against the use of nuclear power and declined to sign the statement other performers like his friend Jackson Browne made in the concert program. His song "Roulette," which he performed at the shows, grew out of an imagined family's flight from the nuclear accident at

Three Mile Island of 1979. But he dropped its inclusion from *The River,* perhaps because he considered it too pointed.[5]

Joel, for his part, was downright dismissive of MUSE. "No Nukes is a bourgeois issue," he told interviewer David Sheff three years later. "I'm not saying I'm a Ronald Reagan pro-nuke, but I understand that we don't have any alternatives."[6] (A half-century later, Joel's comment remains relevant in the sense that many American green-minded progressives, who are disproportionately bourgeois, continue to reject nuclear energy, arguably the most efficient and environmentally friendly approach to sustainability.)

When Joel and Springsteen left high school in 1967, the liberal consensus that had dominated American life was unraveling. One key source of that unraveling was a divide within the Democratic party over the Vietnam War, which both opposed and managed to avoid. But that was pretty much the extent of their political consciousness. Focused on building a career, neither paid much attention to how the prevailing ideological winds were gradually shifting. Richard Nixon was elected president in 1968, large measure by pursuing a veiled political program that implicitly accepted the premises of modern liberalism—he created the Occupational Health and Safety Administration, established Earth Day, and supported the Equal Rights Amendment—while at the same time expanding the Vietnam War and embracing Affirmative Action, not because he sought social justice but instead because he knew it would divide key constituencies in the Democratic party like labor unions and civil rights activists.[7] In his deeply Machiavellian maneuverings in domestic and foreign policy, Nixon may well be the most complex politician in American history in his deft grasp of the nation's rightward drift, even as he proved too clever by half in subverting the democratic process in the Watergate scandal, which proved to be his undoing. Democrat Jimmy Carter defeated his successor Gerald Ford in large measure for his sincere commitment to good government (he was part of the first post-Civil Rights era of Democratic politicians, having defeated segregationist Lester Maddox in 1970). But by the late 1970s, Carter himself was showing unmistakable signs of moving to the right himself, deregulating the airline and trucking industries in 1978 and staking out a hardline stance toward the Soviet Union after the Soviet invasion of Afghanistan in 1979.

These shifting ideological currents were global. The Iranian Revolution of 1978–1979, which brought the first religious fundamentalist regime to power in the Middle East, confounded not only U.S. and Soviet calculations, but also the previous generation of regional leaders, like Saddam Hussein and Muammar Gaddafi, autocrats who nevertheless assumed secular modernization was the path to power in nations like Iraq and Libya. In Great Britain, Margaret Thatcher upended decades of Labor rule in a spirit of neoliberalism that reembraced market principles. Even communist nations like China were reconsidering their political commitments in the name of rapid modernization, as evidenced by Den Xiaoping's famous implied endorsement of capitalist methods in his maxim that "it doesn't matter whether a cat is black or white as long as it catches mice."[8]

Again, there's no indication that any of this mattered very much to Bruce Springsteen or Billy Joel. But both seem to have been jolted by the election of Ronald Reagan to the presidency in 1980. As we've already seen, Springsteen described this development as "terrifying." Joel's most obvious response to this development was "Allentown," a pointed critique of the libertarian economic policies that came to be known as Reaganomics. Springsteen's *Nebraska* was seen, correctly, in a similar light. Even if these records had never been released, it would have been widely assumed that Springsteen and Joel were good liberals, because it was widely (if not always correctly) assumed that pretty much all artists, and pretty much everyone under 35 was.

But—and this is the point of what might seem like a digression from the topic at hand—it is finally impossible to understand why Joel or Springsteen had the impact they did in the 1980s without some consideration of the changing cultural climate in which they were operating at the time. And here's the key to understanding that climate: the conservative winds that were blowing in that decade carried in them a new embrace of tradition, a rededication to the past as a source of vitality that swept through American culture at large.

Nowhere was this new embrace of tradition more obvious than in the realm of popular music. Musicians have always been known for their acuity to new musical trends, and the 1980s certainly had their fair share, ranging from newfangled synthesizer-based bands such as the Human League, Flock of Seagulls, and Eurhythmics that dominated the charts early in the decade, to the emergence of hip-hop as a major pop music genre in the mid-1980s. But a self-conscious dedication to older sounds was also a hallmark of the decade. In the 1970s, there had been bands such as Sha Na Na that were understood to be nostalgia acts. But in the early eighties the Stray Cats wrote and performed a string of hit songs in a 1950s-based rockabilly style, managing to sound fresh and contemporary at the same time. This neo-classical trend was even more pronounced in country music, where a new generation of performers—Dwight Yoakum, Steve Earle, Lyle Lovett, and k.d. lang, among others—set themselves apart from middle-of-the-road country by stripping down their sound to the basics and/or by accentuating styles from an earlier era. Lang fancied herself as the reincarnated voice of Patsy Cline—she called her band the Reclines—though the sheer power of her vocals, coupled with her quirky (and closeted gay) personal style, put her in a class by herself.[9]

This attentiveness to tradition could be as much thematic as it was musical. Over the course of the decade John Cougar Mellencamp wrote paeans to farm life in albums such as *Scarecrow* (1985) and evolved from a fairly straightforward rock musician to one who incorporated Appalachian instruments into his arrangements for *The Lonesome Jubilee* (1987). Even more surprising was the way even avant-garde artists got in on the act. In 1980, the critically celebrated Talking Heads released their landmark album *Remain in Light*, which was heavily influenced by indigenous African music and contains some of the most arresting pop music of the rock era. But by the mid-1980s in albums such as *Speaking in Tongues* (1983), *Little Creatures* (1985), and *True Stories* (1986), lead singer/songwriter David Byrne was celebrating the joys of domesticity and roadside Americana in his own inimitable way ("the future is certain/give us time to work it out," he sings with a gospel choir as his backdrop in "Road to Nowhere"). Laurie Anderson, who was much more avant-garde than even the Talking Heads, titled her 1983 album *United States*; it included tracks with titles like "Yankee See" and "Democratic Way." Neither the Talking Heads nor Laurie Anderson were patriotic in any conventional sense of the term—indeed, some of their music willfully defied national pieties. But in their distinctive ways they rode the wave of engagement with Americana that surged through the body politic.

In this particular context, Joel and Springsteen were both notable for the degree to which they were faithful curators of the nation's musical past. Joel's entire career has been a matter of putting a distinctive topspin on a wide variety of pop idioms. For Springsteen, this commitment to tradition has been more obviously thematic than musical, but the bedrock of his style rests on an African American rhythm & blues foundation that he lovingly maintained long after most black musicians had moved on. When he started to streamline that sound in the late 1970s, the result was tighter alignment with country, folk, and early 1960s rock. In short, his new directions involved rededicating himself to old ones.

It's imperative to remember that whichever way cultural winds may be blowing, there are always people and institutions who resist by whatever means are available to them, and who succeed in maintaining their stance in the face of opposition. In the mid-1980s, there were a series of performers who were genuinely transgressive forces in a conservative era and enjoyed exceptionally high-profile success. The British band Culture Club, for example, scored a string of hits and carved out a queer space in popular culture at a time of considerable hostility toward homosexuality in the United States. The prodigiously talented Prince transgressed a series of racial, sexual, and gender boundaries as a songwriter, guitarist, and electrifying performer in these years. Cyndi Lauper and Madonna carved out sharply different but nevertheless strongly feminist identities that defined the national conversation. (Indeed, the early 1980s was an era of female dominance in pop, as indicated by the high-profile careers of not only these two, but Deborah Harry of Blondie and Stevie Nicks of Fleetwood Mac, among others.)[10] Michael Jackson was a cultural force unto himself, and while there was, and continues to be, a conversation of just what his primary significance was, it's clear that he was not a conventional figure in terms of musical innovation, visual representation, or racial significance. All these people were important in offering alternatives—offering hope—to those who could not, or did not want, to fit into the conventional social categories of the time.

It is of course true that the spirit of an age also leaves a mark even on those who resist it. Many observers considered Madonna's leveraging her sexuality as a form of power to be problematic, if not inimical, to the larger feminist project of the 1980s. Lauper may have shown us that *girls* wanted to have fun, but *women* wanted equal pay for equal work. However undeniably innovative he was, Prince's commercial dominance was challenged by the rise of hip-hop, which he absorbed somewhat uneasily as a generational turnover in pop music was apparent by decade's end. All this said, it would be hard to overstate just how prominent, and how novel, these people were at the time, and how widely their impact resonated beyond the world of popular music. They were broadly recognized cultural icons, all the more important for their perceived progressive power in a conservative age.

Which, paradoxically, made Joel and Springsteen the weirdly normal ones in this gallery of culture heroes. Neither could dance like Michael Jackson, were as sexy as Madonna, or had the striking visual flair of Lauper. Springsteen did embark on a workout regimen circa 1983 that left him looking buff, and his charisma has always been one of his greatest assets. Joel managed to succeed without an obvious surfeit of any of these attributes ("Nobody ever mistook Billy Joel for a matinee idol," Springsteen partisan Dave Marsh once noted.[11]) To a misleading degree, both were understood as "regular guys"—coded as white—and this in turn gave hope to a whole other set of people who valued hard work, tradition, and working-class values while rejecting the rest of the neo-capitalist package that Reagan and his allies were selling in the 1980s. Taken collectively, these pop stars constituted the face of what would later be termed diversity, equity, and inclusion.

Which brings us to the other half of the equation we are exploring here. These people made the impact they did not only because they were talented, or because they embodied ideas and values that either stood out and/or comported with the tenor of their times, but also because of a confluence of three forces that converged in the music industry by the mid-1980s that changed the game and reconstituted the very nature of stardom.

The first is these innovations occurred in record business. In 1980, the industry was in notably poor shape; *Glass Houses* and *The River* were two bright spots in an otherwise disappointing year for Columbia Records in particular.[12] The industry downturn had begun in 1979, when sales fell eleven percent, and bottomed out in 1982, when that label's parent company, CBS, laid off hundreds of employees. This slump was all the more notable given the previously steady growth of the music business in good times and bad, and because the preceding years had been marked by blockbuster releases such as Fleetwood Mac's *Rumors* (1977), as well as the *Saturday Night Fever* (1977) and *Grease* (1978) soundtracks, all of which rank among the bestselling albums of all time. Different reasons were offered for the decline, among them the sharp recession in the wake of the Energy Crisis of 1979, the rise of pirated recording on blank tape, and competition from new media such as video games. There was some belief the industry had reached a saturation point.[13]

As had been true since the late 1960s, the dominant format in the recording business remained the LP, though singles remained important drivers of album sales. There were other formats as well, notably the 8-track tape, which was popular for listening to music in cars, and the pre-recorded audiocassette, which was growing in popularity and which by 1984 overtook the LP as the most profitable of all formats. But in the early 1980s, the arrival of a new configuration offered hope that the industry would receive to be a shot in the arm. Indeed, it did—and changed the dynamics of the music industry as a whole.

That new format was known as the compact disc, also known as CD. A circular 4.75-inch diameter digital optical storage system made from polycarbonate plastic, CDs offered crystalline sound reproduction, and since there was there was no actual contact between the disc and its optical reader (unlike a needle on a record) they never wore out, even if their durability proved more mortal than advertised. Moreover, while the only way you could listen to individual songs on an album out of order was by physically moving the arm of a record player, CDs were programmable, allowing you to hear what you wanted in whatever order you liked. The catch, from a consumer standpoint, is that CDs required new hardware: you had to acquire a CD player in order to hear music in this form. In this regard, the advent of CDs was a little like the advent of color television in the 1960s—or that of video-recording, which was also taking off in the 1980s. Such investments in hardware, in turn, stimulated sales on the software side—not only in encouraging consumers to buy new music in the new format, but also to re-purchase old favorites in the new form. Naturally, there was a price premium involved. Initially, CD costs were absurdly high, though they gradually came down to the point where each cost a few dollars more than a traditional LP.

And what was the first commercially released compact disc? It was Billy Joel's *52nd Street*, which went on sale in Japan in 1982. This was of course years after the LP was released—presumably the idea was to issue an album that already had demonstrated its popular appeal— and is indicative of the slow process by which CDs entered the industry bloodstream. But by March of 1983, there were 800 titles available, and more than 2000 by year's end, with Columbia plunging into the new market with gusto, by setting up a plant to manufacture the discs in Indiana.[14] The first million-selling CD was Dire Straits' 1985 album *Brothers in Arms*, but it took the rest of the decade for CDs to over-take audiocassettes as the most profitable format in the industry. As late as 2012, well into the digital age, CDs still accounted for the majority of album sales.[15]

The second major domain of change in popular music was in the medium of radio. The advent of frequency modulation (FM) to complement amplitude modulation (AM) in the 1960s had resulted in two de facto tracks of broadcasting: AM for pop hits and FM for what came to be known as album-oriented rock (AOR). The latter generally fostered less restricted programming, the least restrictive of which was college radio, where experimentation reigned and many in the industry cut their teeth. Over the course of the 1970s, FM stations became increasingly centralized and corporatized; relatively autonomous disk jockeys like Ed Sciaky of WMMR in Philadelphia, so important to Springsteen's career, became less common. Meanwhile, AM radio also differentiated and specialized with the advent of stations dedicated to new genres like disco and demographically segmented formats such as Adult Contemporary (A/C), which focused on lighter ballads. This approach also had racial implications in intensifying a larger pattern of segregation evident in pop music in the 1970s, a staple theme of rock histories of this period.[16]

Beginning in the mid-1980s, however, a new format—Contemporary Hit Radio (CHR)—emerged and shuffled the programming deck. These stations were much more insistent on playing (and replaying) hits than traditional AOR, which often focused on oldies. On the other hand, CHR was also more diverse in its playlists, allowing for a reintegration of pop on the airwaves, where figures like Prince could jostle alongside white rockers—and, when it came to blistering guitar solos, beat them at their own game. For perhaps the last time in the history of popular music, broadcasting helped create a musical center that fostered a large audience with a shared musical frame of reference.

There was another important implication in the emergence of CHR. Until that time, a pop star could hope for two, maybe three, hit singles from any given album (Joel was unusual in having four with *The Stranger*). But now programmers decided it was more lucrative in terms of luring advertising dollars to go deeper into a hit album than take a risk on an unknown. Such airplay generated momentum that could sustain new releases for years after their release. The conventional wisdom held that one hit single could take an album to the 500,000 gold-record threshold. But three or four could get you to five million. But even that barrier could now be broken. Seven of the nine tracks on Jackson's *Thriller* became hits, with album sales in excess of 38 million. Prince's *Purple Rain*, Lauper's *She's So Unusual,* and Lionel Ritchie's *Can't Slow Down* each had five hits, each selling between ten and twenty million copies of their respective albums globally.[17]

And then there was the last, most transformative piece of this puzzle: music video.[18] The key event here was the advent of Music Television network, known as MTV, which was launched by the Time-Warner media company in 1981. As with any form of cultural innovation, music video had deep roots, dating back to the days where early cartoons were synchronized to jazz recordings. The fusion of music and images was central to the success of the Beatles, dating back to *A Hard Day's Night* (1964), a feature film that featured Fab Four performances. But the form really became recognizably modern in Great Britain with the advent of the British TV show *Top of the Pops* (1964–2006), which featured clips of musical acts performing hit songs.

The immediate precursor of MTV was *Popclips*, a 1980 show hosted by comedian Howie Mandel and broadcast on Nickelodeon, one the first cable channels. The late 1970s and early 1980s were a time of experimentation in cable television, when programming executives were just beginning to offer subscribers niche channels dedicated to specific kinds of programming (like the Weather Channel, launched in 1982). The business model of MTV rested on acquiring free programming from record labels, which they regarded as advertising for their acts. Expectations were modest, but MTV took off rapidly, thanks to engaging graphics, hip video disc jockeys ("veejays"), and, of course a parade of engaging musical acts. In the decade to come, the influence of MTV went far beyond music video, shaping advertising, fashion, and other television programming.

Because they had experience—and an inventory of video to work with—British acts were among the first beneficiaries of MTV, which launched the careers of a series of performers, notably Duran Duran, whose videos were quite cinematic. Veterans like Jackson transferred their varied skill sets easily to the new medium; new acts like Madonna took it with instinctive panache. Among the other implications of MTV's rise was a new emphasis on the individual song as a driver of popularity, which paradoxically fed the rise of hit albums that were now stocked with them.

In the normal order of things, such a situation was not especially propitious for either Joel or Springsteen. They were the products of an older system, one that rested on records sold through relentless touring and AOR radio airplay. "I became a musician partially because of my physical limitations," Joel told *Billboard* in 1994. "I wasn't tall, I don't have Cary Grant looks."[19] (The very reference dates him, even in the context in of the early 1980s.) Springsteen's first music video, "Atlantic City," from *Nebraska*, which debuted in late 1982, is telling in this regard. He's entirely absent from the video, which was shot entirely in black-and-white and depicts, in documentary fashion, the demolition of the famed Marlborough-Blenheim hotel in 1978. He's almost conveying contempt for the new musical order.

But here again, timing worked in favor of the two men. Both were established artists whose careers were peaking. This meant any records they released would get good record company support in terms of promotion, budgets, and the ability to attract talent for any videos they made. Joel's first video was for "Pressure," which was helmed by Australian director Russel Mulcahy. It featured the rapid-cut editing that was *au courant* at the time and visual references to classic movies such as *A Clockwork Orange* and *The Parallax View*.[20] Joel looks a little foolish, but standards were a little more forgiving in the days before appearing on video became an everyday fact of life for performers, and, eventually, everyone else. His second video, "Allentown," also directed by Mulcahy, has the feel of a musical number and is actually quite stylish.

Eventually, Springsteen made his peace with the form and appeared in a series of videos. In some ways, that wasn't difficult, because Springsteen has been obsessed with his visual presentation since at least the time of the *Born to Run* album cover. Springsteen's carefully chosen visual iconography of the 1980s—the leather boots, the denim jacket, the bandana—were not created with MTV in mind, but was greatly magnified by it. The larger point here is that the new cultural form did not prove an obstacle for either man, even if neither was fully at home with it.

Because everything else was coming together. By 1983, the United States was emerging from the severe recession of 1981–1982. The music business had reorganized after years of doldrums. There was a new appetite for the appealingly traditional. And Bruce Springsteen and Billy Joel were each on the cusp of something big.

$$\oint$$

Nineteen eighty-three may well have been the best year of Billy Joel's life. After his divorce from Elizabeth, his motorcycle accident, and the torturous process of recording *The Nylon Curtain,* he decided to take a vacation. His friend Paul Simon convinced him to visit St. Bart's in the winter of 1983. It was there he met supermodel Christie Brinkley, whom he regaled from a barroom piano in a gathering that also included her rising peer Elle McPherson and a teenaged singer named Whitney Houston.[21] Joel actually dated McPherson first, but ultimately bonded with Brinkley, whom he later married and with whom he had a daughter, Alexa Ray—her middle name in honor of Ray Charles. His newfound happiness loosened his creative energies, and he set to work making an album with unusual rapidity. "It was a gas to be writing this stuff, and it just kept coming; you don't fight that," he said. "I think I wrote the whole album in about eight weeks." In the promotional biography that accompanied the new record, he was quoted as saying, "I decided to have as much fun as I could have, and wanted it to *sound* like I was having fun."[22]

The resulting album, *An Innocent Man,* was released in August of 1983. At first glance, it seems like a fairly modest proposition; Joel himself compared it to John Lennon's 1975 collection of oldies, *Rock & Roll,* in which he covered some of the favorite songs of his youth (and discharged some record company obligations in the process). One important difference is that unlike that album, the songs of *An Innocent Man* are originals, each written in honor of performers from the pre-Beatles era of pop. So it is, for example, that the opening track, "Easy Money," evokes the soul music of James Brown—right down to Brown's expertly controlled screeches. "An Innocent Man" conjures up Ben E. King; "The Longest Time" is a pitch-perfect homage to do-wop acts such as the Platters and the Five Satins; "Tell Her About It" is a tribute to Motown. Joel honors local influences in "This Night," which invites comparisons to Dion and the Belmonts, while "Uptown Girl" is downright uncanny in capturing the spirit and letter of Frankie Valli and the Four Seasons. (Actually, as Joel explained, it's an inversion of the group's 1964 hit "Rag Doll," in which the man, not the woman, is the rich half of the couple.[23]) And so on.

There are two things about *An Innocent Man* that make it more than merely derivative. The first is the sheer skill and deceptive simplicity that went into the musical construction of these songs. "It doesn't really ape anything," he explained. It just *feels* like it. There actually isn't a standard chord progression in the LP. It's pretty musically complex. The challenging thing for me was making it seem so simple."[24] One is reminded here of Springsteen's description of Joel's songs as "built like the Rock of Gibraltar"; the chorus of "This Night," for example, is based on the second movement Beethoven's Piano Sonata #8, also known as *Sonata Pathétique*. The execution is also first-rate: the horns are tight, the harmonies are beautifully arranged, and Joel's voice has never sounded better ("I had a suspicion this was going to be the last time I was going to be able to hit those high notes, so why not go out in a blaze of glory," he said of his falsetto in "An Innocent Man"). Like the best cultural works of the 1980s, the album is resonant and fresh at the same time.[25]

The other innovation in *An Innocent Man* is the decisively adult sensibility Joel brings to the proceedings. One of the things that made the music that he honors on the album so compelling is its wonderful sense of innocence—the classic songs of that era are fearlessly wise without being worldly. In his classic book *Mystery Train*, Greil Marcus captures the magic of those 1950s hits: "I feel a sense of awe of how fine their music was," he says of acts like the Monotones, a six-member doo-wop ensemble best known for their 1958 hit "The Book

STEPPING UP

FIGURE 13. Billy Joel photo from *An Innocent Man* photoshoot, 1983. The album would mark his apogee as a pop star. *(Photofest)*

of Love." "I can only marvel at their arrogance, their humor, their delight. They were so sure of themselves."[26] But the man who sings the songs of *An Innocent Man* is both more mature and more vulnerable than the artists he channels. The protagonist of "The Longest Time" is dazzled by the sheer joy of being in love. But that's in part because he knows from hard experience how temporary and fragile such a state can be: "I don't care what consequence it brings / I have been a fool for lesser things." References to "consequences" and "lesser" things imply a history of hurt. The character who sings "An Innocent Man" is certainly not ingenuous; instead, he's a man who's asserting he can chase love in good conscience despite the fears his would-be companion might have about him, fears rooted in experiences he understands ("I've been there"). These are not the kinds of things teenagers typically say to each other.

Similar twists mark the expression of old verities. Part of what made Motown hits like "Shop Around" and "You Can't Hurry Love" so compelling is the way they packaged homespun maternal wisdom in shiny pop packages. Patterned on such songs but written a generation later, "Tell Her About It" implicitly absorbs the lessons of feminism in the way the protagonist counsels a friend to be more expressive in his feelings—to reject the strong silent type archetype that had dominated mid-century versions of masculinity. "Leave a Tender Moment Alone," which has kind of a Burt Bachrach feel to it, explores a man's struggle for comfort with intimacy. At the time and afterwards, Joel made clear that these songs reflected his own efforts to come to terms with outmoded gender roles. "A lot of men my age grew up just as the sexual revolution was getting started, and now that it seems to be winding down, they are confused," he told Stephen Holden of the New York Times in 1986. "I was married for a long time and living on Long Island. When I got divorced and moved back to New York City, it was a Rip Van Winkle experience. I found that the rules had changed, and in many ways my attitudes had become old-fashioned."[27]

Finally, there's self-awareness about the appeal—and the limits—of nostalgia. "Keeping the Faith" lovingly recreates an early sixties adolescence with its references to matador boots ("only Flagg Brothers had them with the Cuban heel"), shark skin jackets, and Old Spice aftershave. The song asserts that youthful experiences are also valuable in terms of their lasting impact ("lost a few fights but it taught me how to lose OK"). But, its narrator says in the bridge, you can't simply live in the past: "You can get just so much from the good life / You can linger too long in your dreams." He reminds his listener that the bad old days weren't always as good as remembered, and that tomorrow isn't as bad as it seems.

An Innocent Man was not Joel's bestselling album—it did not break the 10 million-mark of *The Stranger*—but it made him an incandescent figure in the firmament of eighties pop stars. The album sparked a string of six top forty hits: "Tell Her About It," (his second number one, after "It's Still Rock & Roll to Me"), "Uptown Girl," "An Innocent Man," "The Longest Time," "Keeping the Faith," and "Leave a Tender Moment Alone."

The album also spawned a number of successful videos. The clever "Tell Her About It" depicted Joel as the lead singer in the fictive BJ and the Affordables, performing on the Ed Sullivan Show. It featured a cameo by comedian Rodney Dangerfield, who enjoyed a second lease on life as an unlikely movie star—Joel had originally written "Easy Money" for the movie of the same name with him in mind.[28] "Uptown Girl" was a musical number in which Joel played a greasy mechanic and paramour Brinkley the figure of the title. Producer Jon Small—ex-husband of Joel's ex-wife Elizabeth—hired Michael Peters, who choreographed Michael Jackson's "Beat It" video to help compensate for both Joel and Brinkley's deficiencies, and it became the most watched of his career.[29] "The Longest Time" depicted Joel and his bandmates in the aftermath of their high school graduation; "Keeping the Faith" is a story video about whether Joel was in fact an innocent man. None of these videos have entered the MTV canon, but they got the job done of sustaining the album's momentum. "I thought the whole idea was stupid," he later said of his work on these projects. "But I recognized they were useful promotional tools."[30]

An Innocent Man made Joel a fixture of the airwaves—and record stores at the dawn of the CD era—from the summer of 1983 into the spring of 1985, imprinting him in collective memory as a superstar for generations to come. (The cover, a shot of Joel sitting on a set of cast iron steps on Mercer Street in Soho, has become iconic, and a favorite site for fans to take selfies.[31]) As luck would have it, this was also the moment his peer also reached his own career peak.

$$\text{\clef treble}$$

As with Billy Joel, 1983 found Bruce Springsteen climbing out of a depressive hole. He wasn't working as fast as Joel did on *An Innocent Man*—and his storybook romance with a model wouldn't begin until the following year—but he returned home from his emotionally difficult sojourn in California, began exercising regularly, and visiting an Asbury Park nightclub to pick up the latest musical currents. He spent much of the year working on his next album.[32]

Or, perhaps more accurately, returned to working on the last one. Springsteen was once again generating voluminous material in these months, more than he would ever use. But he found himself turning back to the songs he had written at the time of *Nebraska*, and it was these that turned out to form the core of the new record. There was one song in particular about a Vietnam veteran that proved to be its core. It was, of course, "Born in the U.S.A."

As with Joel, who actually began writing "Goodnight Saigon" in the late 1970s, "Born in the U.S.A." had a long gestation.[33] The immediate cue had come from writer/director Paul Schrader, who in 1981 had sent Springsteen a screenplay of the same name in the hope he would write a song for it (he eventually contributed the theme song for what became *Light of Day* in 1987). Springsteen liked the phrase and incorporated it into a draft of a song he was writing about Vietnam vets.

Joel and Springsteen, who were of draft age at the very height of the Vietnam War, could not but be haunted by it, especially given the growing discourse around the conflict in a series of films released in the late seventies, including *Coming Home* (1978), *The Deer Hunter* (1978), and *Apocalypse Now* (1979). Joel spoke frequently, if vaguely, about friends he had that went overseas, and on at least one occasion told an amusing story about how the building to which he was supposed to report for the draft burned down, singeing his documents.

"Goodnight Saigon," which he described as the result of conversations with vets who encouraged him to write about them, has a collective air (as with "Allentown," it's written with a collective "we" pronoun).[34] Springsteen's experiences, and expressions, are more specific. He played with a drummer, Bart Haynes, who died in the war, and his relationship with (Long Islander) Bobby Muller of Vietnam Veterans of America led to a famous 1981 benefit concert, among other forms of support.[35] In keeping with the prevailing discourse of the time, both Springsteen and Joel avoid taking sides or taking a specific political position in their respective songs, though Springsteen's bristles with implicit condemnation of the indifference and neglect of the jobless former warrior stranded "out by the gas fires of the refinery," an image that likely to have come out of the north Jersey industrial skyline.

The first version of "Born in the U.S.A." was recorded on January 3, 1982, a part of a batch of tunes that functioned as acoustic stenography—as bare-bones version of songs to be fleshed out later. Springsteen concluded that many of these *Nebraska*-fated songs did not work with a band arrangement, but this one was a notable exception. The key to its realization as a full-fledged rock song was a vaguely martial riff that pianist Roy Bittan played on a synthesizer—an instrument that Springsteen had thus far eschewed but which played a major role on the album and in giving his music the sheen it rode onto the pop charts.

Springsteen did not regard the catchiness of the new tune as an unmixed blessing, and "Born in the U.S.A." proved to be something of a political football in the months to come. There's a sharp and ironic contrast between the seeming brightness of the music and the grimness of the lyrics, which tended to be overlooked (though it is not necessarily wrong to interpret the song as a gritty affirmation of resilience in the face of indifference). As has been widely documented, President Reagan invoked the song at a 1984 re-election campaign rally in New Jersey, causing much outrage, and Chrysler chairman Lee Iacocca offered Springsteen an estimated $12 million to use the song an in an ad (he declined). Decades later, Springsteen was still ruminating ruefully about trick-or-treaters in red bandanas coming to his house and singing the song each Halloween.[36]

The other song that gave Springsteen some trouble was the album's first single, "Dancing in the Dark." Springsteen considered the album done in early 1984, when Jon Landau told him it lacked a hit single. An irritated Springsteen responded with a similarly synthesizer-driven pop tune marked by dark lyrics reflecting his struggle to overcome his alienation. "It went as far in the direction of pop music as I wanted to go—and probably a little farther," he later said.[37] "Dancing in the Dark" ultimately landed at number two on the *Billboard* pop chart, unable to dislodge Prince's startlingly original "When Doves Cry" from the top slot.

In between these two songs, the album that came to be known as *Born in the U.S.A.* went through Springsteen's usual set of permutations in which the final product scarcely resembled its early iterations. (One regrettable excision: the lovely, haunting, reverb-rich "County Fair," a vivid slice of small-town life with a melancholy vocal that textures a fleeting moment of happiness.) All of the songs that became side one were derived from *Nebraska*, notably "Child Bride," which underwent a dramatic rockabilly transformation into "Working on the Highway," sidestepping what might be seen as a song about pedophilia, and "Darlington County," a similarly raucous musical short story about a pair of smooth-talking New York operators—"our Pa's each own one of the World Trade Centers"—who find misadventure on a road trip to South Carolina. "Cover Me" was written with Donna Summer in mind, who, despite her disco diva status was also a good rock singer, but Springtseen decided to keep it, giving her "Protection" instead. The title of "I'm on Fire" belied the quiet intensity of Springsteen's inner darkness: "sometimes it's like someone took a knife baby edgy and dull / and cut a six-inch valley through the middle of my skull."

Side two of the album is more of a grab bag of songs. "No Surrender" (added at the last minute) and "Bobby Jean" were both oblique tributes to Van Zandt, who played an important role in the making of the album, but who left the band amid some personal friction with

Springsteen on the eve of its release.[38] "I'm Goin' Down" is an amusing featherweight of a tune about a romantic squabble, while "Glory Days," an anecdotally driven meditation on aging, remains one of the more beloved songs in Springsteen's body of work.

The only track on *Born in the U.S.A.* that has an unmistakably local setting is its closer, "My Hometown," a mournful account of racial tension and deindustrialization populated with childhood memories and Freehold references to Main Street and the recently closed 3M mill there.[39] It's a little passive, and at one point Springsteen planned to drop the song, part of the original *Nebraska* sessions from the album, but was convinced to keep it by co-producer Chuck Plotkin, who argued it worked as a bookend with "Born in the U.S.A."[40]

Springsteen seems to regard *Born in the U.S.A.* as one of his less successful records. He indicated that he tried, and failed, to recapture the intensity of *Nebraska*. "Sometimes records dictate their own personalities and you just have to let them be," he later shrugged.[41] *Born in the U.S.A.* lacks the thematic and/or emotional cohesion of his best work, though the album is sonically distinctive thanks to engineer Bob Clearmountain's mixes, which mark the record as quintessentially 1980s in its luster.

At the time and ever since, there has been a mythology of Springsteen as the reluctant superstar, and it would be unfair to suggest he was not, and is not, sincere about the misgivings that surrounded the hoopla that followed. Certainly, he was far more self-conscious about his pending success than Joel, who had his own reservations but was largely content to do what he needed to take his career to the next commercial level. Springsteen, always mindful of his audience, could be disarmingly direct when he thought it would reflect well on him. As he told Kurt Loder of *Rolling Stone* in December of 1984, "We wanted to play because we wanted to meet girls, we wanted to make a ton of dough, and we wanted to change the world a little bit, you know?"[42] Whatever deliberations may have taken place, it was clear that he had a path forward to big-time success, and, with Landau at the helm of his ship, took it.[43]

His record company was ready and waiting. "I think I hit the studio ceiling," Columbia president Al Teller said. The CEO of CBS, Walter Yetnikoff, was characteristically vulgar. "I don't know if I wet my pants, but I may have," he said. "Sometimes record company executives actually *like* the stuff they're dealing with."[44] The company pulled out all the stops: big promotion budget, Annie Leibovitz photo shoot (Joel had one but didn't like the results),[45] and dance-club friendly extended mixes of "Dancing in the Dark," "Born in the U.S.A.," and "Cover Me" made by producer Arthur Baker. *Rolling Stone* reported in advance of the album's release that a "fun" record was on the horizon.[46]

Born in the U.S.A. proved to be not only one of the biggest albums of the 1980s, but also one of the biggest albums of all time, with global sales of over thirty million copies. It spawned seven top ten singles— "Dancing in the Dark," "Cover Me," "Born in the U.S.A.," "I'm On Fire," "Glory Days," "I'm Goin' Down," and "My Hometown"—a feat only equaled by Jackson with *Thriller* and his sister Janet's *Rhythm Nation 1814* (1989).[47] The first (performance) video, for "Dancing in the Dark," was directed by Hollywood auteur Brian DePalma; the next three, for "Born in the USA," "I'm on Fire" and "Glory Days," were directed by the great independent filmmaker John Sayles. The first of these was marred by bad sound editing, but "I'm on Fire" is a small masterpiece notable for Springsteen's fine acting. "Glory Days" was shot at Maxwell's, a bar in Hoboken, New Jersey, as well as a baseball field in Brooklyn, and remains a classic of the early MTV era.

In 1984–1985, Springsteen became a global icon of, as well as a foil for, the resurgent United States of the Reagan era. The garb that became his signature style—denim, leather, and cotton—signified his solidarity with the American working class in an era of economic transition from an industrial to a service economy. Springsteen was both careful not to demonize Reagan but also to make clear his skepticism of him. "I don't know if he's a bad man," he said in the aftermath of Reagan's invocation of him on the campaign trail. "But I think there's a large group of people whose dreams don't mean that much to him that just indiscriminately get swept aside."[48] In the half-century since, Springsteen has become an international symbol of a "good" American for those who think of themselves as fair-minded but unhappy about the global role of the United States. Which may be why so much of his audience is now European.

Billy Joel's peak commercial moment was essentially 1983–1984, and Springsteen's was 1984–1985. "Dancing in the Dark" was on the *Billboard* chart at the same time as "Leave a Tender Moment Alone" in the summer of 1984, while "Keeping the Faith" jostled with "Born in the USA" in early 1985. Overall, Springsteen had more hits and higher chart positions with his smash than Joel did, though Joel scored his second of three number ones with "Tell Her About It," something Springsteen never did. *Born in the USA* topped the album chart and remained on it for 143 weeks, but *An Innocent Man* landed in the top five and lasted for 111. Springsteen burned brighter. But Joel was sharing a day in the sun in what many observers consider one of the more vibrant moments in the history of popular music.

The two men also shared a landmark moment in pop history, appearing together in "We Are the World." The song, an American answer to the highly successful charity record "Do They Know It's Christmas?" assembled by Boomtown Rats leader Bob Geldof, was recorded under the auspices of USA for Africa. It was written by Lionel Richie and Michael Jackson and produced by Quincy Jones. On January 28, 1985, a who's who of pop music gathered for the recording. Joel sang the first verse with James Ingram and Tina Turner, while Springsteen exchanged lines at the end with Stevie Wonder. In the album that followed, Springsteen contributed a rock version of the Jimmy Cliff classic "Trapped," a rare instance of his engagement with reggae, a genre Joel occasionally engaged.[49]

Both managed to keep that moment going for a little while longer. In July of 1985, Columbia released Joel's *Greatest Hits, Volume I and Volume II*, a two-disc collection that went sold over 10 million copies (over 20 million by industry standards measuring "units") and thus one of the company's bestsellers of all time. A jaunty reggae-styled single, "You're Only Human," in which Joel revisited his own suicidal episode as a way of encouraging resilience in young people, made it into the top ten that summer.

Springsteen's momentum remained strong for over two years following the release of *Born in the U.S.A.* His tour to support the album was an international media event, and his 1984 romance and 1985 marriage to actor/model Julianne Phillips made him tabloid couple comparable to the Joel and the better-known Brinkley. The final single from the album, "My Hometown," peaked in January of 1986. His publicity machine ramped up again later that year for the five-disc set *Bruce Springsteen and the E Street Band Live/1975–85*, which was released in time for the holiday season and generated instant sales in the millions, prompting block-long lines outside record stores.[50] That collection featured a variety of familiar songs as well as a cover of the 1970 Edwin Starr classic "War," which became his eighth straight top ten single.

By that point, the moment was finally over. "I really enjoyed the success of *Born in the U.S.A.,* but by the end of that whole thing, I just kind of felt 'Bruced' out," he said in 1992. "I was like 'Whoa, enough of that.' You end up creating this sort of icon, and eventually it oppresses you."[51]

Although both continued to enjoy commercial and artistic success, Billy Joel and Bruce Springsteen would never be quite so famous again. To some degree, this was a matter of the ever-shifting zeitgeist—rock acts like R.E.M. and U2 were pushing to the fore; hip-hop was beginning to assert its dominance—and to some degree one of personal choice. In 1984, both turned 35: no longer quite young men. Both had moved beyond defining themselves in relationship to the homes and families they left behind. Now they turned to making new ones—on familiar turf.

FIGURE 14. Billy Joel performing in the Soviet Union, July 1987. The tour was a signal event in the accelerating end of the Cold War, and a personal highlight of Joel's career. *(Photofest)*

CHAPTER 7

Family Feuds

Domestic Politics, 1986–1995

A S THIS BOOK has documented, the lives of Billy Joel and Bruce Springsteen have been marked by a series of parallels, intersections, and coincidences that sometimes seem uncanny—the dates of their births, the circumstances of their childhoods, the coinciding peaks and valleys of their careers. But the similarities of their circumstances in the late 1980s and early 1990s are less surprising. Both reached middle age; marriage and child-rearing became an important part of their everyday lives—and everyday life itself took center stage. Perhaps inevitably, their relationship with their respective bands, on which both placed great emphasis earlier in their lives, became strained and then at least partially dissolved. Both continued to record and perform, but their music reflected this new emphasis on domesticity. And a sense of limits, even fragility, that came with aging.

Both were explicit about this. "I like to think that I'll be able to live like a normal human being," Joel told Anthony DeCurtis of *Rolling Stone* in 1986. "I'm not going to be a celebrity forever." Springsteen's reflections were typically more polished, reflecting his greater thoughtfulness—but also an element of self-conscious calculation in constructing his media persona. "Trying to keep the kind of success we had with *Born in the U.S.A.* going would have been a losing game," he said. "A glance at rock history would tell you as much. Artists with the ability to engage a mass audience are always involved with an inner debate as to whether it's worth it, whether the rewards compensate for the singlemindedness, energy, and exposure necessary to meet the demands of the crowd. Also, I felt that a large audience is, by nature, transient. If you depend on it too much, it may distort what you do and who you are. It can blind you to the deeper resonances of your work and your most committed listeners."[1]

Given the similarities in where they had been and where they were headed, there are some significantly ironic differences in the records that followed their mid-1980s heydays. Joel's *The Bridge* and Springsteen's *Tunnel of Love* were both explorations of marriage. Yet while Joel's album had a tortured birth but was marked by a relatively optimistic disposition, Springsteen's came quickly and relatively easily but was clearly the work of a troubled husband. Neither man's marriage lasted. But while the aftermath of *Tunnel of Love* was followed by a second Springsteen nuptial that went on to last for decades, Joel's profession of faith in romance was followed by two more divorces and two more marriages. (Each man fathered three children; Joel's youngest two were born in 2015 and 2017.) On the whole, it would appear that Springsteen has done a better job of managing his demons. But there can be little doubt that both had them, and neither would ever do much more than keep them at bay. Which may be why they managed to retain loyal audiences: they told stories to which aging Boomers (and post-Boomers) could relate.

𝄞

Billy Joel did not particularly want to make a new album in 1986. He was contractually pressured by Columbia to get one out, and the label denied his request for a delay of one to two years. "At the time I was quietly asking myself, 'What are you doing? You're just taking advantage of people liking your old stuff, and the record company's going to market it and hype it—and you know it sucks,'" he told biographer Fred Schruers.[2]

This view is unduly severe. The record that became *The Bridge* is not among his best, and indeed can be seen as part of a larger decline in the overall quality of the work his last years as a recording artist. But it is a competently made record—he once again teamed up with producer Phil Ramone—marked by sophisticated songwriting. Like 52nd *Street*, it has a bit of a jazz flavor in its chord progressions and arrangements, and like that record, it yielded a string of hits.

The core of *The Bridge*, its pun of a title linking musical transitions with personal ones, is a suite of songs about marriage and children. The jazz-guitar styled "This Is the Time" strikes a reflective note about the perishability of happiness, which leads its protagonist to savor the day: "These are the days to hold on to / 'Cause we won't although we'll want to." Though Joel has said that the inspiration of the song came from his relationship with Elle McPherson, it's hard not to believe it was at least also partially grounded in his marriage to Brinkley. "I'm warm from the memory of days to come," he concludes. The album's biggest hit, "A Matter of Trust," is a muscular rock song in which he chronicles the many ways a relationship can go wrong. "But that won't happen to us," he says, "because it's always been a matter of trust." The ballad "Temptation" is a love song for his daughter Alexa Ray. "I can hear my friends say 'Be careful, you're losing your touch,'" he sings, alluding to his ebbing obsession with his career. "But she's such a temptation."[3]

Other tracks allow Joel to build some more strictly musical bridges. When Ray Charles learned Joel had given his daughter the middle name of Ray in his honor, the legendary artist suggested they collaborate, resulting in the bluesy, affectionate duet "Baby Grand." (Though not a pop hit, the song did go top ten on *Billboard's* Adult Contemporary Chart.) "Getting Closer," an ode to self-improvement, features famed Traffic keyboardist and major Joel influence Steve Winwood on the Hammond B-3 organ. The self-mocking "Big Man on Mulberry Street" is a brassy number featuring an ensemble of crack session players that include bassist Ron Carter and tenor sax player Michael Brecker, who appeared on *Born to Run* with his brother

Randy (and contributed the memorable trumpet solo on "Meeting Across the River").

There are songs that do indeed seem like throwaways. "Running on Ice," a caffeinated reggae song inspired by the Police—Joel professed to admire its bassist and vocalist, Sting, who became a friend—but it's essentially a retread of "Pressure" rendered in the first person without that song's edgy irony. (Joel called it "crap."[4]) "Modern Woman," which Joel wrote for the soundtrack of the 1986 comedy *Ruthless People*, was already ascending the pop chart before it showed up on *The Bridge* in July. ("I hated that thing," he later said.[5]) Weakest of all is "Code of Silence," which he was struggling with in the studio when he received a visit from Cyndi Lauper, who helped him finish it and contributed a backing vocal. ("I like her part of the track, anyway."[6]) Again, none of these songs were truly terrible. Actually, they captured the sleek chic of late 1980s pop.

Which may be why, combined with its prior momentum, *The Bridge* was a commercial success. The album made it into the top ten and spawned three hit singles: "Modern Woman" and "A Matter of Trust" (both top ten) and "This is the Time" (top twenty). Joel went on an intermittent tour in 1986–1987, his routine modified to accommodate his wife and daughter. He also continued to be an MTV fixture, notably in the video for "A Matter of Trust," which cleverly played with music history. The performance video showed Joel playing guitar with the band in a basement in Manhattan's East Village. There are two quick cameos of Paul McCartney and Ringo Starr as part of a crowd witnessing the performance, which amounts to a kind of visual pun, given that the Beatles had given a famed impromptu rooftop concert when they were making *Let It Be* that also attracted a curious crowd. Not the first or last time, Joel was linking his heritage to the Fab Four.

As Joel was building *The Bridge*, Springsteen was unwinding in the aftermath of *Born in the U.S.A.* His international tour to support that album, which ran from mid-1984 to late 1985, was the longest of his career. He returned to the house he had bought in the affluent suburb of Rumson, New Jersey, with new wife Julianne Phillips in tow and began to explore domestic life. It did not appear to go well. Based on multiple accounts of the Springsteen marriage, the problem does not seem to be deep interpersonal conflict, but rather mutual incomprehension between two people who had less in common than they thought they did. Springsteen in particular seemed to have trouble settling into the quotidian details of everyday life, resuming his single-life routine and inviting Phillips along for the ride. She was game, but that wasn't sufficient. "I was still emotionally stunted and secretly unavailable," he concluded. The marriage was effectively over in 1988 when Springsteen was caught by paparazzi in Italy canoodling with backup singer Patti Scialfa, who later became his wife, an incident that tarnished his image. Perhaps the most striking thing about the Springsteen-Phillips marriage was the rigorous propriety both maintained after it ended in 1989. "She's a woman of great discretion and decency and always dealt with me and our problems honestly and in good faith," he wrote in his memoir. Phillips, for her part, was similarly circumspect. "The one and only thing I *will* say is that that period was a time of incredible personal growth and introspection for me. And I will forever give that credit to Bruce." Phillips never remarried.[7]

There was no doubt Springsteen would continue his career, whatever the state of his marriage. He built a studio in his Rumson house and began writing songs. But they had a different character. "I'd recently begun writing some new material that, for the first time, wasn't centered on around the man on the 'road' but rather the questions and concerns of the man in the 'house,'" he explained. Though he reported that he was "filled with inner turmoil," the work proceeded quickly—he recorded a batch of songs in approximately three weeks at one point in 1987. As with *Nebraska*, these were songs he made by himself, aided by engineer Toby Scott. While the final product was not as minimalist as that album, Springsteen brought band members in sparingly to "sweeten" some of the songs, which he released that fall as *Tunnel of Love*.[8]

More than *The Bridge*—or more than any previous album Springsteen himself had made—*Tunnel of Love* was a tightly focused album consisting entirely of love songs. The one partial exception, a love song of a different sort, was "Walk Like a Man," a tribute to Douglas Spring-steen set on his son's wedding day. "Well I was young and I didn't know what to do / When I saw your best steps taken away from you," Spring-steen sings, a conciliatory close to the cycle of "father songs" dating back to *Darkness on the Edge of Town* and including "Adam Raised a Cain," "Factory," "Independence Day," and "My Father's House." The other backward glance on the album is the title track, which deals with adult relationship concerns, but does so by using an amusement park as fact and metaphor, inevitably evoking associations of Asbury Park. Indeed, the video for the song was shot there.

A number of songs seem autobiographical without being obviously so. The album opens with "Ain't Got You," in which Springsteen implicitly punctures his own working-class mythology by opening with the acapella line "I've got the fortunes of heaven in diamonds and gold." "All that Heaven Will Allow" is notably lighthearted, both in the context of this album and Springsteen's work generally, while "Brilliant Disguise" and "One Step Up" are expressions of struggle. ("I wanna know if it's you I don't trust / 'Cause I damn sure don't trust myself," he sings during the bridge of "Brilliant Disguise" to a light Latin beat.) The closing track, "Valentine's Day," is more dappled, though finally hopeful, its rolling melody delivered in a soothing ¾ time.

Other tracks seem to fall more obviously into the category of first-person character sketches. In "When You're Alone," an abandoned lover chides his faithless partner when she returns, his measured tone all the more haunting in its almost casual chilliness: "nobody knows honey where love goes / But when it goes it's gone, gone." The narra-tor of "Two Faces," by contrast, is the faithless one, and pays the price for his infidelity by having to witness his woman with another man. "Tougher than the Rest" is marked by a weighty beat and a low laconic vocal that conjure traditional masculinity. But the lyrics define tough-ness in terms of emotional connection and willingness to risk vulner-ability. There's a nod toward gender-bending in the woman character in the song wearing blue, and a video that intersperses gay couples with straight ones.

As with *Nebraska*, the best songs on *Tunnel of Love* unfold like short stories, with a sparse clarity Raymond Carver would envy. "Spare Parts," a pure blues song, tells the story of Janey, who finds herself pregnant—"Bobby said he'd pull out / Bobby stayed in"— and abandoned. In a moment of crisis rendered as a biblical fable, she contemplates leaving her infant behind as a foundling by a river but experiences a moment of grace that empowers her to pull back from the brink of damnation and pawn her wedding ring for "good cold cash." In "Cautious Man," the deeply self-protective Bill Horton finds himself married to a good woman whose love he's not sure he can abide. Here too is a moment of crisis in which he leaves his bed in the dark and lights out the highway. But when he gets there "he didn't find nothing but road," turning back to experience the redemptive power of "God's fallen light." Songs such as these mark Springsteen's gradual but steady re-engagement with the Catholicism of his childhood, no longer regarded with mockery or disdain but rather as a source of strength and wisdom.[9]

Like *The Bridge*, *Tunnel of Love* was well-received by critics and performed well commercially (the sniping that had accompanied earlier Joel releases tapered; Springsteen was lauded for a bracing change in a direction for an album that was notably more intimate than *Born in the U.S.A.*). *Tunnel of Love* topped the album chart three weeks after its release in October of 1987, selling three million copies domestically by the end of the year.[10] Springsteen enjoyed three hit singles: "Brilliant Disguise" and "Tunnel of Love" went top ten, while "One Step Up" made it into the top twenty. The black-and-white video for "Brilliant Disguise" was notable for the way it was rendered in a single, unbroken shot of Springsteen performing the song in a kitchen setting. (It won an MTV Video Award for best editing, which is a bit ironic in that one could argue there wasn't any.) He undertook a tour with U.S. and European legs to support the album.

On one level, it was business as usual for Springsteen and Joel: they were making records, scoring hits, hitting the road. *The Bridge* and *Tunnel of Love* were not as successful as their predecessors, but no one expected them to be. The status of both artists was secure, and both continued to be productive. In keeping with a new emphasis on maturity, the Annie Leibovitz cover of *Tunnel of Love* featured Springsteen in a dress shirt, blazer, bolo tie; Joel's album cover featured an abstract painting.

Yet both men were restless, and both were making significant changes in their lives that went beyond their personal relationships. In one more set of parallels in a lifetime of them, the two were in the process of dismantling their musical families at roughly the same time.

Again, this is not surprising. Rock bands are, almost by nature, volatile organisms. They typically form at formative stages in their members' lives, and given the premium placed on artistic growth, it seems inevitable that members will grow up—and grow apart. The paradigmatic example is of course the Beatles. There are bands that last for decades (here the Rolling Stones come to mind), but always with changes in personnel and in the tenor of member relationships. Springsteen knew early on that he didn't want to be in a band where he wasn't the boss, and while Joel has never stated this as clearly on the record as Springsteen has, his actions are clear enough in that regard.[11] Sooner or later, even the boss is likely to want to dissolve the company. Both did. But they went about it in different ways.

In both cases the process was not immediate. The recording process for *The Bridge* was notably less collaborative than previous Joel records. Rather than have the band together in the studio, he would have Liberty DeVitto come in to play then drums and then leave. Then likewise with Stegmeyer on bass. Brown was around a bit more because the album was more guitar-based than previous Joel albums. Joel was also experiencing some friction with what was now longtime producer Phil Ramone. Indeed, it was the last time they worked together on an album.[12]

Springsteen was proceeding in a similar way on *Tunnel of Love* with the E Street Band. Working with Scott, who turned out the be a key player on the production side, he set up a process he called "Beat the Demo" in which band members were invited to improve on what he had recorded himself in the songwriting process.[13] Roy Bittan and

Max Weinberg saw the most action, but in piecemeal fashion. Danny Federici and Gary Tallent showed up on some of the tracks. But Clarence Clemons's contribution to the album amounted to backing vocals on "When You're Alone." Jon Landau and Chuck Plotkin were listed along with Springsteen as producers, and the full E Street Band was listed in the credits. But this was a record far closer to *Nebraska* in its execution than *The River* or *Born in the U.S.A.* were.

A similar fracturing was discernible on the touring side. Weinberg and Clemons saw the first signs of it toward the end of the *Born in the U.S.A.* tour, when they could feel Springsteen drifting away into the pull of superstardom. ("Things were changing," Weinberg said; "Bruce was changing," said Clemons.) Springsteen seriously considered a solo tour to support *Tunnel of Love,* but decided to bring the band along after all in 1987–1988. He nevertheless shuffled the deck by rearranging the stage layout, adding a horn section, and giving new prominence to Scialfa, reflecting the themes of the album as well as their intensifying personal relationship. There was now an inner circle that stayed in a separate hotel from the rest of the band. E Street morale reputedly improved later in 1988, when Springsteen joined the famous global Amnesty International Tour along with Sting, Peter Gabriel, Tracy Chapman, and Yossou N'Dour. There, more of a spirit of camaraderie among and between the acts prevailed (Springsteen and Sting in particular formed a lasting bond).[14]

Tensions were more overt on the Joel side of the equation. Much of this was financial. While exact figures are hard to come by— Springsteen reported that he never had formal contracts with the band until *Tunnel of Love*—he appeared to share tour proceeds, and that there were at least some stretches when they were on salary.[15] Joel, by contrast, only paid his players when they were on tour or working with him in the studio, which complicated their cash flow. "Billy will never make you rich," Joel's first wife Elizabeth Weber told Liberty DeVitto, as he later reported to Joel biographer Mark Bego.[16] DeVitto, who actually lasted longer with Joel than any of his peers, and who reputedly earned $3 million as Joel's drummer,[17] ended up the most vocal of his critics, appearing, along with Russell Javors, in

Hired Guns, a 2016 documentary on session players. The portrait of Joel—remote and parsimonious—is not flattering.

Joel had his own version of musical activism when he toured the Soviet Union in 1987, an event he considered a highlight of his career. But while the Amnesty International tour seemed to improve the mood of the E Street Band, this one made it worse for Joel's troupe. Excited by the invitation to come the USSR amid signs of an ending Cold War (like the Reykjavik Summit of 1986, among other examples), Joel financed the cost of the tour himself. He seemed to believe the band should work at a discount; they seemed to believe they deserved extra pay, given the eventual payoff in terms of an album, video and other ancillary revenue. An angry David Brown quit; the others—as always, there was a core supplemented by hired players—went along, however grudgingly. The tour seemed to go well, notwithstanding a well-publicized incident in which Joel threw an electric piano from the stage in anger.[18] It also proved a source of inspiration in his future work for his future song "Leningrad." But the live album that followed, *Kohuept* [concert] was not an especially distinguished example of the genre and was notably less successful than *Songs in the Attic,* much less Springsteen's carefully curated *Live / 1975–85.*

The manner in which Springsteen and Joel decisively made their breaks with their teams is a study in contrasts. Springsteen called each member in turn to explain his decision, signing off with a golden handshake of $2 million apiece.[19] In reading through multiple accounts of this moment, it seems clear both that there were hurt feelings along with an acknowledgment of Springsteen's right to do what he did. Joel, by contrast and by his own admission, ghosted his team. When he began work on a new album, he simply didn't call band members to let them know. One player who took the break particularly hard was Stegmeyer, who spent all his free time on the Soviet tour in his hotel room, reputedly because of heavy drinking. After a few years of drifting, he killed himself with a shotgun in 1995.[20]

In some sense, the lives of Springsteen and Joel were beginning to diverge as each turned 40 in 1989. Springsteen literally got his house in order. His first child, Evan, was born in 1990, and he married Scialfa the following year, when she bore him a daughter, Jessica; another son, Sam, was born in 1994. The early Springsteen-Scialfa relationship was tempestuous—which was actually a good sign, as he was finally confronting the issues that had closed him off from the women in his life.[21] His early family routines were largely centered in southern California, punctuated by trips back east. He embarked on an album sabbatical of five years, the longest of his career to that point.

Meanwhile, Joel's life in New York was a mixture of disarray and stasis. He thought he had put his financial woes behind him after his divorce from Elizabeth Weber, but he faced a massive tax bill from the IRS as well as a morass of financial conflicts with her brother Frank, who succeeded Elizabeth as his manager and who appears to have engaged in unethical business practices. Such problems preoccupied Joel well into the new decade.[22] Despite such distractions, he was, for the moment, a happily married father. It was in that context that Joel voiced the role of the Artful Dodger in the 1988 animated Disney film *Oliver and Company* (which restyled the Dickens novel *Oliver Twist* with a canine cast) and contributed a song, "Why Should I Worry?" to the soundtrack. Like Springsteen, he was also on sabbatical, this one three years, the longest of his career.

When he did get down to work on a new album, he replaced Phil Ramone with Mick Jones, founder of the successful hard rock band Foreigner. In the late 1980s, Jones began a career as a producer working for other artists that included the smash 1986 Van Halen album *5150*, the first to feature new lead singer Sammy Hagar as a replacement for the flamboyant David Lee Roth. Jones had impeccable rock credentials (he also worked with the highly regarded hard rock band Bad Company), which Joel was actively seeking, telling a management associate that he was seeking to make a "roadhouse" album.[23]

Storm Front, released in the fall of 1989, was to all outward appearances another typical Joel success. It became his third number one album (after *52nd Street* and *Glass Houses*) and contained his third number one single, "We Didn't Start the Fire" (after "It's Still Rock & Roll to Me" and "Tell Her about It"), which topped the charts for two weeks in December of that year. Another song from the album, "I Go to Extremes," landed in the top ten in 1990, and Garth Brooks's cover of a third song, "Shameless," topped the *Billboard* country chart in 1991 (indicative of the way rock and country began to converge as genres at the turn of the new century, as indicated in the work of Shania Twain, to cite an additional example).

And yet *Storm Front* also revealed a kind of structural weakness in Joel's songwriting in the final years of his recording to his career. This weakness was rooted in his self-image: Joel had always considered himself a rock & roll musician. This identity reflected the musical culture of when he came of age, one he embraced and even insisted upon, to the point of stridency, on *Glass Houses* in general and "It's Still Rock & Roll to Me" in particular. But the peculiar paradox of Joel's career is that he's done most of his best work when his songs emerged in creative friction with other genres—country and bluegrass in "Travelin' Prayer" and "You're My Home"; the American songbook in "New York State of Mind" and "Baby Grand"; jazz in "Zanzibar" and "Big Man on Mulberry Street"; gospel music in "River of Dreams." Joel was never purely imitative in these modes, and a sense of musical ambition led him tweak those genres in subtle but arresting ways in the process of crafting memorable melodies and sophisticated lyrics. This is also—even especially—true when Joel engages with the rock tradition, as he did to impressive effect with the Beatles on *The Nylon Curtain* and doo-wop and other pop genres in *An Innocent Man*. But when left to entirely to his own devices, he tends to produce is straight rock. And more often than not, it's not especially distinguished.

Much of *Storm Front*—the title track, "That's Not Her Style," "State of Grace," "When in Rome"—is forgettable. These songs are competently written and executed ("Storm Front" has a solid R&B groove; "That's Not Her Style" has a bluesy riff), but have not really lodged even in the world of Joel fandom. "I Go to Extremes" and "Shameless" are really solid rock songs with great hooks, but they might have been written and performed by any number of artists with a feel for the genre at the time. (It's ironic that Joel held most tightly to rock at the very moment it is beginning to fade as the dominant genre in pop music.) Even the best rock albums always have their share of filler, but the quotient on this album is more noticeable than on previous Joel records.

There is, to be sure, some solid material here. "And So It Goes," a holdover ballad from *An Innocent Man* sessions, has an emotional directness and vulnerability that characterized that album. (In a 2022 interview with Fareed Zakaria, Joel walked through the chord progression of the song to demonstrate how its dissonant notes complicated what might otherwise seem a simple melody.[24]) But its sparseness would not have fit on *An Innocent Man* as well as it does a meditative closing track on *Storm Front*. Other songs do reflect Joel's ongoing penchant for engaging other genres. "The Downeaster Alexa," a tribute to Long Island fishermen (and a nod to his daughter in the title of a fictive boat), has a strong sense of local color and a melody that evokes a sea shanty. "Leningrad," which grew out of Joel's experiences with a clown he met while touring in the Soviet Union, has an arresting melody that samples Pyotr Tchaikovsky's Violin Concerto in D Major—another example of creative friction, cultural as well as musical. Joel creates a set of parallel lives between himself to suggest the false dichotomies of the Cold War as it came to a close. Indeed, *Storm Front* was released a few weeks before the fall of the Berlin Wall in November of 1989, and as such evinces a strong sense of historical consciousness.

Which brings us to the really pivotal track on the album, "We Didn't Start the Fire." The song has its fans and detractors—among them Joel himself, who described its melody as "a droning mosquito"[25]—but it's an important work in the Joel canon in terms of situating him generationally.

The origins of "We Didn't Start the Fire" date back to a conversation Joel had with John Lennon's son Sean, who attended the same Swiss school as Joel's half-brother Alexander. The adolescent Lennon—he was five at the time of his father's death in 1980—dropped by a Joel recording session at the Hit Factory in New York and got to talking with him about the troubled state of the world. Joel tried to comfort him by pointing out that young people often feel this way.

"Yeah, but at least when you were a kid you grew up in the fifties, when nothing happened," Lennon responded. Joel's riposte: "Are you kidding me?" He proceeded to reel off a litany of events: the Korean War, the Hungarian uprising of 1956, and the racial showdown in Little Rock in 1957. "I've got to write about this," he remembered, scribbling down events and personalities from memory and checking them with an encyclopedia. The song that followed was unusual in that the lyrics came first, to which he retrofitted a country melody he was working on at the time (though there's nothing remotely country about the final product). The title of the song came from a conversation with *Rolling Stone* founder and publisher Jann Wenner, who affirmed it from a series of possibilities Joel tossed out to him.[26]

"We Didn't Start the Fire" is a novelty tune in the sense that it's a seemingly random list of people and events, a couple lines for each year from 1949 to 1963. After that the pace picks up—an implicit argument about the speed of change in the 1960s. ("JFK blown away / What else do I have to say?" is the song's turning point—one not likely to earn consensus among historians that it was all that pivotal, though certainly a watershed event for anyone who lived through it.) Joel blends world historical events like the fall of Dien Bien Phu in 1954 with John Glenn's successful space mission to orbit the earth in 1962. High culture figures like Sergei Prokofiev mingle with pop culture icons such as Marilyn Monroe and sporting events like Sonny Liston's surprise knockout of Floyd Patterson. About the only obvious angle Joel consistently neglects is economics, a characteristic blind spot—anyone who can work in the Panmunjom Peace conference of 1951 could plausibly work in the suspension of the gold standard twenty years later.

The key to "We Didn't Start the Fire" is the climax of its chorus: "We didn't light it, but we tried to fight it." Whether one agrees with this judgment or not, it's important to recognize the force of this line as a historiographic statement—revisionism to the revisionism that blames the United States for the excesses of the Cold War—and one that reflects the fact that Joel, an autodidact, has long been a student of history. (He finally went back to Hicksville High School to claim his diploma, 25 years late, in 1992.[27]) While some may be inclined to view with plausible skepticism Joel's assertion that "we"—presumably Americans of the Baby Boom generation—are not fundamentally to blame for the conflicts of the postwar world, his view does credibly reflect his fundamentally conservative temperament when it has come to major social issues, even as he evinced conventionally liberal opinions that reflect the mainstream of his time. The video for the song, which depicts the arc of a postwar family from marriage to death, captures the way the outside world constantly pressed itself on family domesticity. In any event, it's hard to argue with Joel's concluding assessment of those fires of history: "And when we are gone / It will still burn on and on."

So it was that Joel entered the new decade back in the saddle. Springsteen was slower to return to the fray, and when he did, his work evinced some of the same problems Joel's did. It was only about month after he officially broke up the band that Springsteen had dinner with his presumably ex-piano player, Roy Bittan, who had moved to Los Angeles. Bittan had written music for a piece he thought might work as a Springsteen song, and Springsteen embraced it—and collaboration—with alacrity.[28] A number of demos were recorded, as per his usual method, with Toby Scott in early 1990. But Springsteen soon settled into fiddling mode for over a year, assembling a set of session musicians that included bassist Randy Jackson and Jeff Porcaro, a celebrated drummer who had been a founder of the rock band Toto. His old keyboard player David Sancious also returned to perform on a couple of songs for the first time in almost twenty years. By early 1992 he had an album that was ready to go.

That record, *Human Touch*, remains among his weakest. There's little on it that's truly terrible (though *Billboard* later said the cliché-riddled "Real Man" "might be the worst thing he's ever done").[29] But there's little that stands out, either. As with *Storm Front*, the album is filled with conventional rock songs that are competently performed, yet there's an almost studious air about the way they're executed. "*Human Touch* began as an exercise to get myself back into writing and recording," he explained a few years later in *Songs*. "I wrote in a variety of genres I had always liked: soul, rock, pop, R&B. The record, once again, took awhile because I was finding my way to the songs."[30] The song he co-wrote with Bittan, "Roll of the Dice," is an almost platonically realized version of a classic Bruce Springsteen song— pleasurably familiar in its roaring vocals, chugging guitars, and rolling keyboards—but seemingly trapped in amber. The six and a half-minute title track features some fine guitar playing by Springsteen but offers little beyond a pragmatic approach to romance. "Man's Job," which plays with the intersection of sex and gender, would be considered very dated if it were released today in its emphasis on what some call hetero-normativity. By the early nineties, popular music was moving on, and Springsteen and Joel were beginning to seem old-fashioned. It prob-ably would have been a mistake to chase trends like grunge, let alone hip-hop (though Springsteen flirted with it a few years later in "Streets of Philadelphia"), but it's clear their tide was going out and that younger music fans were finding their pleasures elsewhere.

Still, there was life left in both to make some quality recordings, and each experienced a minor renaissance in the first half of the 1990s. As Springsteen was finishing *Human Touch*, he decided he needed another song, and came up with a stirring, hard-rock account of his son Evan's birth, "Living Proof." Writing that piece seemed to open something up in him, and over the ensuing three weeks he wrote and recorded an entirely new album. The process resembled that of *The River*, when Springsteen thought he had finished that proj-ect only to produce an entirely new disc of material in what became a double album. This time, however, he wanted to release this second set—he called it *Lucky Town*—alongside *Human Touch* as a separate album in its own right.

There was an immediate precedent for this. In September of 1991, the acclaimed hard rock band Guns n' Roses released a pair of albums, *Use Your Illusion I* and *Use Your Illusion II*, on Geffen Records. They rocketed to the top two slots of the charts—with the second install-ment occupying the top slot—and went on to sell a combined 35 mil-lion copies.[31] Springsteen's label, Columbia, had undergone recent changes, now folded under the CBS label after the company was sold to Sony Music in 1988. The company's new president, Don Ienner, considered the questionable commercial merit of releasing the two records simultaneously was less important than honoring one of its more important artists' wishes. And so it was that the two albums were released simultaneously on March 31, 1992.

It's clear why Springsteen wanted to keep *Human Touch* and *Lucky Town* separate. They really are two different records—and *Lucky Town* is far superior to its predecessor in the birth order. Indeed, Springsteen might have benefited from his earlier ruthlessness with his own material by killing *Human Touch* and sticking with *Lucky Town*. It's a more impressive snapshot of his life—and a more impressive testament for what credible middle-aged rock & roll should sound like.

There are a few reasons why. *Lucky Town* is a document of happiness, but happiness of a particular sort. *An Innocent Man* is a record of a man stunned to find himself unexpectedly in love with love, exultant even as his joy is shaded by the fear of hard experience. *Lucky Town*, by contrast, is an account of acquired wisdom, but wisdom expressed in an idiom of spontaneity—the album feels much less labored than *Human Touch*. Springsteen's voice in the opening track, "Better Days," is positively ravaged, but the song is a chronicle of a man who has come out on the other side of self-imposed suffering. "Now a life of leisure and a pirate's treasure don't make much for tragedy," he says. Fortunately, he has been redeemed by the love of his companion—"a woman I can call my friend." The ensuing track, "Lucky Town," exhibits a similarly gritty quality, and similarly hardwon clarity: "I had some victory that was just failure in deceit," he says. Yet, he concludes, "I got some dirt on my hands but I'm building me a home / Down in Lucky Town."

As is often true in Springsteen's work, such moments of grace must be wrested from the mines of sin. A potent sense of cynicism suffuses a number of these songs, notably "Local Hero," "The Big Muddy," and, especially, "Souls of the Departed," which links the violence of the Persian Gulf War of 1990–1991 to that of gang warfare in Los Angeles. "Now I ply my trade in the land of king dollar / Where you get paid and your silence passes for honor," the narrator muses.

Such moments of fierce clarity give the sweeter ones more ballast. "If I Should Fall Behind," an expression of mutual love and vulnerability, is one of the most beloved songs among Springsteen cognoscenti, and one of his personal favorites.[32] "My Beautiful Reward," which closes the album, makes a leap into the mystical—the narrator turns into a flying bird—and reflects the increasingly unselfconscious spirituality flowing through Springsteen's later work, albeit one marked by strongly Catholic dualities.[33]

As he recognized, *Lucky Town* nevertheless remains a minor work in Springsteen's canon. "Both *Human Touch* and *Lucky Town* came out of a moment in which to find out what I needed, I was going to have to let things go, change, try new mistakes—just live," he mused five years later.[34] It's notable that the albums are among the few he gives no real estate in his 2016 memoir.

They were also a commercial disappointment. Though *Human Touch* and *Lucky Town* opened strong, reaching number two and three on the *Billboard* album chart, they sank quickly. "Human Touch" made it to the bottom reaches of the top twenty but was the only hit single from the two albums. The tour that followed was notable for not being a string of sellout dates the way an E Street tour would be, and periodic visits from the old band resulted in audience eruptions that could sound like a judgment.[35] It was hard not to conclude that Springsteen was losing his touch, at least as far as making hit records was concerned.

Joel still had a little fuel in the tank. Though his life was in turmoil—his ongoing financial problems and growing marital difficulties exacerbated by a drinking problem that bedeviled him into the new century[36]—he returned to the studio, this time a converted boathouse on Shelter Island, wedged between the north and south forks of eastern Long Island. Though he once again used DeVitto, and reunited with his saxophonist Richie Cannata, Joel also brought in new players like drummer Zack Alford and multi-instrumentalist Crystal Taliefero, both of whom performed in Springsteen's studio and touring bands of the early nineties. Joel again turned to a new producer, this time Danny Kortchmar. Kortchmar began his career as a guitarist with James Taylor and went on to become a coveted session guitarist associated with west coast acts like Jackson Browne and Linda Ronstadt before turning to a career as a producer that included work with Boz Scaggs, Don Henley, and Neil Young. The album that resulted from the Joel-Kortchmar collaboration, *River of Dreams*, was released in August of 1993.

Like *Storm Front*, *River of Dreams* was a rock-driven album, with some of the same weaknesses. It opens with "No Man's Land," a tediously righteous denunciation of consumer capitalism that could have come from any number of progressive rock bands any time in the previous twenty years. Ditto for "A Thousand Years," a lament for militarism while affirming hope. "Great Wall of China" is a thinly veiled denunciation of Frank Weber, and a rare case of Joel letting his money troubles seep into his work. Kortchmar later expressed pride that "there's no tune on there where Billy's not flat-out doing someone else,"[37] but to the extent that's true it's not necessarily something to be said in the album's favor.

Actually, the songs that *do* pay homage tend to be the ones that pay off. "Shades of Grey" harkens back to Joel's very earliest days as a musician in his hard rock band Attila, evoking the classic 1960s band Cream, and while it's not exactly memorable, it's clever and credible. "All About Soul" is a classic R&B track enhanced by the backing vocals of the pop group Color Me Badd. Apparently about Brinkley, Joel sings it with convincing gusto. Similarly heartfelt is the more original "Lullaby," a musically complex song prompted by Alexa's question to her father about what happens after death. It began as a classical piece and is marked by a complex chordal structure reflective of Joel's musical ambition.

There is one true gem on *River of Dreams*, and it's the title track, which came to him in a dream, refined while taking a shower (where he characteristically tweaked the I-IV-V chord progression in his head).[38] In general terms, the song could be classified as doo-wop, but its origins swirl around a series of related idioms—gospel, spirituals, even South African music: "River of Dreams" is strongly reminiscent of "The Lion Sleeps Tonight," a 1961 hit by the Tokens, which drew on a Zulu melody. Performed in a call-and-response mode (the backing vocals were arranged by Talieferro), the lyrics describe a dream state of fear and longing while touching on transcendence: "I'm not sure about life after this / God knows I've never been a spiritual man." As the song heads to a fade, Joel throws in a few lines from the 1954 Cadillacs version of the doo-wop classic "Gloria." Like the best work on *An Innocent Man*, Joel skillfully captures the elemental joy of earlier pop music while endowing it with a sense of elegance and self-consciousness that adds an additional layer of texture and beauty. "River of Dreams" ranks with his very best work.

The album and song were an instant success. The former entered the *Billboard* pop chart at number one, the first time this happened in Joel's career, and went on to sell in excess of five million copies. The latter peaked at number 3 on the pop singles chart in September of 1993, and continues to be one of his most played songs on the radio. To all outward appearances, Joel was still going strong even as his career as a hitmaker was ending in the fall of 1993. Stephen Holden of the *New York Times*, who had been following Joel's career, not always approvingly, for two decades, hailed his arrival at Madison Square Garden in October, calling him "one of a handful of pop entertainers who need not fear middle-aged obsolescence."[39]

Springsteen also had his final flowering as a hitmaker in the mid-1990s. The prompting for what proved to be one of his biggest hits came from Jonathan Demme, director of the 1993 film *Philadelphia*, starring Tom Hanks as an AIDS-afflicted attorney and Denzel Washington as a homophobic lawyer representing him in a wrongful termination suit. Demme asked Springsteen to write a single, and he came up with the dark, minimalistic "Streets of Philadelphia." The song, sung from the point of view of a physically as well as spiritually sick man, features a dark bank of minor-chord synthesizers against a metronomic drum machine beat that pauses once (in a moment of hope for death) and the barest ray of hope in an organ (that hints at faith against biblical language of Judas's betrayal). The song made it to the top ten in the spring of 1994, and Springsteen won an Academy Award for Best Original Song that year.

Columbia, sensing an opportunity, pressed Springsteen to assemble a greatest hits package on the heels of "Streets of Philadelphia." He had been working on another album, a deeply personal and synthesizer-based record about romantic relationships (a number of these songs eventually appeared on *Tracks* in 1998). Concluding that project wouldn't work, he ditched it and made a U-turn, reassembling the E Street Band and recording a suite of songs. These included "Murder Incorporated" (an outtake from *The River*), "Secret Garden" (from that abandoned album), and two tributes to friendship, "Blood Brothers" and the marvelous "This Hard Land," which might well have been a better way to end *Born in the U.S.A.* They appeared on what became *Greatest Hits*, a motley collection of hit singles, staple FM radio tracks, and new material. The album was released in 1995 and went on to sell over ten million copies.[40] In 1996, Cameron Crowe, a director with an unerring feel about how to use rock music in film, included "Secret Garden" in his generational classic *Jerry Maguire*. It reached the top twenty in early 1997, marking the final notch on Springsteen's belt as a pop star.

Having reassembled the E Street Band, however—for the *Greatest Hits* album, for an appearance on the David Letterman's *Late Show*, and to perform at the Rock & Roll Hall of Fame ceremonies in Cleveland in 1995—Springsteen again walked away. In years to come, he reconvened it for tours and to play on his records, but he maintained his independence, alternatively working alone, with the band, or with bands composed of other people.

Joel, for his part, was beginning a pivot toward live performing that became his primary work as a musician for the next thirty years. He remained in the public eye by launching a high-profile tour with a star of even greater stature than he was: Elton John. John, whose career had launched a few years before Joel's had, and to whom Joel was often compared, has scored seven number one albums and nine number one singles. The first of what became a series of "Face to Face" tours launched in the summer of 1994 with 21 dates mostly on the East Coast. Each brought their bands to play separate sets, bookended with duets facing each other from nine-foot pianos. "I get to sing his songs, he sings my songs, and we sing both of our songs together," Joel explained. In his review of the pair's performance at New York's Giants stadium that July, *New York Times* writer Neil Strauss captured the parallels between the two piano men: "Besides the fact that both have first names as last names, the two pianists are baby-boomers who grew up in planned suburban tract homes with fathers who were for the most part absent. Musically, the two gifted, idiosyncratic artists exist in the nether world between pop and rock, where Broadway show tunes, classical compositions, ragtime, gospel, and rock-and-roll mingle freely. Verbally (though Bernie Taupin wrote many of Mr. John's songs), both are obsessed with mortality and history, the purity of rock-and-roll and the corruption of human beings." Strauss concluded by saying that "Mr. Joel's piano player comes on like a pint of beer and Mr. John's like a cup of tea. On Friday night [three days earlier in what was a weeklong stand at Giants Stadium], however, they discovered that they'd both been working different rooms in the same piano lounge all along."[41]

While Joel was facing outward, Springsteen was turning inward. One of the songs he didn't use from the *Greatest Hits* recording sessions was a piece he called "The Ghost of Tom Joad." A modern updating of John Steinbeck's 1939 novel about the Okie migration to California, the song became the germ of an album of the same name released in 1995 (and followed by a solo tour). Another sparse record in the vein of *Nebraska, The Ghost of Tom Joad* relied on contributions from session players, but most of the instrumentation came from Springsteen himself. The album was a snapshot of working-class America in the Clinton era, with particular attention to Mexican border. *Tom Joad* was also the most multiracial album Springsteen had made, notable for its inclusion of Latin and Asian lives on the margins. In spirit as well as in the location of its creation, the album was decisively Californian, and as such an indication of how far Springsteen had gone from his New Jersey roots. He had planted seeds on the west coast ever since his parents had migrated there a quarter century before, and he had taken root there—far more than Joel, whose sojourn on Los Angeles in the early 1970s had proven temporary.

It's not clear when Billy Joel decided to stop recording popular music—indeed, it appears he himself did not really make an active decision, at least at first. There were hints of it back in the eighties; marriage and fatherhood seemed to prompt musings that he wouldn't be doing it forever, but then and later, it was never entirely clear what a retirement would mean or look like. In his 1985 song "While the Night Is Still Young"—a minor hit included in his *Greatest Hits* package, he sang, "I can see a time coming when I'm gonna throw my suitcase out." As he later told biographer Fred Schruers, "Even though rock and roll was the only thing I ever cared about, I began to think what it might be like not to live that life anymore."[42] It's notable in this context that the last song on *River of Dreams* is "Famous Last Words," which ends in a chorus that can't help but seem prescient: "These are the last words I have to say . . . Now it's time to put this book away."

That book may have closed. But the story wasn't over. And while the lives of Bruce Springsteen and Billy Joel were beginning to diverge in important ways, neither abandoned their local ties or shared experiences. Indeed, with the closing of the American Century—their century—the two returned to their metropolitan base.

FIGURE 15. Bruce Springsteen receives the Presidential Medal of Honor from President Barack Obama, November 2016. The friendship between the two men reflected hopes for racial reconciliation amid a time of polarizing politics. *(Pete Souza/Wikimedia Commons)*

CHAPTER 8

Homing

Legends Take Root, 1996–Present

A T THE TURN of the twenty-first century, Bruce Springsteen and Billy Joel entered a new phase—essentially the second half—of their lives. They had spent a generation near or at the center of American popular music, but now a new generation was coming of age, one with a different set of concerns and pleasures than the ones that shaped their lives. Diversities of race and gender were coming to the fore; the Vietnam War became a distant memory as newer ones took center stage. Joel and Springsteen had become household names. Well into the new century, they continued to be. But who they were perceived to be and the work they perceived to do became increasingly fuzzy and faded in public consciousness. The question both faced was how to deal with such elemental, and at times brutal, facts of life.

Once again, the two found themselves in a similar place, literally and figuratively, as aging stars and New York metropolitans. But here, as elsewhere, they dealt with this status in a somewhat different way. Joel, in effect, decided to essentially end his career as a songwriter and chose to become the leading curator of his own work through public appearances and live performance. Springsteen, by contrast, decided to continue a notably productive career as a recording artist, releasing ten studio albums in the first two decades of the twenty-first century (and a string of live albums, including the notably ambitious *Live in Dublin* in 2007). In recent years, however, his work has also taken on more of a retrospective cast, as his music, like that of Joel, who enjoyed a moment in the footlights of the Broadway stage between 2002 and 2005. Both men have become legacy artists, cherished more for who they were than who they are, dealing with daunting personal challenges as well as enduring the losses that come to all with age. As such they became embodiments of history.

𝄽

The ebbing of Joel's and Springsteen's cultural prominence can be understood in terms of the inevitable shifting of the tides that has characterized popular music for at least a century. Pop is music first and foremost for young people, and by the 1990s Springsteen and Joel were no longer young. Their chosen idiom of rock & roll was also no longer the dominant musical genre. This was the heyday of hip-hop. By this point, it had long since taken on the contours of a musical genre of its own, with a set of conventions and history that defined musical tastes for a generation. But the ebb and flow of such cultural changes were perhaps secondary to more deeply-rooted structural ones that transformed the music industry (along with movies, television, and publishing industries) in the wake of the economic and technological revolution ushered in by the internet. The very meaning of terms like "hit" and "success" were being redefined in entirely new ways.

As discussed, the careers of Joel and Springsteen were the specific result of a series of fortuitous conditions in the music business in the early 1970s, among them profitable record companies willing to make relatively long-term investments in artists, a broadcast industry that blended an emphasis on hits as well as a stable of radio-friendly FM album tracks, and a live concert circuit that interlocked with both as a means of building careers. But at the turn of the century, this system began to unravel.

The most serious blow it sustained was in the record business *as* a business. The invention of Napster in 1999 inaugurated an age of peer-to-peer computer file sharing that made it possible to acquire an entire library of songs instantly and at no-cost, upending the retail model that had governed music ownership since the invention of recorded music at the turn of the twentieth century. Though Napster was shut down as the result of a Record Industry Association of America (RIAA) lawsuit in 2001, and recorded music sales continued to remain the norm for the rest of the decade, it was apparent to all that the writing was on wall for music industry as it had previously been constituted. This posed not only a threat to corporate bottom lines, but also the potential for musicians to envision a career as recording artists, at least as a matter selling their music through standard retail outlets. They had to find other ways of making a living, whether in live performance, licensing their work in other media, or other means.[1]

A similar revolution was taking place in radio. While the broadcasting model on which it emerged in the 1920s was still widespread a century later, radio too experienced disruption in the way producers of content reached listeners. Ever since a series of regulatory and commercial decisions that had been made during back when Herbert Hoover was president, the basic unit of radio broadcasting was local stations (though many were part of national networks).[2] By the end of the century, however, the Internet allowed listeners to conquer distance, and it now became possible to listen to any station anywhere on one's computer (or, later, phone). Yet even as this happened, the very notion of broadcasting itself was splintering, as listeners began to fragment into specialized niches that could deliver the programming they wanted whenever they wanted it. The advent of satellite radio created a cable-TV model whereby listeners could access the content of their choice on a subscriber basis (notably E Street Radio, a SiriusXM station in which one could hear Springsteen music 24/7). Streaming services such as Spotify allowed listeners to create personalized playlists, often incorporating algorithms that predicted what they might like, in ways considered more satisfying than traditional broadcast formats. Now it was streams, at least as much as sales or airplay, that determined what was considered a hit. And hits were, to a much greater degree than in Springsteen or Joel's heyday, far more demographically siloed than they were in the mid-twentieth century, when hits were songs considered part of a shared national culture.

The only side of this triangle that was unbroken by the early twenty-first century was touring. Actually, it had become more important, and in some cases more profitable, than ever. Once, tours had been promotional tools to promote records—that's how Joel and Springsteen built their careers. Now, it was the other way around, as live shows became the most obvious (and in most cases only) way a musician could make a living. Unlike recording and radio, this development was decisively advantageous to those acts who had already established audiences, especially older audiences able to pay premium prices for live experiences that were now promoted as having a special cache in an age of on-demand digital delivery. Springsteen and Joel consistently ranked among the highest grossing concert acts of the century, and this was the way both maintained a sense of cultural currency. But while Springsteen continued to do it as a globetrotting act with an increasingly cosmopolitan accent, Joel became a commuter—though he only went to work about once a month, and got back and forth by helicopter.

$$\text{\textflatsign}$$

In 1996, Bruce Springsteen came home to New Jersey—where, his peripatetic tendencies notwithstanding, he has been based ever since. He made the move for family reasons. "My oldest boy was going into first grade, and we just decided we didn't want to raise the kids in L.A.," he told biographer Peter Ames Carlin. "Patti and I wanted the children to have a more normal upbringing." The Scialfa-Springsteens bought a compound in Colts Neck, a wealthy shore town about 50 miles south of Manhattan, and ten miles east of Freehold (though symbolically a good deal further away). "We lived in a nice neighborhood, and [the kids] went to good schools, but outside of that they grew up around dry cleaners, hunters, people who did all sorts of things. So really, the intent was to create as real a life for the kids as possible, and we liked it."[3]

Springsteen's life in suburbia was shockingly normal for those who witnessed it. "The stories have the ring of folk legends," Carlin, who spent time with Springsteen, reported. "There he is on Main Street on Freehold's weekly Kruise Night, his son perched on his shoulders as they watch the vintage hot rods drive past. See that guy in the Range Rover with the car seats in back? That's Bruce Springsteen dropping his kids off at school. An hour later he's in sweats in the Gold's Gym at the mall, straining through his weight room regimen as the trainer barks encouragement. By midafternoon, he'd be back at school, arriving early enough to sit on the hill above the playground to watch the kids running and swinging through recess. 'That's my boy down there,' he boasted, pointing out his eldest to a friend."[4]

The move was more than purely practical, however. "You get a little older and when one of those crisp fall days come along in September and October, my friends and I slip into the cool water of the Atlantic Ocean," he said in his induction speech to the New Jersey Hall of Fame in Newark on May 4, 2008. "We take note that there are a few less of us as each year passes. But the thing about being in one place your whole life is that they're still all around you in the water . . . And on the beach there's a whole batch of new little kids running away from the crashing surf like time itself. That's what New Jersey is for me. It's the repository of my life on Earth."[5]

Joel's attachment to his native Long Island was similarly deep—indeed, since his own return from Los Angeles in the mid-seventies, he has spent most of his life there since. Joel has owned a series of homes in Manhattan and on the east end of the Island, but his steadiest residence been his compound on Centre Island, a peninsula jutting out from Oyster Bay in eastern Nassau County. (It's the one featured on the cover of *Glass Houses*; it was burglarized in 2020.[6]) Like Springsteen, Joel has been quietly active in philanthropic causes, notably Charity Begins at Home, an informal umbrella organization through which he has funded a variety of causes. He also became a businessman, teaming up with a partner to found the Long Island

Boat Company in 1997. He also opened a custom motorcycle shop in 2010.[7]

Like Springsteen, Joel kept a relatively low professional profile in the second half of the 1990s. But while this was a period of relative quietude for Springsteen, Joel's personal life was in upheaval. His marriage to Christie Brinkley unraveled in 1994, though the two remained friendly and committed to raising their daughter Alexa. Joel went through a series of relationships in the years that followed, avoiding a third marriage. He continued to tour—citing financial concerns as a reason in the aftermath of his multiple management debacles—and in contrast to the more family-oriented approach that had characterized his conduct when his marriage was solid and Alexa was young, he increasingly indulged in destructive alcoholic binges. He launched another "Face to Face" tour with Elton John in 1998–1999, and while the two men seemed to have genuine warmth for each other, John (who had come out on the other side of his own addictions) was impatient with Joel's self-indulgence and dismayed by his sudden decision to cancel dates in England. Joel's alcohol consumption remained an issue over the course of the coming decade.[8]

Despite these setbacks, Joel was clearly thinking about—and making an active effort to build—a legacy. Back in 1989, he accepted an invitation from Long Island University to teach a master class for students there, and in the years that followed, he made regular appearances in Q&A sessions, notably a full-fledged lecture tour in 1996. He seemed to savor the chance to explain his work, sometimes making points by illustrating them on the piano.[9]

At the turn of the century, Joel's body of work, like Springsteen's, was disseminated through a series of albums largely comprised of previous work. In 1997, Columbia issued *Greatest Hits Volume III*, which included a string of Joel songs since *The Bridge* and three cover tunes: Carole King's "Hey Girl," Leonard Cohen's "Light as the Breeze," and Bob Dylan's "To Make You Feel My Love" (which Dylan did not release himself until a career renaissance in his album *Time*

Out of Mind later that year). In 1998, Springsteen released *Tracks*. a four-CD set of outtakes and unused material from the previous quarter century, and followed it two years later with *Live in New York City*, a collection which included the new songs of "Land of Hope and Dreams," and "American Skin (41 Shots)," a commentary on the murder of Guinean immigrant Amadou Diallo by police officers in 1999. The song was part of a broader move toward avowed progressive politics on Springsteen's part—he spoke out against the 1996 California Proposition 209, which ended Affirmative Action in that state[10]— that became more pronounced in the decades that followed, as will be discussed below. Regular repackages of Springsteen's and Joel's work have become common in the twenty-first century. Both were included in Columbia's "Essential" series for its most important catalog artists, for example, largely as collector's items but also as a means of introducing younger people to their work.

In 1999 both Springsteen and Joel were inducted into the Rock & Roll Hall of Fame, voted in the first year they were eligible. Springsteen was inducted by Bono (with whom Joel had gone on a pub crawl the year before); Joel by Ray Charles. Both inductees used much of their speeches to thank their bands—Joel noted that some members of his touring squad, like Crystal Taliefero, would soon be joining Springsteen on tour. But Joel could not help allowing an edge of aggrievement into his speech. He noted his humble roots in Levittown—"not exactly the soul of America"—asserting "it sucked" along with his childhood belief that there's "gotta be something better than this." That something was music on the radio. Joel correctly noted the racial covenants preventing African Americans from living in Levittown, and the role of black artists in shaping his vision from afar, almost making it sound he was as much a victim of segregation as they were. "I know I've been referred to as derivative," he said. "Well, I'm damned guilty. I'm derivative as hell." But he said, if originality was really the standard in popular music, "there wouldn't be any white people here." He was sincere and meant well. But Joel's defensiveness compromised his graciousness.[11]

Laurels like industry awards are sometimes an indication of fading relevance, but as the new century began both Springsteen and Joel continued to press ahead with their creative lives. In his induction speech, Joel jokingly referred to the dread of Columbia executives because he was now writing classical music. In 2001 he released *Fantasies and Delusions*, a collection of pieces performed by the British-Korean pianist Richard Joo, who was recommended to him by Joel's half-brother Alexander, the Viennese conductor. The album was an indication of Joel's deeply rooted conservative musical temperament, as the suite of pieces evoked the melodic richness of late Romantic composers such as Sergei Rachmaninoff and Claude Debussy rather than recent 20th century modernists. *Fantasies and Delusions* performed well on the *Billboard* classical music chart, occupying the top spot and selling over 200,000 copies in the next decade.[12] But Joel has not released anything further in this vein.

His body of work got an unexpected new lease on life from an unlikely quarter: choreographer Twyla Tharp, an artist who really did have one foot planted in modernism. Tharp approached Joel in the year 2000, pitching an ambitious work of dance based on his music. She began her effort to do this by asking Joel whatever happened to Brenda and Eddie of "Scenes from an Italian Restaurant," and Anthony of "Movin' Out." Joel didn't have an answer.[13] While skeptical Tharp's idea could work, he nevertheless gave his blessing, and Tharp constructed an extended dance piece based on these characters—and James, from the *Turnstiles* song of the same name—tracing their experiences before and after the Vietnam War. The setting of "Scenes from an Italian Restaurant" was moved back to the early sixties, Brenda leaves Eddie for Tony, and James gets killed in Vietnam (Tharp has this happen during "We Didn't Start the Fire"; another crucial song, positioned as a depiction of Post-Traumatic Stress Syndrome, is "Goodnight Saigon"). The show uses dozens of Joel compositions, concluding on a hopeful note with "I've Loved These Days."[14]

The result of Tharp's labors, *Movin' Out*, is customarily called a jukebox musical, though this is not quite accurate. Nor are the terms opera or recital. It is instead a loosely plotted suite of songs performed by dancers who do not sing. In a reversal of the usual staging, the musicians perform above the stage rather than in a pit. The show, which underwent some tweaking in Chicago, opened on Broadway in 2002, and ran for over three years. National and international tours followed. Joel won win a Tony Award for his orchestration of *Movin' Out* the following year.

Following another cluster of concerts with Elton John in the winter and spring of 2003, Joel was literally and figuratively offstage for much of the next three years, during which time personal problems bubbled into public view. He had a series of traffic accidents in 2004–2005, and while none were officially attributed to alcohol, his drinking problems flared again, leading him to two stints of rehab in 2002 and 2005 (the latter at the famed Betty Ford Center). He resumed a touring regimen again in 2006, and spent much of the next eight years on the road, including clusters of shows with John in 2009–2010. One particular high note was "Last Play at Shea," a pair of July 2008 concerts Joel performed at the New York Mets stadium in Queens before it closed. The shows featured an array of stars who appeared with him, including Tony Bennett, Garth Brooks, John Mayer, Steven Tyler, Roger Daltrey, John Mellencamp, and—especially prized by Joel—Paul McCartney.

Instability continued to characterize Joel's personal life. He went through a number of relationships and another marriage to food writer Katie Lee from 2004 to 2009. An ensuing relationship with Morgan Stanley executive Alexis Roderick culminated in his fourth wedding in 2015, presided over by Joel's friend, New York governor Andrew Cuomo. The couple's daughter Della Rose was born a month later; another child, Remy Anne, followed in 2017. It appeared his life had settled down at least somewhat as he crossed the threshold into his seventies two years later. Back surgery in 2021 resulted in a 50-pound weight loss, improving his physical health.[15] By this point, Joel was deep into his residency at Madison Square Garden, a record-setting experience that consolidated his legacy and cemented his association with greater New York.

At the turn of the new century, Bruce Springsteen was also cementing his association with greater New York. He did so in what ranks among his greatest works, about one of its greatest tragedies.

$
$

The anecdote has become part of Springsteen lore—"a Bruce story," to use the terminology of devotees. In the aftermath of September 11, 2001 terrorist attacks on the World Trade Center and the Pentagon, Springsteen was pulling out of a parking lot in Sea Bright, New Jersey, when a fellow motorist drove by and rolled down his window. "We need you!" he shouted from the moving car and disappeared without awaiting a reply.[16]

Metro Jersey residents—the heart of Springsteen country—needed all the help they could get in those dark days. Springsteen was at home with Scialfa when the first plane hit the first tower. He watched the second one hit on live television. Springsteen quickly realized that many of the victims from the attacks on the World Trade Center were commuters from northeastern New Jersey. "The local communities were hit pretty hard," he told a reporter. "There were 150-plus casualties from Monmouth County alone. You would drive by the church every day and there was another funeral."

Springsteen was shaken—and moved to act. "When that guy yelled out, 'Bruce, we need you,' that was a tall order, but I knew what he meant," Springsteen recalled 15 years later. "I turned to the only language I've ever known to fight off the night terrors, real and imagined, time and again. It was all I could do."[17]

In the days that followed, he was one of a number of artists who made gestures of solidarity, which included making a live recording of himself singing "Thunder Road" to be played at a victim's funeral (which he did not attend out of fear of becoming a distraction). Springsteen and Joel both appeared in a fundraising telethon that was aired around the world on September 21. Joel performed "New York State of Mind"; Springsteen debuted a new song, "My City of Ruins," written in a Curtis Mayfield mold similar to the new song he included in *Live in New York City,* "Land of Hopes and Dreams." Both are marked by incantatory power that fuses the black gospel tradition and Springsteen's Catholic faith. "My City of Ruins" was in fact written about Asbury Park. But it took on new meaning in the wake of the 9/11 attacks, and suggestive of the ways the fates of New York and New Jersey were entwined.

Actually, 9/11 catalyzed what had been an incomplete and drifting set of songs that Springsteen had been working on following a national and international tour with the E Street Band in 1999–2000. But he hadn't been happy with the results. "It just didn't add up," he said. "There are many listenable bad records that hold your attention because they are not dull. They may have been written, constructed, arranged, and produced in a way that holds the ear. It may not be art, but it's admirable craft." He and Jon Landau realized they were no longer on the cutting edge, and belatedly took the advice of Columbia Records president Don Ienner, who suggested he work with Brendan O'Brien, a producer who had made records with Pearl Jam and Rage Against the Machine, and who had expressed an interest in working with Springsteen. They'd had a few preliminary meetings before 9/11 occurred. Afterward, a galvanized Springsteen went to Atlanta, where O'Brien was based, and began working on the album that became *The Rising,* which was released in July of 2002.[18]

With the possible exception of *Tunnel of Love, The Rising* is the most conceptually focused album Springsteen has ever made. But while that album was centered on marriage, this one explores the many facets of grief. As is his wont, Springsteen makes no explicit references to 9/11 (though a couple songs come close), instead allowing the songs to take on resonances that extend beyond that specific event. Some of the older tracks—"Nothing Man," a monologue by what appears to be figure haunted by survivor's guilt, actually dates back to 1994—take on new meanings. "Waitin' on a Sunny Day," a staple of Springsteen's recent tours, was also written earlier, but aptly suggests the struggle to escape bereavement. So does "Lonesome Day," which opens the album in a song where its narrator finds himself bewildered by loss and a belated recognition of how little he really knew his loved one. ("It's all right, all right, all right," he sings, straining to console himself, in a song in which Springsteen pulls off an impressive falsetto.) The one unabashedly joyous song, "Mary's Place," was written to evoke the raucous spirit of Springsteen's *Wild, Innocent and E Street Shuffle* days. But in this context takes on a charged air of catharsis.[19]

Other songs on *The Rising* showed Springsteen self-consciously trying to stretch himself, musically and otherwise. With the help of his old friend and producer Chuck Plotkin, he connected with Pakistani singer Asif Ali Khan and his group to record "Worlds Apart," a rock song with Middle Eastern vocals and percussion.[20] The ensuing track, "Let's Be Friends (Skin to Skin)," is a what appears to be an implicit paean to interracial romance in the mode of Sly and the Family Stone, a style that is not exactly in Springsteen's wheelhouse, but one he gamely attempts in the name of a broader ecumenicalism. These songs jostle with more generic ones like "Further Up the Road" and "Countin' on a Miracle," which fall under the "listenable bad records" category he described.

The most impressive tracks on *The Rising*, and the ones that really stitch it together, are those what were written in the wake of 9/11. "The Fuse" and "You're Missing" probe the experience of confronting emptiness ("Coffee cups on the counter, jackets on the chair / Papers on the doorstep, but you're not there," goes one verse from the latter). "Paradise" contrasts visions of the afterlife between a Palestinian suicide bomber, a Navy wife mourning a husband killed at the Pentagon, and a third character swimming in a liminal space between life and death.[21] And "Empty Sky," with its percussive, suspended chords, cites the Plains of Jordan—site of the destroyed city of Sodom— while evoking both the longing of loss and a thirst for vengeance: "I want a kiss from your lips / I want an eye for an eye."

The towering bookends of *The Rising* are two songs that appear at either end of the album. Both engage one of the most dramatic moments in the catastrophe: rescue workers who died in the quest to save others, using the fact and metaphor of ascension to document their glory. The album's second track, "Into the Fire," is a gorgeous hymn that mourns the loss of beloved hero with an incantatory chorus that in turn invokes strength, faith, hope, and love. The shattering title track, which is the thirteenth song, tells the story of a firefighter who responds to the call and climbs ever higher into darkness. Springsteen sings the second verse in a voice laced with fear as his ascending protagonist senses the newly dead and the presence of God: "May their precious love bind me / As I stand before your fiery light." The ensuing lines have him expressing love for his wife and children, as his life becomes a dream "like a catfish dancing on the end of my line." Amid the devastation, he sees a sky of love and tears, glory and sadness, mercy and fear, memory and shadow, longing and emptiness before the music finally breaks into blessed fullness and a new life amid a triumphant choir of voices. He has risen.

The Rising was Springsteen's first true E Street Band album since Born in the U.S.A., and was greeted as such with significant media attention. It instantly topped the Billboard album chart and remained there for three weeks in the days before the iPod, released months earlier, accelerated the transformation of music listening and sales into a digital realm. New York Times film critic A.O. Scott reviewed the album for Slate in a piece headlined "the poet laureate of 9/11."[22] Indeed, it may well be that The Rising is the most significant work of popular culture to come from that event.

The Rising followed an interregnum of seven years between 1995 and 2002 when Springsteen had not released a studio album, the longest stretch of his career. But it inaugurated a stretch of steady professional activity in which he released ten albums in the next twenty years. He also toured extensively, give 236 performances of his one-man Broadway show over 471 days, and wrote a 500-page memoir.[23] Though much of this work went unnoticed except by all but his most devoted fans, it represents a stretch of productivity that would tax an artist half his age.

It's here, when they entered late middle age, when Springsteen's life and work finally began to diverge from that of Joel, both in his relative stability—punctuated by debilitating bouts of depression—and his ongoing dedication to new creative expression. Joel remained active as well, but mostly as a live performer, and one who tended to stay close to home. Springsteen, who had always been less musically adventurous than Joel, now struck out in some new directions while also staying close to his roots, even as he roamed the globe with tours that stretched across five continents.[24]

The music Springsteen wrote and performed through the first decade of the twenty-first century varied in nature and quality. *Devils and Dust* (2005) is a minimalist album along the lines of *Nebraska* and *The Ghost of Tom Joad*, and like the latter has a strong southwestern flavor. Of particular note is the dramatic title track, written in the aftermath of the U.S. invasion of Iraq and narrated from the point of view of an American soldier warily eyeing an approaching vehicle and unsure whether it's occupied by friend or foe. "Reno" is an unusually graphic depiction of a visit to a prostitute, and the closing track, "Matamoros Banks," narrates the death of an undocumented immigrant backward in time. Perhaps the most tender song on the album is "Jesus Was an Only Son," a track that reflects Springsteen's Catholic engagement (in most Protestant denominations, Jesus is interpreted as having brothers and sisters). The album, like most of Springsteen's work at this point, leapt to the top of the charts upon release, but faded quickly after his core fan base snapped up copies.[25]

In 2006–2007, Springsteen made a foray into folk music. *The Seeger Sessions* was his first album consisting of cover tunes, all popularized by legendary singer and ethnomusicologist Pete Seeger. They range from nineteenth century folk classics such as "Old Dan Tucker" and "Mary Don't You Weep" to Civil Rights gospel standards such as "We Shall Overcome" and "Eyes on the Prize." The following year Springsteen issued *Live in Dublin*, a 23-track album in which many of these songs and some of Springsteen's own are performed with a band of 17–20 members, including a full brass section that he had first used in 1997 and continue to convene in the years that followed.

Like Joel, Springsteen toured regularly—at times it seemed continuously—in the twenty-first century. The difference, both from Joel and in the way he used to work, is that Springsteen now wrote songs while on the road. Some of such material, along songs he worked on at home in Rumson, coalesced in his 2007 album *Magic*, perhaps the most underrated in Springsteen's body of work.

In one sense, *Magic* stands out as the purest straight rock album Springsteen made since *Born in the U.S.A.* It's a full, regular, E Street Band record—the last featuring a full complement of charter members, as keyboard player Danny Federici died in 2008. (He was honored with "The Last Carnival," a song Springsteen included on his next album.) *Magic* is a medley of a dozen songs without an obvious thematic thread the way records such as *Nebraska*, *Tunnel of Love*, or *The Rising* did—which is one of the things that makes it so satisfying. Among its gems are "Radio Nowhere," a razor-sharp, metallic song about the quest to find connection and redemption on the airwaves, and "Girls in Their Summer Clothes," a tribute to the Beach Boys, and one which, like the greatest of Beach Boys records, has a dark subtext that its gorgeous melody and harmonies doesn't quite hide. The song's unreliable narrator, Bill, a denizen of the actual Tony's Grill in Freehold, tells us things been a little tight, even as he unconvincingly asserts things are going to go his way. "Beautiful thing, maybe you could save my life," he says of the waitress Shaniqua, enchanted by and objectifying her at the same time. (The two of course are not that far apart.[26])

But *Magic* is also indicative of the way politics was becoming an increasingly apparent facet of Springsteen's songwriting, and this is one more way in which he was diverging from Joel, who still considered himself a Democrat but continued to adopt a more diffident approach to controversial issues. Back in 2000, "American Skin (41 Shots)"' had provoked actual controversy—Mayor Rudolph Giuliani, New York Police Department commissioner Howard Safir, and NYPD union leader Patrick Lynch condemned it, with Bob Lucente, leader of the Fraternal Order of the Police, dubbing Springsteen "a floating fag"[27]—though it seems safe to say that any fair-minded reading of the song, which includes a police perspective, would not find it especially partisan. Springsteen's political statements on *Magic* are for the most part allusive, even elusive. But a close listening makes clear that he was no fan of President George W. Bush, whose war in

Iraq became the most divisive foreign policy issue in the United States since Vietnam. The title tragic, "Magic," can be heard simply as the monologue of a trickster, though there's something distinctly reminiscent of the oracular pronouncements of Defense Secretary Donald Rumsfeld in repeated lines "This is what will be."[28] The deceptively cheerful "Livin' in the Future" is a sprightly song about a failed love affair, but as Springsteen biographer Peter Ames Carlin notes, references to pistols, gunmetal skies, Election Day and the taste of blood after a kiss have an allegorical air.[29] Another standout song on the album, "Long Walk Home"—the video features Tony's Grill, and the lyrics mention Sal's Grocery in Freehold—is a melancholy reflection on cultural change. "That flag flying over the courthouse means certain things are set in stone," the narrator recalls his father saying, noting its affirmation of what the community will, and won't, do (a line that can be read more than one way). The one explicitly political song on *Magic* is the ponderous "Last to Die," a reference to Democratic political candidate, Vietnam vet, and antiwar protester John Kerry, who in 1971 asked a famous rhetorical question: "How do you ask a man to be the last man to die for a mistake?" Springsteen had endorsed Kerry, and also performed live at a campaign rally on his behalf the night before the 2004 presidential election.

By 2008, Springsteen was clearly identified in the public eye as a liberal Democrat, and his many fans who weren't typically ignored or made allowances for what was now an obvious partisan orientation. He gave an unsolicited endorsement to Barack Obama, who was surprised and pleased. "I'm not usually impressed by celebrity endorsements," Obama said. "I *like* the guy. I've got a bunch of his music on my iPod. I *really* like him."[30] It was the beginning of what proved to be a significant friendship.

Springsteen teamed up with Joel for a "Change Rocks" benefit concert for Obama in New York that October, where the two performed a "A Matter of Trust" in what was clearly intended to be recast as a political statement.[31] Springsteen as was also chosen as a performer for Obama's inauguration in 2009, where he played "The Rising" at the Lincoln Memorial with a gospel choir, and joined Pete Seeger for a rendition of "This Land Is Your Land." Later that year, Springsteen was among the honorees of the Kennedy Center, awarded to Americans who have made distinguished contributions to the arts. Joel joined that elite circle four years later.

It was while he was making appearances on Obama's behalf in 2008 that Springsteen debuted a new song, "Working on a Dream," that captured the optimism of the moment, cast as it was against the financial crisis of 2007–2008 that had been a key factor in Obama's election. The album that followed in 2009, *Working on a Dream*, may well be his weakest. It's a little ironic that a man who viewed the pop hooks of "Dancing in the Dark" with ambivalent suspicion was now crafting some of his catchiest tunes, albeit ones rooted in mid-1960s rather than forty years later. "This Life" is another tribute to the Beach Boys; in what may a bit of a *Nylon Curtain* moment, Springsteen invokes the *Revolver*-era Beatles in "Life Itself" and "Surprise Surprise." But the songs tend to evaporate on contact. Others simply don't work: "Queen of the Supermarket" is a well-intentioned, but mawkish, tribute to a working-class woman that harkens back to his misstep on "Mary Queen of Arkansas" on his debut. The album also includes as a bonus track, "The Wrestler," an original song for the 2008 film of the same name directed by Darren Aronofsky and starring Mickey Rourke in an Oscar-winning performance.

The one true standout in *Working on a Dream* is the album's opening track, "Outlaw Pete," a fully realized short story saturated in the cinematic history of the Western. (It furnished the basis of a children's 2014 children's book illustrated by Frank Caruso.) "Outlaw Pete" tells the story of a lifelong criminal trying to go straight, an effort complicated by a vengeful lawman who tells him "you think you have changed but you have not." A mythic—and perhaps politically incorrect—meditation on the power of nature over nurture, the song takes a lovely turn in its conclusion, which pivots to the perspective of Pete's half-Navajo daughter, "skin so fair," who "braids a piece of Pete's buckskin chaps in her hair." An eight-minute epic—its relentless four-note descending melody offset at the end by a guitar solo that ascends to break free of it—"Outlaw Pete" is the kind of epic song Springsteen had not recorded since the days of "Jungleland."[32]

Speaking of which: *Working on a Dream* was the swan song for Clarence Clemons, whose sax is prominent here but who died from complications of a stroke in 2011. (Springsteen was at his bedside when Clemons drew his last breath.[33]) He was replaced by his nephew, Jake Clemons. Max Weinberg's son Jay also filled in for his father on some of the dates on the *Working on a Dream* tour. With Federici missing, the E Street Band was changing. But many of its core components remained intact, and Steve Van Zandt had long since been back in the fold, notwithstanding his commitments to the hit HBO series *The Sopranos* (1999–2007), in which he played a gangster. The E Street Band remained one of the most beloved ensembles in popular music, and indeed was inducted into the Rock & Roll Hall of Fame in its own right 2014.

Springsteen reached what may have been his apogee in the public eye at the 2009 Super Bowl, where he and the E Streeters were given a coveted half-time performance slot reserved for the most beloved of pop entertainers. His fourteen-minute set consisted of "Tenth Avenue Freezeout," "Born to Run," "Working on a Dream" (an assertion of his ongoing relevance), and "Glory Days." And yet, even as he persisted as a household name, it was apparent to Springsteen that his new material wasn't connecting with audiences the way his older music did.[34] During the *Working on Dream* tour, he began doing did what Joel had for years: tacking back toward fan favorites. He now began performing different albums, in their entirety and in order, on different nights.

Joel would probably endorse Springsteen's description of touring as "my truest form of self-medication." But that wasn't always an available option for either man, and in these years Springsteen, like Joel, continued to be stalked by darkness within. Joel dealt with it by self-medicating, at times disastrously, with alcohol. Since late 2003, Springsteen relied on antidepressants, which worked well for him, but which needed occasional adjustment. In late 2009, he and his psychiatrist of 25 years decided to stop using the one he was on (and the psychiatrist died shortly thereafter). Springsteen went into a tailspin from which he recovered with the help of a new doctor and new medication. But depression continued to hover in the years ahead.[35]

In 2012, Springsteen released *Wrecking Ball,* an album that was meant to be a reckoning for America but became a kind of reckoning for him. Recorded with a new producer, Ron Aniello, known for working with figures as varied as Shania Twain (who Jon Landau managed) to Sixpence None the Richer, *Wrecking Ball* has a notably darker air than *Magic* or *Working on a Dream,* and has a thematic focus along the lines of *The Rising.* This time, the subject is the legacy of the 2008 financial crisis and its lingering impact on American life. Though, once again, the album avoids naming specific issues or targets, Springsteen's class politics are more pointed here than any previous album. (You have to go back to his 1986 song "Seeds"— "Long limousine shiny and black / You don't look ahead, you don't look back"—to find anything as pointed, and that track never appeared on an album.) Animated by militant Celtic overtones, and a rousing penny whistle, "Death to My Hometown" seethes with animosity that the melancholy "My Hometown" entirely lacks. "Jack of All Trades," which begins as a seemingly innocuous waltz, nevertheless contains notes of ominous dissonance and ends with its day laborer narrator stating, "If I had a gun, I'd find the bastards [such as bankers who grow fat] and shoot them on sight." The dark colors of *Wrecking Ball* are ably deepened by guitarist Tom Morello of Rage Against the Machine, who appears on a number of tracks, and who went on tour with Springsteen. They may also reflect Springsteen's inner state, as his bleak, seemingly autobiographical "This Depression," with its slow, sledgehammer beats, suggests. But there are notes of resilience here as well, notably the title track, in which Springsteen channels the inner voice of the soon-to-be-demolished Giants Stadium, home for many of his performing triumphs. The album ends on a hopeful note with "We Are Alive," in which the souls of the Great Railroad Strike of 1877, a Civil Rights worker killed in 1963, and a contemporary undocumented immigrant who perished in south-western desert live on "to carry the fire and light the spark."

"*Wrecking Ball* was received with a lot less fanfare that I thought it would be," Springsteen mused four years later. "I was sure I had it. I still think I do and did." It's not exactly that the album did badly—it debuted at number one, his tenth time reaching that status. President Obama used the leadoff track, the anthemic "We Take Care of Our Own," as a campaign song. But, as was the norm now, the album cooled quickly, which in part reflected the more mercurial state of the pop charts in an age of fading sales and more the more precise measures of SoundScan. But there was more to it than that, as Springsteen recognized, including the fact that there was a price to be paid for politicking. "I came to terms with the fact that in the States, the power of rock music as a vehicle for these ideas had diminished. A new kind of super-pop, hip-hop, and a variety of other exciting genres had become the hotline of the day, more suited to the current zeitgeist. I can't complain." Still, it was hard. "I thought this was one of my most powerful records and I went out l went out looking for it all."[36] He has reason to think so, and indeed it seems likely the *Wrecking Ball* will be remembered by Springsteen fans as among the strongest of his late work.

The forces of gravity were asserting themselves now. Joel had sensed them, and acceded to them, decades before. No titan of modern popular music—not Sinatra, not Elvis, not Dylan or Paul McCartney—could produce hits for more than a generation. Such figures could enjoy success as elder statesmen for another one, but increasingly the emphasis was on the elder, not the statesman. By the time he reached his sixty-fifth birthday in 2014, Springsteen was fading as unmistakably surely as Joel was.

Still he pressed on. That year Springsteen released *High Hopes*, his eighteenth studio album. It was one that suggested he treading water, however. The record features a number covers, including the title track, and a pair of songs, "American Skin" and "The Ghost of Tom Joad," that had been released in other forms. Still other tracks were holdovers from prior sessions. Aniello was again producing, in tandem with O'Brien, and Morello was on hand to enliven the proceedings. But the album is among Springsteen's most forgettable, even as, yet again, it debuted at number one, in a moment when sales mattered less than ever as an index of popularity (radio airplay was virtually non-existent).

Now, whether as a matter of choice or perceived necessity, Springsteen entered retrospective mode. In 2016, he published the memoir he spent seven years writing himself, *Born to Run*, which of course was an important source for this book and is quoted throughout. *Born to Run* quickly topped the bestseller lists and critically celebrated for its grace and candor. It was accompanied by *Chapter and Verse*, an album of his earliest as well as best known songs.

Springsteen then played what might be termed his *Movin' Out* card and mounted his own stage show, *Springsteen on Broadway*, which ran at the 975-seat Walter Kerr Theatre to packed houses in 2017–2018. *Springsteen on Broadway* had a notably different vibe than his legendary concerts, not only because of the venue's relatively tiny size. However carefully rehearsed—and they were indeed planned quite intricately—Springsteen's E Street shows were festive affairs notable for their sense of spontaneity. This show, by contrast, was truly a stage show, intricately executed on an intimate scale. (Its origins derived from a performance for about one hundred people he gave for departing members of the Obama administration at the White House in the final month of the president's term.[37]) Springsteen, who graciously declined to enter the Tony Awards competition for the show, nevertheless received a special award for *Springsteen on Broadway*. Robert DeNiro, who attended the show—and who reputedly transformed Springsteen's playful concert line "Are You Talkin' To Me?" into the ominous rhetorical question of Travis Bickle in the 1976 Martin Scorsese film *Taxi Driver*[38]—denounced President Donald Trump, praised Springsteen, and said he regarded the real title of the show as *Jersey Boy*.[39] Fittingly, the man who presented him with the honor at the Tonys was Joel.

Springsteen could still try something new, even if he reached back to do so. In 2019, he released *Western Stars,* in which he returned to his now-familiar California side in a fresh way with a collection of songs in the vein of pop craftsmen like Glen Campbell and Burt Bachrach. It was a surprising but compelling move with some fine country tracks, among them the title song, "Tucson Train," and "There Goes My Miracle" (notable for its strong vocal). A documentary film to accompany the album was produced for theatrical release, undoubtedly hampered by the Covid-19 pandemic.

In 2020, Springsteen offered his fans the musical version of his memoirs in the form of *Letter to You,* in which he includes a rousing version of the song he played for John Hammond a half-century earlier, "If I Was the Priest," as well as another song, "Janey Needs a Shooter," he wrote with the late, great Warren Zevon, who included it on his 1978 album *Bad Luck Streak in Dancing School. Letter to You* also includes a series of songs like "One Minute You're Here" and "Ghosts," which serves as a requiem for vanished friends, and others, like "Land of a Thousand Guitars," that conjure the world of his childhood. While unmistakably nostalgic, the album also works on its own terms as a classic rock album, one of the better ones Springsteen has made in the twenty-first century. He performed a number of the songs from *Letter to You* during his 2023 international tour.

The retrospective mood continued in his recordings. In November of 2022, Springsteen released *Only the Strong Survive,* his second collection of covers. Like *Letter to You,* this one had been recorded during the COVID pandemic, and like previous projects, this one only came after he discarded previous material. This time the focus was not his relatively late discovery of folk music, but rather his early encounter with soul music. Springsteen had always prided himself on being something of a rock ethnomusicologist, and *Only the Strong Survive* is chock full of obscure gems like Frank Wilson's 1965 Motown rarity "Do I Love You? (Yes I Do)" and Frankie Valli's "The Sun Ain't Gonna Shine No More," which became a minor hit for the Walker Brothers in 1966. In a promotional video for the album, Springsteen explained that it was meant to be a showcase for his voice, an instrument he had tended to give short shrift given the imperatives of his songwriting for most of his career.[40] It's a modest record, but a spirited one. *Only the Strong Survive* was dubbed "Vol. I," leaving the door open for future installments.

He and Joel were old men now. They were legends, and, for now, living ones.

Conclusion

Swift Currents

As it turns out, well, most of us are from
suburbia. That's a lot of what America is.

—Billy Joel, 1998

SUMMER 2010. Dad is driving his high-school aged son and his
girlfriend to an unremembered destination. Stopped at a light.
That vaguely annoying song is on the radio again. Hackneyed references to *Romeo and Juliet* and *The Scarlet Letter*, apparently untethered
from those classics. "Who *is* this?" he asks, unable to keep irritation out
of his voice.

"That's Taylor Swift," the girlfriend replies.

Ah yes: Taylor Swift. Nashville darling, by way of eastern Pennsylvania. Dad has heard about her. Another teen sensation. Back at home,
he listens to the song—the archetypically named "Love Story"—while
reading the lyrics. Very old-fashioned; boy needs matrimonial blessing from dad. Riddled with clichés. On the other hand, there's something undeniably ingenuous about it: the character experiencing
these things for the first time. That faintly sexual ache in her voice.
And the deft opening line that puts the whole thing in a retrospective
frame: "We were both young when I first saw you." Yes, there's something there.

A few months later—fall leaves, football games, son's senior year—
Taylor Swift releases *Speak Now*. Dad is impressed. The Beatlesque
title track, right down to the hand-clapping. That line in "Mine": "You

made a rebel of a careless man's careful daughter." The skillfully compressed "Story of Us," which doesn't so much end as sever. It's official: Dad is a fan.

And he remains one for the next decade: *Red* in 2012. *1989* in 2014. *Reputation* in 2017. *Folklore* and *Evermore* in 2020. *Midnights* in 2022, with its evocation of Frank Sinatra's classic *In the Wee Small Hours* sixty-eight years before. Each one a carefully sculpted album, in the classic sense of the term. Finely chiseled songs that encapsulate and extend generations of pop history. "She knows music and she knows how to write," Billy Joel says of Swift in 2021. "She's like that generation's Beatles. ("I don't really know how to process words like that from someone like him," Swift says in response. I'm a huge fan of his; that's an icon saying that."[1])

Others note Swift's similarities with Bruce Springsteen, whose daughter took him to see a Swift show when she was in college, and whose songs he describes as "really, really well-built and well-made."[2] As critic Emily St. James noted in *Vox*:

> Both musicians love songs about a kind of white Americana that's never really existed but that the central characters of which feel compelled to chase anyway. They use those songs to tell stories about those people and the places they live. They're terrifically good at wordplay. Both are fascinated by the ways that adolescence and memories of adolescence continue to have incredible power for adults. Both are amazing at crafting bridges that take already good songs to another level. And both write songs featuring fictional people whose lives are sketched in via tiny, intimate details that stand in for their whole selves.[3]

Taylor Swift has something else in common with Billy Joel and Bruce Springsteen: she's aging. She is of course forty years younger than they are, but the sixteen-year-old of her debut album in 2006 is now edging toward middle age. Sixteen-year-olds of the 2020s all know who she is, but, well, she's no Lil Nas X or Olivia Rodrigo (who regards Swift as a role model).[4] Taylor Swift may not be an old-fashioned girl, but she's gotten dated.

Not as dated as Springsteen and Joel, of course. For some of us, this can be hard to accept. There was a time, seemingly not long ago, when they were the very embodiment of youth. Not only *their* youth, but that of a nation reborn in a crucible of depression and war and embarking on a golden age. Part of what made it so was the absorptive power of a global colossus in which even those from the hinterlands could cross barriers, literal and figurative, and occupy a place at the center of American culture. These realities have not entirely disappeared, as the success of Swift—and the dominance of the suburban culture that so decisively shaped Joel and Springsteen—attests. But its mortality, and theirs as well as ours, is harder to ignore.

Still, music won't go away. Nor will music that's loved and remembered and passed down from generation to generation. But such receding fragments will be harder to recognize and place in context as memories of them grow fainter. As Springsteen wrote in "Independence Day," "Soon everything we've known will just be swept away."

But not yet. We inhabit a perishable eternal now. The knowledge of that perishability is an ache and a spur to savor the moment. We will be right to have loved the sound of lives well lived.

ACKNOWLEDGMENTS

THIS BOOK BEGAN with a phone call I was reluctant to take. In January of 2022, Peter Mickulas of Rutgers University Press suggested we talk about a manuscript I'd written that he could not publish because its subject—everyday life in the late American empire, which is to say the world we inhabit at this moment—fell outside his bailiwick as executive editor. Peter wanted to talk about where else I might shop the project, a conversation I didn't particularly want to have because I'd already surveyed the publishing landscape and concluded that I had reached a dead end. But Peter pressed for us to have a chat, and I felt I owed it to him to uphold my end of his kindness. We ran through a set of what I already knew would be fruitless options, and rang off.

In the weeks that followed, I found myself thinking about what *did* fall in Peter's bailiwick. (One area was sociology, which I had thought was a plausible, if admittedly unorthodox, prospect for that empire manuscript.) Another was regional studies of the Mid-Atlantic centering on New Jersey. I'd written about Bruce Springsteen, and had once planned to write on Billy Joel, both of whom hailed from the region. And that's how—very suddenly—this book snapped into place. It was drafted over a period of six months in 2022. That never would have happened without Peter.

Once launched, I had a lot of other help along the way. My old friends Wally Levis and Andy Meyers talked through my ideas. Springsteen biographer Peter Ames Carlin, who in 2011 took me on an unforgettable tour of Bruce Springsteen's Freehold, gave me a useful read of the manuscript. So did Tom Perrotta and June Skinner Sawyers, who has compiled an impressive body of Springsteen work of her own. Ken Womack showed me around Asbury Park, and my beloved high school social studies teacher—and Levittown native—Pete White pointed out the landmarks of Billy Joel's Hicksville.

This is the fifth book I've written for Rutgers University Press, which has been my haven in an often-heartless publishing world. I have ongoing debts to publisher Micah Kleit, editorial director Kimberly Guinta, and sales and marketing director Jeremy Grainger. I appreciate the production work, once again, of Westchester Publishing Services, in particular production editor, Kristen Bettcher, who has ushered a number of my books into print, and copy editor Jennifer Apt. Thanks also to Charles Brock, who designed the cover. It's great to have the privilege of working with top-tier talent.

Since 2020, when I arrived amid the COVID-19 pandemic, I have had the good fortune to work at Greenwich Country Day School and be a part of the founding of its upper division. I savor the company and support of my colleagues, notably Adam Rohdie, Chris Winters, Andrew Ruoss and Lauren Waller, and benefited from conversations with performing arts teachers Sarina Bachleitner and Jonathan DeVries. Gregory Grene, who migrated to GCDS from our old home at the Ethical Culture Fieldston School, was a musical companion, in more ways than one. (He is, truly, a prodigal talent.) Having such a firm institutional foundation has made sustaining my scholarly passions possible for one more round. My thanks to all in the GCDS community.

This book, like a number of previous ones, was substantially written at the Starbucks coffee shop in Dobbs Ferry, New York. I was gladdened by the proficiency and good will of the staff there and the camaraderie of a community that buoyed me for the last decade.

My family continues to be my mainstay source of sustenance, even as the lives of my four children—Jay, Gray, Ry, and Nancy—sail into the open seas of adulthood. My wife Lyde remains by my side. My final words of thanks are, once more, to her.

Jim Cullen
Hastings-on-Hudson, New York
May 2023

NOTES

Introduction

Epigraphs: https://www.danspapers.com/2016/01/watch-alec-baldwin-interview
-billy-joel-in-east-hampton/; https://www.youtube.com/watch?v=Wt7TKLqX
_SE (March 28, 2023).

1. Enid Nemy, "To Be Thin, Beautiful and Cheek-to-Jowl," *New York Times*,
December 14, 1977: https://www.nytimes.com/1977/12/14/archives/to-be-thin
-beautiful-and-cheektojowl.html; David Cook, "What's with the Bridge and
Tunnel Label?" Street Easy Reads website, September 27, 2018: https://streeteasy
.com/blog/bridge-and-tunnel/.

2. Henry Luce's 1941 essay "The American Century," is reprinted in *Diplo-
matic History* 23:2 (1999): 159–171. http://www-personal.umich.edu/~mlassite
/discussions261/luce.pdf.

3. Charlie Gillett, *The Sound of the City: The Rise of Rock & Roll* (1970; New
York: Pantheon, 1983).

4. The story of "Will You Still Love Me Tomorrow?" is recounted in Ken
Emerson, *Always Magic in the Air: The Bomp and Brilliance of the Brill Building
Era* (New York: Penguin, 2005), 90–91. See also the entry of the song at the
Fandom website: https://popular-music.fandom.com/wiki/Will_You_Love
_Me_Tomorrow. King notes Owens feared the song was "too country" in a
Tweet: https://twitter.com/carole_king/status/1329444915600912392?lang=es.

5. You can hear this May 15, 1971 performance at https://www.youtube.com
/watch?v=ZBs3jXi78kA. Springsteen's description of the girl groups' influence is
quoted in Clinton Heylin, *E Street Shuffle: The Glory Days of Bruce Springsteen
and the E Street Band* (New York: Viking, 2013), 9.

6. Getting precise figures on record sales can be surprisingly tricky, not only because there doesn't seem to be an easily available definitive source, but also because numbers depend on how you count them (each disc in multiple album sets are sometimes counted, for example) and because figures are constantly updated. Although one hesitates to regard it as definitive, Wikipedia seems to have done a good job of tabulating and confirming sales figures. See "List of best-selling music artists": https://en.wikipedia.org/wiki/List_of_best -selling_music_artists#cite_note-cert-1.

7. Joel was the subject of an academic conference at Colorado College in 2016; there have been a series of "Glory Days" conferences for Springsteen at Monmouth University in 2005, 2009, and 2012; a symposium marking the fortieth anniversary of his 1978 album *Darkness on the Edge of Town* was held there in 2018. Articles on Springsteen as a queer artist include Martha Nell Smith, "Sexual Mobilities in Bruce Springsteen: Performance as Commentary," *South Atlantic Quarterly* 90:4 (Fall 1991), 833–854; and Natalie Adler, "Our Butch Mother, Bruce Springsteen," in *Long Walk Home: Reflections on Bruce Springsteen*, edited by Jonathan D. Cohen and June Skinner Sawyers (New Brunswick: Rutgers University Press, 2019), 155–161. Two important studies of Springsteen fandom include Daniel Cavicchi, *Tramps Like Us: Music and Meaning Among Springsteen Fans* (New York: Oxford University Press, 1998) and Lorraine Mangione and Donna Luff, *Mary Climbs In: The Journeys of Bruce Springsteen's Women Fans* (New Brunswick: Rutgers University Press, 2024).

8. Bruce Springsteen, *Born to Run* (New York: Simon & Schuster, 2016), Fred Schruers, *Billy Joel: The Definitive Biography* (New York: Crown Archetype, 2014).

9. Barack Obama and Bruce Springsteen, *Renegades: Born in the USA* (New York: Crown, 2021), 7, 132.

10. *Extraordinary with Fareed Zakaria*, May 13, 2022: https://www.youtube .com/watch?v=jou9SovPY6g.

11. Hannah Dailey, "Olivia Rodrigo Is 'Still Crying' After Performing With Billy Joel: 'Biggest Honor Ever'" *Billboard*, August 25, 2022: https://apple.news /AZdHStiqFTT2aF-Q2tiCn5A.

12. Nick Paumgarten, "The Thirty-Three-Hit Wonder," *The New Yorker*, October 27, 2014: https://www.newyorker.com/magazine/2014/10/27/thirty -three-hit-wonder.

13. In his 2020 podcasts with Barack Obama, Springsteen estimated that two-thirds of his audience is now European, with the other third American. See *Renegades*, 262; Keith Caulfield, "Bruce Springsteen Becomes First Act with Top-Five Charting Albums in Each of the Last Six Decades with *Letter to You*," *Billboard*, November 2, 2020: https://www.billboard.com/pro/bruce -springsteen-makes-history-with-letter-to-you/.

14. For one example, see, Joan Hanauer, "Quote of the Day: Billy Joel," UPI archives, August 16, 1982: https://www.upi.com/Archives/1982/08/16/QUOTE -OF-THE-DAY-Billy-Joel/3028398318400/.

15. For a list of these shows, see http://www.coveredbybrucespringsteen.com /viewcover.aspx?recordID=69; Samantha Maine, "Billy Joel Takes Blame for Bruce Springsteen's Motorbike Breakdown," *New Musical Express*, November 27, 2016: https://www.nme.com/news/music/billy-joel-takes-blame-for-bruce -springsteen-bike-break-down-1876427.

16. Chuck Klosterman, *Sex, Lies and Cocoa Puffs: A Low Culture Manifesto* (New York: Scribner, 2003), 42–55; Klosterman, "The Stranger," New York *Times* Magazine, September 15, 2002: https://www.nytimes.com/2002/09/15/magazine/the -stranger.html; "Billy Joel: Oh, the Squandered Genius!" *Slate*, November 29, 2005: https://slate.com/culture/2005/11/the-squandered-genius-of-the-piano-man.html.

17. Ron Rosenbaum, "The Worst Pop Singer Ever: Why, Exactly, Is Billy Joel So Bad?" *Slate* January 23, 2009: https://slate.com/human-interest/2009/01/the -awfulness-of-billy-joel-explained.html.

18. Fred Ahrens, "Billy Joel, Bard of the Burbs," Washington *Post*, April 23, 1998: https://www.washingtonpost.com/archive/lifestyle/1998/04/23/billy-joel -bard-of-the-burbs/9c2cbce6-aa8d-44e5-b6cc-32954d389e9b/.

19. Christgau's piece, "Yes, There Is a Rock Critic Establishment (But Is that Bad for Rock?)" is reprinted on his website, robertchristgau.com: https://www .robertchristgau.com/xg/rock/critics-76.php; Knobler and Mitchell's piece is included in the anthology *Racing in the Street: The Bruce Springsteen Reader*, edited by June Skinner Sawyers (New York: Penguin, 2004), 29–39.

20. Henry Edwards, "If There Hadn't Been a Bruce Springsteen, Critics Would Have Made Him Up," New York *Times*, October 5, 1975: https://www.nytimes .com/1975/10/05/archives/if-there-hadnt-been-a-bruce-springsteen-then-the -critics-would-have.html; Mary Harron, "No One's Fault," *New Statesman*, November 19, 1982, 29–30. For more on Springsteen's conservatism, see Jim Cullen, "Bruce Springsteen's Ambiguous Musical Politics in the Reagan Era," *Popular Music and Society* 16:2 (Summer 1992), 1–22, and Cullen, "Summer's Fall: Springsteen in Senescence," in Cohen and Sawyers, 189–199.

21. Klosterman, "The Stranger."

22. To cite one example, Joel went into a well-publicized rage that led him to throw an electric piano off the stage in anger at his lighting crew in Russia in 1987; see Schruers, 186. Springsteen biographer Peter Ames Carlin was surprised to witness Springsteen erupt in rage during a rehearsal for a 2012 show. See *Bruce* (New York: Touchstone, 2012), 456. Over the years, both men have been sued by their employees, and while there are at least two sides to such stories, it's clear that neither man was necessarily a hero to their valets.

Chapter 1 New York State of Mind

1. For an excellent study of the way the Erie Canal literally changed the course of American history, see Peter Bernstein, *Wedding of the Waters: The Erie Canal and the Making of a Great Nation* (rpt; New York: Norton, 2006).

2. Howard Taubman, *The Making of the American Theater* (New York: Coward McCann, 1965), 27–29; 51.

3. For a brief overview of the emergence of theatrical culture in the early nineteenth century, see Jim Cullen, *The Art of Democracy: A Concise History of Popular Culture*, second ed. (1996; New York: Monthly Review Press, 2002), Chapter 2; and Cullen, *A Short History of the Modern Media* (Malden, MA: Wiley Blackwell, 2014), also Chapter 2. The best single-volume treatment of early theater in America remains David Grimsted, *Melodrama Unveiled: American Theatre and Culture, 1800–1850* (1968; Berkeley: University of California Press, 1987).

4. Important studies of minstrelsy include Robert Toll, *Blacking Up: The Minstrel Show in Nineteenth Century America* (New York: Oxford University Press, 1974); Eric Lott, *Love and Theft: Blackface Minstrelsy and the American Working Class* (New York: Oxford University Press, 1993); and Yuval Taylor and Jake Austen, *Darkest America: Blackface Minstrelsy from Slavery to Hip-Hop* (New York, W.W. Norton, 2012).

5. W. T. Llamon, *Raising Cain: Blackface Performance from Jim Crow to Hip-Hop* (Cambridge, MA: Harvard University Press, 1998). See especially pp. 1–4 on Catherine Market, and 60–66 on the culture of canalling.

6. Lawrence Levine, *Highbrow/Lowbrow: The Emergence of Cultural Hierarchy in America* (Cambridge, MA: Harvard University Press, 1988), 85–98; Robert Toll, *On with the Show: The First Century of Show Business in America* (New York: Oxford University Press, 1976), 41–45. Barnum devotes a chapter (XVII) to the Jenny Lind tour in his memoir *Struggles and Triumphs* (1869; New York: Penguin, 1981), 170–182.

7. Lawrence Levine, "The Folklore of Industrial Society: Popular Culture and Its Audiences," *American Historical Review* 97:5 (December 1992): 1369–1399. The piece was later published in Levine, *The Unpredictable Past: Explorations in American Cultural History* (New York: Oxford University Press, 1993), 291–320.

8. For more on this, see Robert Fishman, *Bourgeois Utopias: The Rise and Fall of Suburbia* (New York: Oxford University Press, 1989).

9. On the etymology of "rubes" and similar terms, see Nancy Groce's superb compendium *New York: Songs of the City* (1999; New York: Billboard Books, 2003), 23–24. You can see a clip of Alistair Cooke explaining the New Rochelle imbroglio and a performance from the show in the 1959 *Omnibus* episode on You Tube: https://www.youtube.com/watch?v=G83Oroai-oU.

10. Groce, 23,123.

11. Ian T. McAuley, "New Rochelle's Long Black History," New York *Times*, February 20, 1983: https://www.nytimes.com/1983/02/20/nyregion/new -rochelle-s-long-black-history.html.

12. Christopher Gray, "Tracing Scott Joplin's Life Through His Addresses," New York *Times*, February 4, 2007: https://www.nytimes.com/2007/02/04 /realestate/04scap.html; "Scott Joplin in New York: A Ragtime Mystery," The Bowery Boys podcast, February 23, 2019: https://www.boweryboyshistory.com /2019/02/scott-joplin-in-new-york-a-ragtime-mystery.html.

13. For a good brief biography, see James Kaplan, *Irving Berlin: New York Genius* (New Haven: Yale University Press, 2019). Philip Furia, who is also a Berlin biographer, wrote the excellent overview *The Poets of Tin Pan Alley: A History of America's Great Lyricists* (1990; New York: Oxford University Press, 1992). For a fine cultural study of "White Christmas," see Jody Rosen, *White Christmas: The Story of an American Song* (New York: Scribner, 2002). "God Bless America" angered Woody Guthrie, who wrote "This Land is Your Land" as a response (and later inspiring Springsteen to incorporate it into his live shows). See Joe Klein, *Woody Guthrie: A Life* (1980: New York: Delta, 1999), 140–145. Springsteen biographer Dave Marsh, who recognizes the affinities in the two songs, describes the circumstances of Springsteen's discovery of "This Land is Your Land" in his 1979 biography *Born to Run*, folded into his two-volume, expanded work *Two Hearts: The Definitive Biography, 1972–2003* (New York: Routledge, 2004), 278–279. You can see Berlin perform "God Bless America" on *The Ed Sullivan Show* in 1968 on YouTube: https://www.youtube .com/watch?v=B0BZ89rw3zM.

14. On the emergence of radio and records and their relationship with each other, see Cullen, *A Short History of the Modern Media*, 120–123; 191–195 and *The Art of Democracy*, 182–183.

15. You can see a video, complete with their wry banter, on YouTube: https:// www.youtube.com/watch?v=n9kfdEyV3RQ.

16. Gary Giddins, *Bing Crosby: A Pocketful of Dreams, The Early Years, 1903–1940* (rpt; New York: Back Bay Books, 2002), 239–240.

17. Giddins, 154, 269, 297.

18. The literature on Frank Sinatra is immense. His pre-eminent biographer is James Kaplan. See *Frank Sinatra: The Voice* (New York: Doubleday, 2010) and the second volume, *Frank Sinatra: The Chairman* (New York: Doubleday, 2015). For excellent compendia of writings on Sinatra, *see Legend: Frank Sinatra and the American Dream*, edited by Ethlie Ann Vare (New York: Boulevard Books, 1995) and *The Frank Sinatra Reader*, edited by Steven Petrov and Leonard Mustazza (New York: Oxford University Press, 1995). New York journalist Pete Hamill,

who knew Sinatra, is the author of an evocative book-length essay, *Why Sinatra Matters* (New York: Little, Brown, 1998).

19. Nancy Sinatra, *Frank Sinatra: My Father* (rpt; New York, Pocket Books, 1986), 13. For a consideration of Sinatra in his cultural milieu, see Jim Cullen, "Fool's Paradise: Frank Sinatra and the American Dream," *Popular Culture in American History*, 2nd ed., edited by Cullen (Malden, MA: Wiley-Blackwell, 2013), 186–210.

20. You can see the clip on YouTube: https://www.youtube.com/watch?v =BFsnMl3UqIA.

21. For an analysis of the song and a clip of Joel performing it, see the unofficial Billy Joel website "One Final Serenade": https://www.onefinalserenade.com /all-my-life-2007-single.html.

22. John Lahr, "Sinatra's Song," *The New Yorker*, October 26, 1997: https:// www.newyorker.com/magazine/1997/11/03/sinatras-song/amp; Rafael Pocaro, "Bruce Springsteen Reveals the Song He Would Listen to for the Rest of His Life," rock&rollgarage.com: http://rockandrollgarage.com/bruce-springsteen -reveals-the-song-he-would-listen-to-the-rest-of-his-life/; Clip of Springsteen at the 2008 New Jersey Hall of Fame Ceremony, YouTube: https://www.youtube .com/watch?v=4hAAehP6UxM; Springsteen on *The Late Show with Stephen Colbert*, November 21, 2021: https://www.youtube.com/watch?v=SN-EollIYGo; Bruce Springsteen, *Born to Run* (New York: Simon & Schuster, 2016), 418–421. (The chapter is titled "King of New Jersey," a title conferred on Sinatra by Jack Nicholson, also a Jersey native.)

23. Much of the material in the preceding and following paragraph comes from Cullen, *A Short History of the Modern Media*, 202.

24. As with Frank Sinatra, there is a robust discourse surrounding the career of Elvis Presley. The definitive biography is that of Peter Guralnick: *Last Train to Memphis: The Rise of Elvis Presley* (New York: Little, Brown, 1994), and *Careless Love: The Unmaking of Elvis Presley* (New York: Little Brown, 1999). The "Elvis" of rock criticism is Greil Marcus; see his classic essay on Presley, "Presliad," in *Mystery Train: Images of America in Rock & Roll Music*, 6th ed. (1975; New York: Plume, 2015).

25. For more on this, see Peter Ames Carlin, *Sonic Boom: The Impossible Rise of Warner Bros. Records* (New York: Holt, 2021).

26. David Sheff, "The Playboy Interview: Billy Joel," *Playboy*, May 1982, posted at davidsheff.com: https://www.davidsheff.com/billy-joel.

27. Springsteen, *Born to Run*, 41.

28. For a superb overview of these songwriters and their metropolitan backgrounds see Ken Emerson, *Always Magic in the Air: The Bomp and Brilliance*

of the Brill Building Era (New York: Penguin, 2005). Emerson discusses the integration of Latin sounds in particular in Chapter 9 (pp. 121–140).

29. Bruce Springsteen, liner notes for *The Promise*, a collection of *Darkness on the Edge of Town*-era outtakes released in 2010.

30. For YouTube clips of these performances, see https://www.youtube.com /watch?v=9hJOweovH_s and https://www.youtube.com/watch?v=cUSMkd ZK06I.

31. On the challenges Springsteen faced in this regard, see Marsh, 76–77.

Chapter 2 Hard Times, Boom Years

1. Fred Schruers, *Billy Joel: The Definitive Biography* (New York: Crown, 2014), 20. On Springsteen's genealogy, see Peter Ames Carlin, *Bruce* (New York: Touchstone, 2012), 5–8.

2. Bruce Springsteen, *Born to Run* (New York: Simon & Schuster, 2016), 9.

3. Jonathan Schifman, "Are There Any Original Levitt Houses Left in Levittown?" *Newsday*, August 25, 2017: https://www.newsday.com/long-island /are-there-any-original-levitt-houses-left-in-levittown-j65196. Special thanks to my old high school teacher, Pete White, a Levittown resident who took me on a tour of the neighborhood in July of 2022. As per the article, it's clear that most of the original homes have been modified, many of them beyond recognition, which includes Joel's home at 20 Meeting Lane.

4. Jim Cullen, *Democratic Empire: The United States Since 1945* (New York: Blackwell-Wiley, 2016), 33.

5. Cullen, *Democratic Empire*, 30–31. On heating, see, for example, an exultant Springsteen noting a new family home actually had it in Carlin, p. 20 and another such description on p. 34. Gas jets feature in his opening monologue in "Growing Up" as featured in his 1986 album *Live 1975/85*.

6. "Reader's Poll: Best Billy Joel Songs of All Time," *Rolling Stone*, December 5, 2012: https://www.rollingstone.com/music/music-lists/readers-poll-the -best-billy-joel-songs-of-all-time-16758/10-goodnight-saigon-225613/; Barack Obama and Bruce Springsteen, *Renegades: Born in the USA* (New York: Crown, 2021), 69; Springsteen, *Born to Run*, 101.

7. Landon Jones, *Great Expectations: America and the Baby Boom Generation* (rpt; New York: Ballentine, 1981), 1–3. James Patterson, *Grand Expectations: The United States, 1945–1974* (New York: Oxford University Press, 1996).

8. Scott Sandage, *Born Losers: A History of Failure in America* (Cambridge, MA: Harvard University Press, 2005), 5.

9. Alexis de Tocqueville, *Democracy in America,* Book II, Chapter 19, "That Almost All Americans Follow Industrial Callings: https://www.marxists.org /reference/archive/de-tocqueville/democracy-america/ch31.htm#:~:text=In%20 this%20respect%20they%20share,same%20time%20those%20who%20govern.

10. Comment translated in *The Joel Files,* an important independent 2001 documentary about the Joel family history directed by Beate Thalberg: https:// www.youtube.com/watch?v=qE-_rpjmEFE. In a notable gesture of magnanimousness, Joel and his half-brother Alexander agreed to meet with the heirs of the Neckermann family that impoverished his grandparents; the scene is captured in the documentary.

11. Hank Bardowitz, *Billy Joel: The Life and Times of an Angry Young Man* (2006; Milwaukee: Backbeat Books, 2011), 2; Schruers, 8–20.

12. Schruers, 20; Bardowitz, 6.

13. Bardowitz, 8; Schruers, 22–23, 28; "Billy Joel's Mother Dies at 92," *The Hollywood Reporter* (Associated Press), July 16, 2014: https://www .hollywoodreporter.com/news/music-news/billy-joels-mother-dies-at-719073/. "Togetherness," a term that was in widespread use in the 1950s, has been widely discussed in scholarly discourse. See, for example, Laura J. Miller, "Family Togetherness and the Suburban Ideal," *Sociological Forum* 10:3 (September 1995): 393–418. Elaine Tyler May elaborates on the general concept in *Homeward Bound: American Families in the Cold War Era,* Fourth Ed. (1988; New York: Basic, 2017).

14. Bardowitz, 5–6; Schruers, 26, 30.

15. Schruers, 29–30.

16. Carlin, 1–6.

17. Carlin, 4–7.

18. Schruers, 22–25.

19. "Their deep love and attraction and yet the dramatic gulf between my mother and father's personalities was always a mystery to me . . . My mother and her two sisters have an unending faith in people, are social creatures who will merrily make conversation with a broom handle. My father was a misanthrope who shunned most of humankind." *Born to Run,* 37.

20. Barack Obama and Bruce Springsteen, *Renegades: Born in the USA* (New York: Crown, 2021), 13.

21. Springsteen, *Born to Run,* 8–9.

22. Carlin, 10–15.

23. Springsteen, *Born to Run,* 26–28; 498–500.

24. My thanks to Peter Ames Carlin for relating Springsteen's bedroom mirror stories in an email correspondence of July 26, 2022. On Joel and Elvis, see Bardowitz, 10.

25. Cullen, *Democratic Empire*, 60.

26. Rutgers 250 (1766–2016) website: https://ucmweb.rutgers.edu/250/our -history.htm#:~:text=In%201945%20and%201956%2C%20state,New%20 Jersey%2C%20a%20public%20institution.

27. Dave Marsh, *Bruce Springsteen: Two Hearts* (New York Routledge 2004), 23. This "definitive biography" by a journalist and critic who has had more access to Springsteen than any other, is in fact a combination and extension of two previous works: *Born to Run: The Bruce Springsteen Story* (New York: Ballantine, 1979), and *Glory Days: Bruce Springsteen in the 1980s* (New York: Pantheon, 1987). On Joel's schooling, see Schruers, 45–46; Bardowitz, 22, 307.

28. Carlin, 39, 46–47, 107.

29. Jon Pareles, "Bruce Springsteen on Broadway: The Boss on His 'First Real Job,'" New York *Times*, September 27, 2017: https://www.nytimes.com/2017/09 /27/arts/music/bruce-springsteen-broadway.html.

30. Springsteen, *Born to Run*, 154.

31. Schruers, 65–67.

32. Marsh, *Two Hearts*, 35. Marsh is particularly good at cataloging Springs- teen's early rock influences, which pepper his narrative and can be gleaned from the index. On Joel's early influences, see Schruers, 32–33.

33. Jody Rosen, "The Squandered Genius of the Piano Man," *Slate*, Novem- ber 29, 2005: https://slate.com/culture/2005/11/the-squandered-genius-of-the -piano-man.html; Springsteen cites the influence of R&B figures like King Curtis and his Van Morrison in *Born to Run*, 145, 155.

34. June Skinner Sawyers, "The Town that Bruce Built," *Chicago Tribune*, January 25, 2004: https://www.chicagotribune.com/news/ct-xpm-2004-01-25 -0401240201-story.html.

35. The best treatment of the city can be found in Daniel Wolff, *Fourth of July, Asbury Park: A History of the Promised Land*, revised ed. (2005; New Brunswick: Rutgers University Press, 2022). The water tower memory, which comes from an interview Wolff had with Springsteen, can be found on p. 115.

36. Springsteen devotes a chapter to the Upstage in *Born to Run* (104–113). The pre-eminent chronicler of the Asbury Park scene of Springsteen's youth generally is Robert Santelli. See his piece "Remembering the Upstage in *Backstreets: Springsteen—The Man and His Music*, a collection of pieces from the fanzine edited by Charles R. Cross (New York: Harmony Books, 1989), 36–40. Santelli is also the author of the keepsake volume *Greetings from E Street: The Story of Bruce Springsteen and the E Street Band* (New York: Chronicle Books, 2006).

37. For an overview of the Shore Sound and its best-known local practitioners, see Santelli's "Twenty Years Burning Down the Road: The Complete History of Jersey Shore Rock 'n' Roll" in *Backstreets*, 23–33.

38. Wolff, 114–124.

39. Springsteen, *Born to Run*, 108.

40. Springsteen, *Born to Run*, 117.

41. Carlin, 61.

42. Springsteen, *Born to Run*, 138, 149.

43. Rock historian Clinton Heylin, who has explored Springsteen's early history in part by drawing on Sony archives, contests this story, and argues that Springsteen and biographers greatly exaggerated how exploitative Appel was, instead emphasizing the upfront financial risks he ran in taking Springsteen on. See *E Street Shuffle: The Glory Days of the E Street Band* (New York: Viking, 2013), 45, 121–143.

44. For Appel's version of his dispute with Springsteen, see Marc Eliot's well-documented book *Down Thunder Road: The Making of Bruce Springsteen* (1992; New York: Simon & Schuster, 2008). Another good treatment of their dispute, attuned to the foibles of all parties, can be found in Fred Goodman, *The Mansion on the Hill: Dylan, Young, Geffen, Springsteen and the Head-on Collision of Rock and Commerce* (New York: Times Books, 1997), 275–298. As an indication of their durable reconciliation, Peter Ames Carlin describes a backstage scene with Appel, to whom Springsteen dedicated the show in 2009. For Springsteen's retrospective tribute to Appel, see *Born to Run*, 257–259.

45. Clive Davis, *The Soundtrack of My Life* (New York: Simon & Schuster, 2013), 145. Davis recounts his early encounters with Joel and Springsteen sequentially on pp. 144–147.

46. On Ripp's background, and the circumstances surrounding the release of *Cold Spring Harbor*, see Schruers, 72–81, and Bordowitz, 43–45.

47. Bordowitz cites the 25-cent/$20 million figure on p. 72. Schruers uses similar but not identical figures on p. 98.

48. Bordowitz, 63; Schruers, 99.

Chapter 3   Points of Departure

1. Victor Fiorillo, "How Philadelphia Made Billy Joel," *Philadelphia*, August 9, 2015: https://www.phillymag.com/things-to-do/2015/08/09/how-philadelphia-created-billy-joel/; Dan DeLuca, "Who Broke Springsteen in Philly?" *Philadelphia Inquirer*, September 29, 2016: https://www.inquirer.com/philly/blogs/inthemix/Who-broke-Bruce-Springsteen-big-in-Philly.html.

2. Fred Schruers, *Billy Joel: The Definitive Biography* (New York: Crown, 2014) 100; L.C. Greene, "Michael Stewart, Pop Music Pioneer, Dies at 57," *The Daily Bulletin* (Ontario, CA), November 15, 2002: https://groups.google.com/g/alt

.obituaries/c/KFY5En1iEus; "*Piano Man* by Billy Joel," *Classic Rock Review,*
January 29, 2013: https://www.classicrockreview.com/2013/01/1973-billy-joel
-piano-man/; Jack Breschard, review of *Piano Man, Rolling Stone,* March 14, 1974:
https://www.superseventies.com/joelbilly1.html.

3. Bill Friskics-Warren, "Eric Weissberg, 'Dueling Banjos' Musician, Dies at
80," New York *Times,* March 23, 2020: https://www.nytimes.com/2020/03/23
/arts/music/eric-weissberg-dies.html.

4. Ken Bielin, *The Words and Music of Billy Joel* (Santa Barbara, CA: Praeger,
2011), 27.

5. Chuck Klosterman, "The Stranger," New York *Times* Magazine, September 15, 2002: https://www.nytimes.com/2002/09/15/magazine/the-stranger
.html.

6. You can see him do this with a wicked wit during his session with James
Lipton's *Inside the Actor's Studio:* https://www.youtube.com/watch?v=ELuZxvs
UByQ.

7. Schruers, 97.

8. Hank Bardowitz, *Billy Joel: The Life and Times of an Angry Young Man*
(2006; Milwaukee, WI: Backbeat Books, 2011), 74.

9. Schruers, 101.

10. Schruers, 82–83; Bardowitz, 59–60; "Billy Joel: 'Ain't No Crime,'" https://
www.onefinalserenade.com/aint-no-crime.html. The website says the Belushi-
Joel parodies occurred in 1977, but Joel first appeared on *Saturday Night Live* in
February of 1978.

11. Schruers, 84–85.

12. The interview is available on Facebook: https://www.facebook.com/watch
/?v=10154331340507996.

13. Laura Sinagra, "Showing the Fans that He's in Control," New York *Times,*
January 25, 2006: https://www.nytimes.com/2006/01/25/arts/music/25joel.html
?smid=em-share; Bardowitz, 74.

14. Schruers, 353. The three "Dollars" movies are *A Fistful of Dollars* (1964), *For
a Few Dollars More* (1965), and *The Good, the Bad, and the Ugly* (1966), whose
main theme features what is probably the most famous musical phrase in the
history of the western. Joel also cited the Newman brothers, Alfred and Lionel,
who wrote film scores; their nephew, Randy Newman, was one of the great
singer-songwriters of the 1970s and 1980s. See Joel's liner notes in *Songs in the Attic.*

15. Joel notes the bartender angle in the liner notes from *Songs in the Attic.* See
also Glenn Gamboa, "Billy Joel's 'The Ballad of Billy the Kid' Is about a Bartender," *Newsday,* August 4, 2015: https://www.google.com/search?q=ballad+of
+billy+the+kid+newsday&rlz=1C5CHFA_enUS905US905&oq=ballad+of+bill

y+the+kid+newsday&aqs=chrome..69i57j69i60.7491j0j4&sourceid=chrome&ie
=UTF-8&safe=active&ssui=on.

16. Bardowitz, 62; "Reader's Poll: The Best Billy Joel Songs of All Time," *Rolling Stone*, December 5, 2012: https://www.rollingstone.com/music/music-lists/readers -poll-the-best-billy-joel-songs-of-all-time-16758/10-goodnight-saigon-225613/.

17. "Best Billy Joel Songs of All Time."

18. Greil Marcus, *Mystery Train: Images of America in Rock ''n' Roll Music*, 6th ed. (1975; New York: Plume, 2015), 97. The second sentence actually refers to Randy Newman, a songwriter notable for his long career of singing from the point of view of deeply unpleasant people, revealing their essence from the inside.

19. John Rockwell, "Pop Music: Theatricality Marks Billy Joel Songs," New York *Times*, February 23, 1974: https://www.nytimes.com/1974/02/23/archives /pop-music-theatricality-marks-billy-joel-songs.html; Schruers, 103–104.

20. Schruers, 104–105.

21. Schruers, 107.

22. Bob Egan, Pop Spots website: http://www.popspotsnyc.com/streetlife _serenade/; Brian Hagiwara page, AllMusic website: https://www.allmusic.com /artist/brian-hagiwara-mn0001287160.

23. "'Roberta' by Billy Joel," Songfacts website: https://www.songfacts.com /facts/billy-joel/roberta.

24. Stephen Holden, review of *Streetlife Serenader*, *Rolling Stone*, December 5, 1974: https://www.rollingstone.com/music/music-album-reviews/streetlife -serenade-107113/.

25. Schruers, 107; https://www.brucespringsteen.it/DB/mn.aspx?yr =1974&mt=12. Bardowitz includes *Billboard* data on the respective albums' performance in a table on p. 288.

26. Dan Epstein, "Inside Bruce Springsteen's *Greetings from Asbury Park, NJ*: 10 Things You Didn't Know," *Rolling Stone*, January 5, 2018: https://www .rollingstone.com/feature/bruce-springsteens-greetings-from-asbury-park-n-j -10-things-you-didnt-know-204206/.

27. Peter Ames Carlin, *Bruce* (New York: Touchstone, 2014), 133.

28. Dave Marsh, *Two Hearts: Bruce Springsteen: The Definitive Biography, 1972–2003* (New York: Routledge, 2004), 58–59; Clive Davis, *The Soundtrack of My Life* (New York: Simon & Schuster, 2013), 146; Springsteen, *Born to Run*, 183.

29. Bangs's review of *Greetings from Asbury Park, NJ*, first published on July 5, 1973, can be found *in Bruce: The* Rolling Stone *Files* (New York: Hyperion, 1996), 32–33. https://web.archive.org/web/20080620004208/http://www.rollingstone .com/artists/brucespringsteen/albums/album/107193/review/5943460 /greetings_from_asbury_park_nj.

30. Springsteen, *Born to Run*, 177.

31. Davis, 146–147.

32. Rob Kirkpatrick, *The Words and Music of Bruce Springsteen* (New York: Praeger, 2007), 17; June Skinner Sawyers, *Tougher than the Rest: 100 Best Bruce Springsteen Songs* (New York: Omnibus, 2006), 10.

33. Kirkpatrick, 16.

34. Carlin, 110, 121.

35. The piece, "Who Is Bruce Springsteen and Why Are We Saying All these Wonderful Things about Him" appears in *Racing in the Street: The Bruce Springsteen Reader*, edited by June Skinner Sawyers (New York: Penguin, 2004), 29–39.

36. Springsteen, *Born to Run*, 183–186–187.

37. Carlin, 166.

38. Bruce Springsteen, *Songs* (1998; New York: HarperCollins, 2003), 23.

39. Carlin, 162.

40. Carlin, 164; "E Street Band," Bruce Springsteen Wiki: https://brucespringsteen.fandom.com/wiki/E_Street_Band; Chris Jordan, "How the E Street Band Got Its Name," *Asbury Park Press*, February 20, 2017: https://www.app.com/story/entertainment/music/2017/02/20/bruce-springsteen-how-e-street-band-got-its-name/98157104/. Springsteen explained the origins of the band's name at a "Conversation with Bruce Springsteen" event at Monmouth University in January of 2017. Clemons's recollection comes from *Big Man: Real Life and Tall Tales* (New York: Grand Central Publishing, 2009), 56.

41. Carlin, 162–163.

42. Springsteen, *Songs*, 25.

43. Springsteen, *Songs*, 25–26

44. Carlin notes that such songs were omitted because "they didn't fit into the movie Bruce imagined himself writing and directing." *Bruce*, 163.

45. Springsteen, *Songs*, 25; *Born to Run*, 191.

46. Springsteen, *Songs*, 26.

47. Springsteen, *Born to Run*, 193.

48. Marsh, 92. Part I of *Two Hearts* was originally published as *Born to Run: The Bruce Springsteen Story* (New York: Dell, 1979).

49. Springsteen, *Songs*, 27.

50. This analysis draws on Jim Cullen, *Born in the U.S.A.: Bruce Springsteen and the American Tradition* (New York: HarperCollins, 1997), 107–108.

51. David Horovitz, "Bruce Springsteen's Kibbutz Violinist," *The Jerusalem Post*, October 22, 2007: https://www.jpost.com/Arts-and-Culture/Music/Bruce-Springsteens-kibbutz-violinist.

52. Carlin, 167.

53. Robert Hilburn, *Springsteen* (New York: Rolling Stone Press, 1985), 58; Swartley's essay appears in *Stranded: Rock and Roll for a Desert Island,* edited by Greil Marcus (1978; New York, Da Capo, 2007); Marsh, *Two Hearts,* 84, 118.

54. Landau's review of May 22, 1974 is reprinted at TheBoots.net website: http://web.archive.org/web/20030202021626/http:/home.theboots.net /theboots/articles/future.html; the ad is reprinted as part of a piece by Mike Barnes, "Springsteen: Born to Run," *Hi-fi news and Record Review*: https://www .hifinews.com/content/springsteen-born-run.

55. Marsh, 118; Carlin, 166.

56. Bardowitz, 77, 79; Marsh, 83; Carlin, 178.

57. See Christgau's pages on Springsteen and Joel on his website, "Robert Christgau, Dean of American Rock Critics," www.robertchristgau.com. (The boast is not an idle one.)

58. Carlin, 168.

59. Bardowitz reports Joel's wife and manager Elizabeth stating that he had a net worth of about $8000 as late as 1977 (75). Springsteen told Tom Hanks that by the time he turned thirty in 1980, he had been audited by the IRS and had about $20,000 to his name—a paltry figure for a man who by that point had become a star. (Both men lived relatively well, however, even if they burned through revenue as fast as they earned it. See Yohana Desta, "Bruce Springsteen Remembers His Post-*Born to Run* Tax Troubles," *Vanity Fair,* April 28, 2017: https:// www.vanityfair.com/hollywood/2017/04/bruce-springsteen-tom-hanks -tribeca.

Chapter 4   Arrivals

1. Bruce Springsteen, *Born to Run* (New York: Simon & Schuster, 2016), 239.

2. Hank Bardowitz, *Billy Joel: The Life and Times of an Angry Young Man,* revised ed. (2006; Milwaukee: Backbeat Books, 2011), 90; Fred Schruers, *Billy Joel: The Definitive Biography* (New York: Crown, 2014), 113.

3. Schruers, 114.

4. Springsteen, *Born to Run,* 235.

5. John Rockwell, "Billy Joel Sings the Praises of New York," New York *Times,* December 10, 1978: https://www.nytimes.com/1978/12/10/archives/billy-joel -sings-the-praises-of-new-york-billy-joel.html.

6. See for example, Stephen Gillon and Cathy Matson, *The American Experiment: A History of the United States,* 3rd ed. (Boston: Cengage, 2008), whose thirty-third chapter is titled "The Age of Limits, 1974–1979." The phrase turns up elsewhere in the literature of the period.

7. Rockwell.

8. Bardowitz, 70, 84.; The Spector quote, part of a Timothy White interview with Joel first published on September 4, 1980 in *Rolling Stone* as "Billy Joel is Angry," appears in *The Rolling Stone Interviews, 1967–1980* (New York: St. Martin's Press/Rolling Stone Press, 1981), 417. On the E Street Band's participation, see Peter Ames Carlin, *Bruce* (New York: Touchstone, 2014), 232–233.

9. Julie Lasky, "Highland Falls, N.Y.: A Cozy Community Next Door to West Point," New York *Times*, July 25, 2018: https://www.nytimes.com/2018/07/25/realestate/highland-falls-ny-a-cozy-community-next-door-to-west-point.html.

10. Schruers, 117–118; Joel describes the background of the song in a Q&A he rendered in Nuremberg, Germany, in 1995: https://www.youtube.com/watch?v=vvOnuPYiUzw.

11. Bardowitz, 84.

12. Schruers, 114; Joel told Greyhound story to Howard Stern in an interview for his radio show in a clip that is no longer available. For a description, see Jason Scott, "Behind the Song: Billy Joel, 'New York State of Mind,'" *American Songwriter*, circa 2020: https://americansongwriter.com/behind-the-song-billy-joel-new-york-state-of-mind/.

13. Schruers, 115; Bardowitz, 84.

14. Joel explained the source of the song to an Australian interviewer in 1976, which can be seen at https://www.youtube.com/watch?v=m2ozPH6vgUk. See also Schruers, 40–41.

15. Tom Wolfe, "The Me Decade and the Third Great Awakening," *New York*, August 23, 1976: https://nymag.com/news/features/45938/.

16. Schruers, 131; See Robert Christgau's assessment at https://www.robert christgau.com/get_album.php?id=7125.

17. Schruers, 122–127; Walter Yetnikoff, *Howling at the Moon: The Odyssey of a Monstrous Music Mogul in an Age of Excess* (New York, Broadway Books, 2004), 107–108.

18. Springsteen, *Born to Run*, 256; the book he cites is Marc Eliot's *Down Thunder Road: The Making of Bruce Springsteen* (1992; New York: Simon & Schuster, 2008), which, as Springsteen notes, includes court depositions that he sardonically calls "fun and fascinating bedtime reading."

19. Carlin, 173.

20. Nick Hornby, *Songbook* (New York: Riverhead, 2003), 11.

21. Bruce Springsteen, *Songs* (1998; New York: HarperCollins, 2003), 45–46.

22. "Bruce was writing about a song per day. It was crazy," Danny Federici remembered of Steel Mill days. "It got so I didn't want to go to rehearsal, because every time there'd be this mess of new songs to learn." See Louis Masur, *Runaway Dream: Born to Run and Bruce Springsteen's American Vision* (New York: Bloomsbury, 2013), 55.

23. Springsteen, *Born to Run*, 207; *Songs*, 44.

24. Springsteen, *Songs*, 208.

25. Carlin, 186.

26. Stevie Van Zandt, *Unrequited Infatuations* (New York: Hachette, 2021), 81.

27. Carlin, 185–187; James R. Petersen, "The Ascension of Bruce Springsteen," *Playboy*, March 1976, reprinted at the Greasy Lake website: https://www.greasylake.org/v6/display_article.php?Id=7&headline=The+Ascension+of+Bruce+Springsteen&publication=Playboy&concert_date=&release_title=.

28. Clarence Clemons and Don Reo, *Big Man: Real Life and Tall Tales* (New York: Grand Central Publishing, 2009), 225.

29. Carlin, 200; Dave Marsh, *Two Hearts: The Definitive Biography* (New York: Routledge, 2004) 149; Maureen Orth, Janet Huck and Peter S. Greenberg, "Making of a Rock Star," *Newsweek*, October 27, 1975, 57–61; Jay Cocks, "Backstreet Phantom of Rock," *Time*, October 27, 1975, 48–58 (both of these pieces are reprinted in June Skinner Sawyers, *Racing in the Street: The Bruce Springsteen Reader* (New York: Penguin, 2004), 53–73.

30. Marsh, 139.

31. Springsteen, *Born to Run*, 209.

32. Eve Zibart, "'Bruuuuce! Bruuuuce!'" *The Washington Post*, August 13, 1978: https://www.washingtonpost.com/archive/lifestyle/1978/08/13/bruuuuce-bruuuuce/8e8a1edd-dfdd-4620-b75b-129d970487d5/.

33. Masur, 47.

34. Masur, 75.

35. Carlin, 231–233. In a footnote on p. 231, Carlin reports that the band actually voted in Springsteen's absence about whether to split up, which resulted in a 3–3 tie. His account relies most heavily on the memory of Van Zandt, who writes about the incident in *Unrequited Infatuations*, 107–109. Van Zandt presents himself, as indeed he appears to be in a number of situations, as a mediator of sorts and the man who facilitated the deal with Barsalona. Precisely gauging Van Zandt's role in Springsteen's career is difficult, in part because he came and went a number of times over the years. But it's clear that he played a role in keeping Springsteen grounded in his Jersey roots.

36. Bardowitz, 99.

37. Joel's comments included in the Columbia Records bio for *An Innocent Man*; Bardowitz, 90–92.

38. Billy Joel, "Billy Joel Pays Tribute to Phil Ramone: He Was the King," *Rolling Stone*, April 3, 2013: https://www.rollingstone.com/music/music-news/billy-joel-pays-tribute-to-phil-ramone-he-was-the-king-183052/.

39. You can see the clip at https://www.youtube.com/watch?v=wYI9D
_vrNnc. For other renditions of this of-told tale, see Joel's tribute to Ramone in
Rolling Stone cited above and Schruers, 130–131.

40. Schruers, 127.

41. For more detail, see Bob Egan's page on *The Stranger* cover at Pop Spots:
https://www.popspotsnyc.com/billy_joel_the_stranger/.

42. You can see the ad, and get background information on it, from Jamie
Bologna, "Anthony Martignetti, the 'Anthony!' of Prince Spaghetti Ads, Has
Died," WBUR Radio Boston: https://www.wbur.org/radioboston/2019/10/23
/prince-ad-50th-boston-north-end-italian-food.

43. Andy Greene, "Billy Joel's *The Stranger* at 40: A Track-by-Track Guide,"
Rolling Stone, September 29, 2017: https://www.rollingstone.com/music/music
-lists/billy-joels-the-stranger-at-40-a-track-by-track-guide-199703/movin-out
-anthonys-song-199732/.

44. The song refers to "Mr. Cacciatore's on Sullivan Street," a fictive reference
to a real restaurant, since closed, known as Napoli's. See Scott A. Rosenberg,
"Billy Joel's New York Connections Run Deep," *Newsday*, January 26, 2014:
https://www.newsday.com/news/new-york/billy-joel-s-new-york-city
-connections-run-deep-c46973.

45. Rob Sheffield, "Billy Joel's Garden Residency Begins with Salty Jokes and
Sing-Alongs," *Rolling Stone*, January 28, 2014: https://www.rollingstone.com
/music/music-news/billy-joels-garden-residency-begins-with-salty-jokes-and
-sing-alongs-235577/.

46. Joel explained this in a "Master Class" at Princeton in 1994. You can see it
on You Tube at https://www.youtube.com/watch?v=MnfqSBzEcw8 https://
www.rollingstone.com/music/music-news/billy-joels-garden-residency-begins
-with-salty-jokes-and-sing-alongs-235577/.

47. Bardowitz, 98; Glenn Gamboa, "Billy Joel Talks 'Scenes from an Italian
Restaurant': I Couldn't Do a Show without It," *Newsday*, August 1, 2015: https://
www.newsday.com/entertainment/music/billy-joel-talks-scenes-from-an
-italian-restaurant-i-couldn-t-do-a-show-without-it-i86873.

48. Bardowitz, 98; Gamboa, "Billy Joel Talks 'Scenes from an Italian
Restaurant.'"

49. Joel, Princeton Master Class, 1994.

50. Joel, Princeton Master Class, 1994.

51. Lydia Hutchinson, "The Story Behind Billy Joel's 'Only the Good Die
Young,'" *Performing Songwriter*, May 9, 2012: https://performingsongwriter.com
/only-good-die-young/. You can see a clip of the Joel/Springsteen performance
on YouTube: https://www.youtube.com/watch?v=iX_y3_bt-8U.

52. Dan Barry, "Just the Way He Is," New York *Times*, July 13, 2008: https://www.nytimes.com/2008/07/13/arts/music/13barr.html?pagewanted=1.

Chapter 5   Through Glass, Darkly

1. Springsteen writes candidly about his failures in relationships during the late 1970s and early 1980s in the "Downtime" chapter of his memoir *Born to Run* (New York: Simon & Schuster, 2016), 271–274.

2. Hank Bardowitz, *Billy Joel: the Life and Times of an Angry Young Man* (2006; Milwaukee: Backbeat Books, 2011), 102; Fred Schruers, *Billy Joel: The Definitive Biography* (New York: Crown, 2014, 2014), 140.

3. Jessie Katz, "Carly Simon Admits that 'You're So Vain' Is About Warren Beatty, *Billboard*, November 18 2015: https://www.billboard.com/music/music-news/carly-simon-youre-so-vain-warren-beatty-6769186/.

4. You can see the Florida State Q&A on YouTube at https://www.youtube.com/watch?v=OL25RnHqnGo; A story based on the Stern interview is posted as "Billy Joel Dreams in Music": https://web.archive.org/web/20120503063104/http://www.howardstern.com/rundown.hs?j=n&d=1289797200.

5. Bardowitz, 104–105; Schruers, 140; Jean François Petit, "Zanzibar Café, New York: Home of Cab Calloway, the HideHo Blog, October 2, 2009: http://www.thehidehoblog.com/blog/2009/10/zanzibar-cafe-new-york-home-of-cab-calloway.

6. Schruers, 140.

7. For one version of the controversy, see Bardowitz, 107–108.

8. Peter Ames Carlin, *Bruce* (New York: Touchstone, 2012), 255–261; Dave Marsh, "Bruce Springsteen Raises Cain," *Rolling Stone*, August 24, 1978: https://www.rollingstone.com/music/music-features/bruce-springsteen-raises-cain-2-179332/.

9. Bruce Springsteen, *Born to Run* (New York: Simon & Schuster, 2016), 266. Among those who believed that Springsteen threw away his best work in this period is Clinton Heylin. *See E Street Shuffle: The Glory Days of Bruce Springsteen and the E Street Band* (New York: Viking, 2013), Chapter 5 (144–170).

10. Carlin, 237.

11. Anthony DeCurtis, "What Springsteen Kept to Himself," New York *Times*, November 4, 2010: https://www.nytimes.com/2010/11/07/arts/music/07darkness.html.

12. The Jim Miller piece is excerpted at https://www.enotes.com/topics/bruce-springsteen/critical-essays/jim-miller-2.

13. Carlin, 247. The cover of *The Promise* appears to come from those photoshoots.

14. Bruce Springsteen, *Songs* (1998; New York: HarperEntertainment, 2003), 65.

15. Carlin, 32.

16. Springsteen, *Born to Run*, 264–265.

17. Springsteen, *Born to Run*, 270.

18. Bardowitz, 126; David J. Criblez, "Forty Years Later, Billy Joel's *Glass Houses* Is Still a Classic," *Newsday*, June 12, 2020: https://www.newsday.com /entertainment/music/glass-houses-billy-joel-40th-anniversary-d70856.

19. Bardowitz, 127; John Rockwell, "Pop: Five Nights of Billy Joel at the Garden," New York *Times*, June 25, 1980: https://timesmachine.nytimes.com /timesmachine/1980/06/25/111250154.html?pageNumber=69.

20. Paul Nelson, review of *Glass Houses*, *Rolling Stone*, May 1, 1980: https://web .archive.org/web/20080228143909/http://www.rollingstone.com/artists /billyjoel/albums/album/241142/review/5942679/glass_houses.

21. Bardowitz, 129.

22. On Joel's relationship with Frank Weber, see Schruers, 126; 195–216.

23. Schruers, 160–161; Ellan Cates, "Piano-Playing Rock Superstar Billy Joel Suffered a Fractured Right Wrist," United Press International, April 16, 1982: https://www.upi.com/Archives/1982/04/16/Piano-playing-rock-superstar-Billy -Joel-suffered-a-fractured-right/9931387781200/#:~:text=NEW%20YORK%20 %2D%2D%20Piano%2Dplaying,completely%2C%20his%20doctor%20said%20 Friday.

24. Springsteen performed the song at the Musicians United for Safe Energy Concerts of September 1979. You can see a clip on YouTube: https://www .youtube.com/watch?v=eFE78WbrZjc.

25. Robert Hilburn, *Springsteen* (New York: Rolling Stone Press/Charles Scribner's Sons, 1985), 138.

26. Carlin, 278; Walter Yetnikoff with David Ritz, *Howling at the Moon: The Odyssey of a Monstrous Music Mogul in an Age of Excess* (New York: Broadway Books, 2004), 121; Springsteen, *Born to Run*, 277–278.

27. Springsteen, *Songs*, 98.

28. Springsteen, *Born to Run*, 276. It wasn't necessarily easy to achieve this effect. An early mix of the album seemed to actually bury the vocals in the view of Jimmy Iovine, and Springsteen and mixer Chuck Plotkin agonized over getting it right. See p. 280.

29. Springsteen's acceptance speech is included in *Springsteen on Springsteen: Interviews, Speeches, and Encounters,* edited by Jeff Burger (Chicago: Chicago Review Press, 2014). Quote appears on p. 284.

30. Springsteen, *Born to Run*, 278–279; Carlin 271–272, "Meet Virginia Springsteen Shave, Bruce Springsteen's Sister on Whom One of His Songs Was Based!" *Hollywood ZAM*, November 1, 2021: https://hollywoodzam.com

/virginia-springsteen-shave-bruce-springsteens-sister-on-whom-one-of-his
-songs-was-based/.

31. Paul Nelson, "Let Us Now Praise Famous Men," *Rolling Stone*, December 11,
1980: https://www.rollingstone.com/music/music-album-reviews/the-river-97028/.

32. Sirach 44:1–2 in https://biblia.com/bible/nrsv/sirach/44/1-15. Catholic
translations of this passage are worded differently: "I will now praise the godly,
our ancestors in their own time." See the United States Conference of Catholic
Bishops translation: https://bible.usccb.org/bible/sirach/44.

33. James Agee and Walker Evans, *Let Us Now Praise Famous Men* (1941;
Boston: Houghton Mifflin, 2001).

34. Nelson, "Let Us Now Praise."

35. Dave Marsh, *Two Hearts: The Definitive Biography, 1972–2003* (New York:
Routledge, 2004), 229.

36. Carlin, 279; Nelson, "Let Us Now Praise."

37. Carlin, 280.

38. John Lennon praises Springsteen's 'Hungry Heart' in final interview hours
before his death, beatleshistorian.com, August 22, 2016: https://beatleshistorian
.com/?p=655; Jonathan Cott, "John Lennon: The Last Interview," *Rolling Stone*,
December 23, 2010: https://www.rollingstone.com/feature/john-lennon-the-last
-interview-179443/. Cott waited 30 years to release the transcripts of the interview,
which he decided not to publish in the immediate aftermath of Lennon's death.

39. Springsteen, *Born to Run*, 297; 301–310. Springsteen described the site of
the breakdown as taking place somewhere in the middle of the country, but has
also described it as taking place in California. See the transcripts of his podcasts
with Barack Obama, *Renegades: Born in the USA* (New York: Crown 2021), 63.

40. Springsteen, *Born to Run*, 299.

41. Carlin, 294.

42. Springsteen, *Songs*, 136.

43. Carlin, 292.

44. Yetnikoff made the remark to Fred Goodman as reported in *The Mansion
on the Hill: Dylan, Young, Springsteen, and the Head-on Collision of rock and
Commerce* (New York: Times Books, 1997), 338.

45. Carlin, 297.

46. "It's about anybody who's ever had a hangover," Joel told interviewer David
Sheff in his *Playboy* interview of 1982. "Wake up in the morning and you're so
hung over saying, 'You stupid idiot. You had to be a big shot.' I did a lot of
personal research for that song." https://www.davidsheff.com/billy-joel.

47. Jay Cocks, "Against the American Grain: and Bruce Springsteen Billy Joel
Risk Big and Score Big," *Time*, November 15, 1982: http://content.time.com/time
/subscriber/article/0,33009,949664-1,00.html.

48. You can see the *Nylon Curtain* video excerpt at https://www.youtube.com /watch?v=Pqc4U8uWTRU.

49. Schruers, 150.

50. Schruers, 151.

51. Joel, *Complete Albums Collection* video.

52. On the influence of "A Day in the Life" on "Goodnight Saigon," see the series of clips included in the web page on the song at the One Final Serenade website: https://www.onefinalserenade.com/goodnight-saigon.html.

53. Schruers, 154–155; Joel, *Complete Albums Collection* video.

54. Marsh, *Two Hearts*, 276.

55. Bardowitz, 145.

Chapter 6   Right Time

1. Joel discusses this in the *Extraordinary with Fareed Zakaria* CNN+ interview in May of 2022: https://www.youtube.com/watch?v=jou9SovPY6g.

2. Fred Schruers, *Billy Joel: The Definitive Biography* (New York: Crown, 2014), 151.

3. Bruce Springsteen, *Born to Run* (New York: Simon & Schuster, 2016), 51, 327.

4. Peter Ames Carlin, *Bruce* (New York: Touchstone, 2012), 127.

5. On "Roulette" and the MUSE concerts, see Carlin, 271–273; Dave Marsh, *Two Hearts: The Definitive Biography, 1972–2003* (New York: Routledge, 2004), 213–217. On the subversiveness of pop music, see Neil Strauss, "Human Touch: Bruce Springsteen Reflects on His Music, Life Without the E Street Band, and the Glory of Rock and Roll," *Guitar World*, September 1995, in *Springsteen on Springsteen: Interviews, Speeches, and Encounters*, edited by Jeff Burger (Chicago: Chicago Review Press, 2014), 196.

6. David Sheff, "The Playboy Interview: Billy Joel," *Playboy*, May, 1982: https://www.davidsheff.com/billy-joel.

7. On Nixon's calculations regarding Affirmative Action, see Michael Lind, *The Next American Nation: The New Nationalism and the Next American Revolution* (New York: Basic, 1995), 188ff.

8. For a good overview of the tremendous ideological shift occurring across the globe in this period, see Christian Caryl, *Strange Rebels: 1979 and the Birth of the 21st Century* (New York: Basic, 2013).

9. This discussion is derived from Jim Cullen, *Democratic Empire: The United States Since 1945* (Malden, Mass.: Wiley Blackwell, 2016), 222–223.

10. Carlin, 315.

11. Dave Marsh, "Billy Joel and the Miracle of 52nd St.," *Rolling Stone*, December 14, 1978: https://www.rollingstone.com/music/music-news/billy-joel-the -miracle-of-52nd-street-38352/.

12. Much of the following analysis derives from Jim Cullen, *1980: America's Pivotal Year* (New Brunswick, NJ: Rutgers University Press, 2023), 80–81.

13. Michaelangelo Matos, *Can't Slow Down: How 1984 Became Pop's Blockbuster Year* (New York: Hachette, 2020), 3; Recording Industry Association of America database: https://www.riaa.com/u-s-sales-database/ January 27, 2021); Peter Tschmuck, "The Recession in the Music Industry: A Cause Analysis," Music Business Research: https://musicbusinessresearch.wordpress.com/2010 /03/29/the-recession-in-the-music-industry-a-cause-analysis/#:~:text =Between%201977%20and%201980%2C%20sales,sold%20between%201978%20 and%201980.

14. Matos, 19–20.

15. Heather Kelly, "Rock On! The Compact Disc Turns 30," CNN.com, October 12, 2012: https://www.cnn.com/2012/09/28/tech/innovation/compact -disc-turns-30/index.html#:~:text=Story%20highlights&text=On%20October %201%2C%201982%2C%20the,to%20the%20next%20hot%20medium.

16. See, for example, Jack Hamilton, *Just Around Midnight: Rock & Roll and the Racial Imagination* (Cambridge, MA: Harvard University Press, 2016). Hamilton traces the white appropriation of black music as intensifying over the course of the 1960s, a process he regards as largely complete by the early 1970s. He uses the Springsteen/Clarence Clemons relationship as a particularly insidious example of the dynamic (pp. 13–14).

17. Marsh, 444.

18. The next three paragraphs draw on Cullen, *Democratic Empire*, and Jim Cullen, *The Art of Democracy: A Concise History of Popular Culture* (1996; New York: Monthly Review Press, 2002), 277–281.

19. Mark Bego, *Billy Joel: The Biography* (New York: Thunder's Mouth Press, 2007), 212.

20. For an analysis, see "Stylus Magazine's Top 100 Music Videos of All Time": http://stylusmagazine.com/articles/weekly_article/stylus-magazines-top-100 -music-videos-of-all-time.html.

21. For accounts of this trip, see Schruers, 164–168 and Bego, 196–198. Different accounts suggest the album was written in as little as six weeks—whatever the interval it was notably fast, especially for him.

22. Schruers, 172; Hank Bardowitz, *Billy Joel: The Life and Times of an Angry Young Man* (2005; Milwaukee: Backbeat Books, 2011), 151.

23. Schruers, 174.

24. Bardowitz, 151.

25. Bardowitz, 151–152; Nick Paumgarten, "The Thirty-Three Hit Wonder," *The New Yorker*, October 20 2014: https://www.newyorker.com/magazine/2014/10 /27/thirty-three-hit-wonder.

26. Greil Marcus, *Mystery Train: Images of America in Rock 'n' Roll Music,* sixth revised edition (1975; New York: Plume, 2015), 3.

27. Stephen Holden, "Billy Joel Reaches Out to Embrace Pop," New York *Times,* August 3, 1986: https://www.nytimes.com/1986/08/03/arts/recordings -billy-joel-reaches-out-to-embrace-pop.html.

28. Bego, 205.

29. Schruers, 175; Bego, 213.

30. Schruers, 175.

31. https://www.onefinalserenade.com/album-page—an-innocent-man.html.

32. Carlin, 299–302.

33. Joel mentions this in a 1982 audio interview with Ed Sciaky available at the One Final Serenade website: https://www.onefinalserenade.com/goodnight -saigon.html.

34. See Joel's 1996 Q&A at the University of Akron, included at the One Final Serenade website.

35. On Springsteen's relationship with Muller, see Marsh, *Two Hearts,* 309–313.

36. For one account of the song's tumultuous history, see Jim Cullen, *Born in the USA: Bruce Springsteen and the American Tradition* (New York: HarperCollins, 1997), Chapter 1. Springsteen mentions the trick-or-treaters both in *Songs* (164) and *Born to Run* (314). Marsh discusses the matter on pp. 479–489; the $12 million figure is cited on p. 624.

37. Springsteen, *Songs,* 166.

38. Springsteen devotes a chapter to the subject to the subject in *Born to Run,* 313–317. For Van Zandt's version, which is largely consonant, see *Unrequited Infatuations: A Memoir* (New York: Hachette, 2021), 153–156.

39. Springsteen notes the autobiographical character of the track in *Songs,* p. 166.

40. Carlin, 303.

41. Springsteen *Songs,* 167; *Born to Run,* 317.

42. Kurt Loder, "The Rolling Stone Interview: Bruce Springsteen," included *in Bruce: The Rolling Stone Files,* edited by Park Puterbaugh (New York: Hyperion, 1996), 154.

43. Fred Goodman, who stakes out a critical stance on the relationship between art and commerce, describes Landau's shrewd, if unsentimental, role in shaping Springsteen's commercial success, especially with *Born in the U.S.A.* See *The Mansion on the Hill: Dylan, Young, Springsteen, and the Head-on Collision of Rock and Commerce* (New York: Times, Books, 1997), 332–352.

44. Carlin, 307.

45. Bardowitz, 153.

46. Christopher Connelly, "'Fun' Springsteen Album, Tour Due," *Rolling Stone*, June 7, 1984, in *The Rolling Stone Files*, 139–140.

47. Carter Alan, "Springsteen's *Born in the USA* Scores 7 Top Ten Hits," Classic Rock 107WZLX, June 4, 2018: https://wzlx.iheart.com/featured/carter-alan /content/2018-06-04-springsteens-born-in-the-usa-scores-7-top-10-hits/. Carter Alan was one of five charter veejays on MTV at the time of its debut in 1981.

48. Loder, 155.

49. Gavin Edwards, "'We Are the World': A Minute-By Minute Breakdown," *Rolling Stone*, March 6, 2020: https://www.rollingstone.com/music/music -features/we-are-the-world-a-minute-by-minute-breakdown-54619/. Springsteen recorded another reggae song he wrote himself, "Part Man, Part Monkey," in 1990; it was included on his 1998 collection *Tracks*.

50. Carlin, 329–330.

51. Jim Henke, "The Rolling Stone Interview: Bruce Springsteen Leaves E Street," *Rolling Stone*, August 6, 1992: https://www.rollingstone.com/music /music-news/bruce-springsteen-leaves-e-street-the-rolling-stone-interview -172718/.

Chapter 7   Family Feuds

1. Anthony DeCurtis, "The Rolling Stone Interview: Billy Joel," *Rolling Stone*, November 6, 1986: https://www.rollingstone.com/music/music-features/billy -joel-the-rolling-stone-interview-107567/; Bruce Springsteen, *Songs* (1998; New York: HarperEntertainment, 2003), 189.

2. Fred Schruers, *Billy Joel: The Definitive Biography* (New York: Crown, 2014), 182–183.

3. Schruers, 184–185.

4. DeCurtis, Schruers, 183.

5. Hank Bardowitz, *Billy Joel: The Life and Times of an Angry Young Man* (2006; Milwaukee: Backbeat Books, 2011), 157.

6. Schruers, 185.

7. Bruce Springsteen, *Born to Run* (New York: Simon & Schuster, 2016), 351–352; Peter Ames Carlin, *Bruce* (New York: Touchstone, 2012), 344.

8. Springsteen, *Born to Run*, 348–349.

9. For more on the religious trajectory of Springsteen's music, see Jim Cullen, *Born in U.S.A.: Bruce Springsteen and the American Tradition* (New York: Harper-Collins, 1997), Chapter 6. The subject is also engaged in Cullen, "Summer's Fall: Springsteen in Senescence," in *Long Walk Home: Reflections on Bruce Springsteen*, edited by Jonathan Cohen and June Skinner Sawyers (New Brunswick: Rutgers University Press, 2019), 189–199.

10. Carlin, 339.

11. "I've always believed that the E Street Band's continued existence—and it's now been forty-plus years since its inception—is partially due to the fact that there was little or no confusion amongst its members," Springsteen wrote in 2016 after having dissolved and reconstituted the band a number of times since 1989. "Everyone knew their job, their boundaries, their blessings and limitations. My bandmates were not always happy with the decisions I made and may have been angered by some of them, but nobody doubted my right to make them. Clarity ruled and allowed us to forge a bond based on the principle that we worked together, but it was my band." See *Born to Run*, 149–150.

12. Schruers, 183. Ramone and Joel would team up one more time to record the Sinatraesque "All My Life" in 2007.

13. Carlin, 335.

14. Carlin, 327, 341, 348; Springsteen, *Born to Run*, 350.

15. In 2021, Weinberg reported the E Street Band would share as much as $2.8 million a night. See "Bruce Springsteen's Drummer—the Legendary Max Weinberg": https://drummagazine.com/bruce-springsteen-drummer/#:~:text =How%20much%20does%20Springsteen%20pay%20the%20E%20Street%20 Band%3F&text=The%20amount%20varied%20from%20tour,equally%202.8%20 million%20per%20night.

16. Mark Bego, *Billy Joel: The Biography* (New York: Thunder's Mouth Press, 2007), 230.

17. Joel biographer Fred Schruers makes this assertion on p. 315.

18. Billy Joel Has a Tantrum, New York *Times*, July 28, 1987: https://www.nytimes .com/1987/07/28/arts/billy-joel-has-a-tantrum.html#:~:text=Apparently%20 angered%20when%20a%20film,hurled%20it%20to%20the%20floor.

19. This figure has been widely reported. See "Bruce Springsteen's Drummer"; Elif Ozden, "The Reason Bruce Springsteen Gave $2 Million to Each E Street Band Member," Rock Celebrities, October 27, 2021: https://rockcelebrities.net /the-reason-bruce-springsteen-gave-2-million-to-each-e-street-band-member/.

20. Schruers, 188–189; Bardowitz, 165–166.

21. Springsteen, *Born to Run*, 372.

22. Bardowitz does the best reporting on this. *See Angry Young Man*, 163–180, ff.

23. Schruers, 199.

24. See *Extraordinary with Fareed Zakaria*, a CNN+ interview from May of 2022: https://www.youtube.com/watch?v=jou9SovPY6g.

25. Bego, 250; Schruers, 201.

26. Schruers, 199–200; Bardowitz, 168–169; Bego, 252.

27. "Mom, don't worry. I can finally pull myself out of this dead-end job I have and start working on a career with a real future," he quipped in a speech. See the

account of the event reported by Nadine Brozan in the *New York Times* on June 26, 1992: https://www.nytimes.com/1992/06/26/style/chronicle-419092.html.

28. Carlin, 359–360.

29. Kenneth Partridge, "Bruce Springsteen's *Human Touch* and *Lucky Town* at 25: *Are These Unloved Albums Truly that Bad?*" *Billboard*, March 31, 2017: https://www.billboard.com/music/rock/bruce-springsteen-human-touch-lucky-town-albums-7736729/.

30. Springsteen, *Songs*, 216.

31. "11 Facts You Didn't Know about GN'R's *Use Your Illusion* Albums," Triple M, February 27, 2017: https://www.triplem.com.au/story/11-facts-you-didn-t-know-about-gnrs-use-your-illusion-albums-17714.

32. Springsteen, *Songs*, 218–219.

33. For more on the Catholic dimension of Springsteen's songwriting, see Jim Cullen, *Born in the U.S.A: Bruce Springsteen and the American Tradition* (New York: HarperCollins, 1997), Chapter 6.

34. Springsteen, *Songs*, 218.

35. Carlin, 371–372.

36. Mark Bego reports Liberty DeVitto saying Joel drank heavily touring tours of the period (282–283). In his authorized biography, Schruers is more elliptical, and discussed Joel's use of cocaine, heroin, and marijuana with him, but describes alcohol as Joel's "drug of choice" (233).

37. Schruers, 219.

38. Schruers, 226.

39. Stephen Holden, "A Pundit of Suburbia," New York *Times*, August 8, 1993: https://www.nytimes.com/1993/08/08/arts/recordings-view-billy-joel-a-pundit-of-suburbia.html; "Piano Man at the Garden," October 4, 1993: https://www.nytimes.com/1993/10/04/arts/review-rock-piano-man-at-the-garden-with-supporting-cast.html.

40. Carlin, 378–392; Springsteen, *Born to Run*, 398; Springsteen, *Songs*, 262.

41. Bardowitz, 189–191; Neil Strauss, "Elton John and Billy Joel: So Alike, So Different," New York *Times*, July 25, 1994: https://www.nytimes.com/1994/07/25/arts/pop-review-elton-john-and-billy-joel-so-alike-so-different.html.

42. Schruers, 179.

Chapter 8   Homing

1. For a good cultural analysis of the role of the internet in transforming musical experience, see Chuck Klosterman's chapter on the subject in *The Nineties: A Book* (New York: The Penguin Press, 2022), 129–164.

2. For a brief overview of radio's history, see Jim Cullen, *A Short History of the Modern Media* (Malden, MA: Wiley-Blackwell, 2014), Chapter 4.

3. Peter Ames Carlin, *Bruce* (New York: Touchstone, 2012), 391.

4. Carlin, 391–392.

5. Bruce Springsteen, New Jersey Hall of Fame Induction Speech, in *Springsteen on Springsteen: Interviews, Speeches, and Encounters* (Chicago: Chicago Review Press, 2014), 331.

6. "Billy Joel's Long Island Home Burglarized; Motorcycles Damaged," CBS News New York: https://www.cbsnews.com/newyork/news/billy-joel-home-burglarized/.

7. Mark Bego, *Billy Joel: The Biography* (New York: Thunder Mouth Press, 2007, 199–203; Rick Murphy, "'The Piano Man' Becomes 'The Boat Man,'" the *New York Times*, November 30, 1997: https://www.nytimes.com/1997/11/30/nyregion/the-piano-man-becomes-the-boat-man.html; "20th Century Cycles Opens Its Doors in Oyster Bay," billyjoel.com, November 11, 2010: https://www.billyjoel.com/news/20th-century-cycles-opens-its-doors-oyster-bay/.

8. Fred Schruers reports that Joel's battles with Frank Weber "had wiped him out financially, and now the road owned him." See *Billy Joel: The Definitive Biography* (New York: Crown, 2014), 230. While this may be an exaggeration, it is certainly the case that Joel was far less wealthy than he might have been had his business affairs been managed more scrupulously in the previous twenty years. On his drinking problems, including the pub crawl with U2 mentioned in the next paragraph, see pp. 231–241.

9. Hank Bardowitz, *Billy Joel: The Life and Times of an Angry Young Man* (2006; Milwaukee: Backbeat Books, 2011), 166–67; Schruers, 307–308; https://concerts.fandom.com/wiki/Billy_Joel_Concerts_1990s.

10. Sonia Nazario, "Celebrities Urge Defeat of Prop. 209," Los Angeles *Times*, October 28, 1996: https://www.latimes.com/archives/la-xpm-1996-10-28-mn-58696-story.html.

11. You can see the speech on YouTube: https://www.youtube.com/watch?v=9C9RQUrHhHo. Springsteen's can be seen there as well: https://www.youtube.com/watch?v=kmdRGzfRPoo.

12. Bardowitz, 206.

13. Schruers, 137–138; Nicole Perradoto and Juan Ferero, "Hybrid Vehicle Billy Joel and Twyla Tharp's *Movin' Out* Is a New Breed of Musical Theater," *Buffalo News*, February 3, 2004, updated July 23, 2020: https://buffalonews.com/news/hybrid-vehicle-billy-joel-and-twyla-tharps-movin-out-is-a-new-breed-of-musical/article_55c2f97d-f1be-5e58-8aa1-0acb647b3158.html.

14. You can see a complete performance on YouTube: https://www.youtube.com/watch?v=4cj8x8VnaPk.

15. Kirsten Fleming, "Billy Joel Shows Off 50-pound Weight Loss Onstage," *New York Post*, November 8, 2021: https://nypost.com/2021/11/08/billy-joel -shows-off-50-pound-weight-loss-on-stage/.

16. This and the next three paragraphs on Springsteen in 9/11 draws on the Afterword of the 2005 edition of Jim Cullen, *Born in the U.S.A.: Bruce Springsteen and the American Tradition* (1997; Middletown: Wesleyan University Press, 2005), 193–194; Bruce Springsteen, *Born to Run* (New York: Simon & Schuster, 2016), 437–440, and Carlin, 407–408. The definitive study of "Bruce stories"—an ethnographic study of Springsteen fandom—is Daniel Cavicchi's *Tramps Like Us: Music and Meaning among Springsteen Fans* (New York: Oxford University Press, 1998).

17. Springsteen, *Born to Run*, 443.

18. Bruce Springsteen, *Songs* (1998; New York HarperEntertainment, 2003), 303–304; *Born to Run*, 438–441.

19. Springsteen, *Born to Run*, 442–443; *Songs*, 305–306.

20. Springsteen, *Songs*, 306.

21. Springsteen, *Born to Run*, 442.

22. A.O. Scott, "The Poet Laureate of 9/11," *Slate*, August 6, 2002: https://slate .com/culture/2002/08/bruce-springsteen-the-poet-laureate-of-9-11.html.

23. Nick Corasaniti, "Springsteen Reopens Broadway, Ushering in Theater's Return," New York *Times*, June 27, 2021: https://www.nytimes.com/2021/06/27 /theater/bruce-springsteen-broadway.html#:~:text=It%20was%20a%20line%20 from,particularly%20these%20days%2C%20us.%E2%80%9D. *Springsteen on Broadway* ran between October of 2017 and 2018. As the *Times* story indicates, Springsteen performed a post-Covid limited run in 2021.

24. For a world map of Springsteen shows around the world, see https://www .setlist.fm/stats/concert-map/bruce-springsteen-2bd6dcce.html?year=2014.

25. Carlin, 422.

26. For a more extended reading of this song, see Jim Cullen, "Summer's Fall: Springsteen in Senescence," in *Long Walk Home: Reflections on Bruce Springsteen*, edited by Jonathan Cohen and June Skinner Sawyers (New Brunswick: Rutgers University Press, 2019), 189–199.

27. For a good treatment of the controversy, see Carlin, 401–406.

28. Rumsfeld was famous for statements about known knowns, unknown knowns, and unknown unknowns. In 2004, journalist Ron Suskind quoted a senior advisor to President Bush—since cited as VP Dick Cheney and political guru Karl Rove—scorning the "reality-based community" and asserting "We're an empire now, and when we act, we create our own reality." See Suskind, "Faith, Certainty and the Presidency of George W. Bush," New York *Times*, October 17,

2004: https://www.nytimes.com/2004/10/17/magazine/faith-certainty-and-the-presidency-of-george-w-bush.html.

29. Carlin, 425–426.

30. Obama quoted in Carlin, 427.

31. You can see a video of their performance at http://www.coveredbybrucespringsteen.com/viewcover.aspx?recordID=69.

32. For a fuller blog post reading of "Outlaw Pete," see Jim Cullen, "Outlaw Pete: Springsteen Makes a Western," American History Now, February 4, 2009: http://amhistnow.blogspot.com/2009/02/among-many-virtues-in-bruce.html.

33. Barack Obama and Bruce Springsteen, Renegades: Born in the USA (New York: Crown, 2021), 137.

34. Carlin, 439–440.

35. Carlin, 455; Springsteen, Born to Run, 484–487.

36. Springsteen, Born to Run, 469–470.

37. Obama and Springsteen, 91, 104.

38. Caroline Madden, "The Famous Taxi Driver line You Probably Didn't Know Was Improvised," SlashFilm, February 22, 2022: https://www.slashfilm.com/766949/the-famous-taxi-driver-line-you-probably-didnt-know-was-improvised/.

39. Rebecca Rubin, "Robert DeNiro Slams Trump at the Tonys: 'F—Trump,'" Variety, June 10, 2018: https://variety.com/2018/legit/news/robert-de-niro-trump-tonys-1202839957/.

40. https://www.youtube.com/watch?v=usSLCdiRoAw.

Conclusion

Epigraph: Fred Ahrens, "Billy Joel, Bard of the Burbs," Washington Post, April 23, 1998: https://www.washingtonpost.com/archive/lifestyle/1998/04/23/billy-joel-bard-of-the-burbs/9c2cbce6-aa8d-44e5-b6cc-32954d389e9b/.

1. Melissa Ruggieri, "Billy Joel Says Taylor Swift is the Beatles of Her Generation: 'She Knows Music,'" USA Today, November 3, 2021: https://www.usatoday.com/story/entertainment/music/2021/11/03/billy-joel-50-years-return-madison-square-garden-residency-taylor-swift-adele-olivia-rodrigo/6197569001/; "Taylor Swift on Who 'All Too Well' Is About," Extra, November 12, 2021: https://extratv.com/2021/11/12/taylor-swift-on-who-all-too-well-is-about-plus-her-new-short-film/.

2. Gem Aswad, "Bruce Springsteen Takes Us on a Guided Tour of His iTunes Playlist," Variety, October 4, 2017: https://variety.com/2017/music/news/bruce-springsteen-a-guided-tour-of-his-itunes-folder-playlist-1202580076/.

3. Emily St. James, "Taylor Swift Is the Millennial Bruce Springsteen," *Vox*, July 31, 2020: https://www.vox.com/culture/2020/7/31/21340926/taylor-swift -folklore-millennial-bruce-springsteen (June 12, 2022).

4. Frankie Dunn, "Olivia Rodrigo on Heartbreak, Taylor Swift and Her TV Obsession," *i-D*, January 14, 2021: https://i-d.vice.com/en_uk/article/pkdmz8 /olivia-rodrigo-interview-about-drivers-license-taylor-swift-and-disney -hsmtmts. The relationship between the two became a little more complicated when Rodrigo was accused of failing to credit Swift (and Hayley Williams of Paramore) for sampling their songs in her work. See "Olivia Rodrigo Gives Up Millions of Dollars in Royalties to Taylor Swift and Hayley Williams After Being Accused of Copying Their Songs," *Buzzfeed News*, September 2, 2021: https:// www.buzzfeednews.com/article/benhenry/olivia-rodrigo-paramore-good-4-u -taylor-swift-deja-vu.

INDEX

Note: Page numbers in *italics* refer to illustrations. Page numbers followed by n refer to notes.

ABOUT THE AUTHOR

JIM CULLEN teaches history at the recently founded upper division of Greenwich Country Day School in Greenwich, Connecticut. He is the author or editor of twenty books, among them *The American Dream: A Short History of an Idea That Shaped a Nation, Born in the U.S.A.: Bruce Springsteen and the American Tradition,* and *1980: America's Pivotal Year.* His essays and reviews have appeared in the *Washington Post, CNN.com, USA Today, Rolling Stone,* and the *American Historical Review,* among other publications. A father of four, Jim lives with his wife, Sarah Lawrence College historian Lyde Cullen Sizer, in Hastings-on-Hudson, New York.